DATA ARCHITECTURE: A PRIMER FOR THE DATA SCIENTIST

DATA ARCHITECTURE: A PRIMER FOR THE DATA SCIENTIST

Big Data, Data Warehouse and Data Vault

W.H. INMON
DANIEL LINSTEDT

AMSTERDAM • BOSTON • HEIDELBERG • LONDON • NEW YORK • OXFORD
PARIS • SAN DIEGO • SAN FRANCISCO • SINGAPORE • SYDNEY • TOKYO

Morgan Kaufmann is an imprint of Elsevier

Executive Editor: Steven Elliot
Editorial Project Manager: Kaitlin Herbert
Project Manager: Punithavathy Govindaradjane
Designer: Mark Rogers

Morgan Kaufmann is an imprint of Elsevier
225 Wyman Street, Waltham, MA 02451, USA

ISBN: 978-0-12-802044-9

British Library Cataloguing-in-Publication Data
A catalogue record for this book is available from the British Library

Library of Congress Cataloging-in-Publication Data
A catalog record for this book is available from the Library of Congress

For information on all MK publications
visit our website at www.mkp.com

Working together
to grow libraries in
developing countries

www.elsevier.com • www.bookaid.org

Dedication

To Dr Ernest Lockridge
Yale University, Ohio State University
With great affection from your student (who was definitely not a star at Yale)

CONTENTS

PREFACE

A while back there was a cartoon going around that showed different perspectives of an airplane. From an armaments perspective the plane had heavy armor all over it. From a weaponry perspective the plane had cannon and rockets everywhere. From a bombing perspective the plane was armed with all sorts of bombs. From a pilots perspective the plane was sleek and highly maneuverable. From an engineer's perspective the plane had all sorts of widgets and knobs and gizmos.

The problem with each of these perspectives was that they were completely different and at odds with each other. At the end of the day the airplane was a compromise of each perspective. None of these perspectives was optimized at the expense of the others' in the actual final product.

Data is pretty much the same way. There are different perspectives of data by different groups of people. One group wants to handle huge volumes of data. Another group wants to access detailed data almost instantaneously, through online access. Another group wants to have data tightly controlled with a great deal of integrity. And yet another group wants their own "personal" data where they can easily and quickly create and manipulate their own version of the data using the computer.

Each group of people with their own perspective, in their own world, has a valid viewpoint. But data cannot satisfy all the perspectives and all needs at once.

Data is a complex thing. There are many facets to data. And, many uses of data.

This book is about the larger architectural issues that surround and encompass data. It attempts to represent ALL the uses and ALL the perspectives of data found in the organization or corporation. This book attempts to balance ALL the needs and perspectives of data in a rational, fair fashion.

This book starts with the greatest perspective of data that is possible within the corporation. It starts with the understanding that there is a wide diversity of data found in the corporation. But, to use that data effectively the organization must treat the data according to circumstances.

Some books are "how-to" books – manuals. Some books are stories – fiction and non-fiction. Some books are entertainment – pure escapism. This book is a descriptive book – a "what" book – a book about a large and complex architecture. Data forms a mosaic and is different from organization to organization. It describes data at a high architectural level and then delves into clear and understandable details to make sure you are clear about what is being said.

There is a lot of confusion today about data (as there has been for as long as there has been a computer), most of it caused by vendors of technology. Technology vendors are wont to make wild and unfounded claims. They are prone to exaggerate and to overstate their case. But perhaps worst of all, technology vendors are likely to suffer from a myopia from which only they should suffer. Technology vendors are prone to present a very narrow-minded view of the larger world view of data. Technology vendors are likely to present a view of the world as if they are the only technology that exists or ever will exist. And that just is not realistic. This severe case of vendor-borne myopia causes great confusion.

The claims of Big Data are such it is easy to get lost trying to comprehend what the reality and possibilities of Big Data are. This book is about perspective: How does Big Data fit into a world of decision making? There are several important perspectives taken into account by this book – how are corporate decisions being made today, how should corporate decisions be made, and how – with Big Data – might corporate decisions be made.

Some of the major topics found in this book include:

Corporate data – the vista of information across the entire corporation. There are many different types of data found in the corporation. The book lays out one perspective of data and describes – at a very high level – how that data is used (and is not used) in the decision-making process of the corporation.

Big Data – what is it and how can it enhance decision making in the corporation. There are different definitions of Big Data. This book takes a very pragmatic view of Big Data then discusses some salient characteristics of it. The most salient characteristic – one not discussed by the vendors – is that of the difference of repetitive and non-repetitive Big Data. Profound differences between repetitive and non-repetitive Big Data is herein called the "great divide." This book is worth buying for no other reason than simply to understand this "great divide" and its implications to the decision-making ability of the corporation.

Data warehouse – the need for corporate integrity of data. One day, corporations awoke to the fact having data was not the same thing as having believable data. They awoke to discover the meaning of "data integrity." That was the day the enterprise data warehouse (EDW) was born. With an EDW, corporations had the bedrock data on which to make important and trustworthy decisions. Prior to the EDW, corporations had plenty of data, but the data was not believable.

Data vault – the need for managing the change of data over time. Data warehouses evolved over time. The ultimate in the evolution of data warehousing was the discipline and structure known as the "data vault." There were and are many reasons to have the data vault as the backbone of the systems that require integrity.

Operational systems – the need to run the corporation's day-to-day business. For all the needs of managing very large data volumes and for data integrity requirements, there is (and will continue to be) a need to have systems that run and enhance the day-to-day operations of the organization.

Architecture – how the different types of data and the different needs for data are fitted together, in a holistic and a cohesive way. It is one thing to recognize the different needs of perspectives of data in the corporation. It is another thing to envision how the different types of data fit together in a cohesive, holistic manner.

Upon reading this book the reader will have an idea how all forms of data in the corporation fit together. The purpose of this book is to present a high level, holistic view of ALL corporate data and how the different data forms can work together in a constructive manner.

This book is for managers, architects, business persons, and technicians. Anyone involved in the decision making of the corporation will find this book useful. Of special interest is the "data scientist." To a data scientist, this book is like an atlas, where the different continents and the different seas of the world have been mapped out. No more do data scientists have to go exploring a world thought to be flat. No more does the data scientist have to painfully learn by trial and error the shape of islands and continents.

Many years ago at Yale University my English teacher my freshman year was Dr Ernest Lockridge. Dr Lockridge taught me my only English composition course I have ever had. Neither Dr Lockridge nor myself had any idea what was ahead. Fifty-three books later I can only be grateful for the instruction and inspiration. If my memory does not fail me (and it dims after all these years) I believe Dr Lockridge was the first person to call me "Mr Inmon." It caught my attention then and it still does today.

My lifelong thanks to Dr Ernest Lockridge.

WHI/DL

March 25, 2014

ABOUT THE AUTHORS

Bill Inmon – the "father of data warehouse" – has written 53 books published in nine languages. Bill's latest adventure is the building of technology known as textual disambiguation – technology that reads raw text in a narrative format and allows the text to be placed in a conventional database so that it can be analyzed by standard analytical technology, thereby creating unique business value for Big Data/unstructured data. Bill was named by *ComputerWorld* as one of the ten most influential people in the history of the computer profession. Bill lives in Castle Rock, Colorado. For more information about textual disambiguation refer to www.forestrimtech.com.

Dan Linstedt is an internationally known expert in data warehousing and business intelligence. He's worked in the field for more than 23 years, and continues to help Fortune 50 clients and government customers around the world in their pursuit of business information (BI) excellence. He's an expert in Big Data, unstructured data systems, and performance and tuning. He's also the author and inventor of the Data Vault Model and Methodology. He currently works with government agencies and major financial industries as a mentor for their enterprise BI initiatives. You can learn more about Data Vault at http://learndatavault.com.*

*Data Vault 2.0 is introduced as a best practice methodology and approach for dealing with Big Data and NoSQL solutions.

CORPORATE DATA

In today's world it is easy to get lost when dealing with data. There are many different types of data and each type of data has its own peculiarities and idiosyncrasies. Products, vendors, and applications become so focused on their own specific world that the larger picture of how things fit together often gets lost. It oftentimes is useful to step back and look at the larger picture to gain a proper perspective.

The Totality of Data Across the Corporation

Consider the totality of data found in the corporation. A simplistic depiction of the totality of data found in the corporation is seen in Figure 1.1.1.

The totality of data represented here includes everything to do with data of any kind found in the corporation.

There are many ways to subdivide the totality of data in the corporation. One such way (but hardly the only way) to subdivide the data found in the corporation is to divide the totality of data into structured data and unstructured data, as seen in Figure 1.1.2.

Structured data is the data that has a predictable and regularly occurring format of data. Typically structured data is managed by a database management system (DBMS) and consists of records, attributes, keys, and indexes. Structured data is well defined, predictable, and managed by an elaborate infrastructure. As a rule most units of data in the structured environment can be located very quickly and easily.

Unstructured data, conversely, is data that is unpredictable and has no structure that is recognizable to a computer. As a rule, unstructured data is rather clumsy to access, where long strings of data have to be sequentially searched (parsed) in order to find a given unit of data. There are many forms and variations of unstructured data. Perhaps the most commonly occurring form of unstructured data is text. However, by no stretch of the imagination is text the only form of unstructured data.

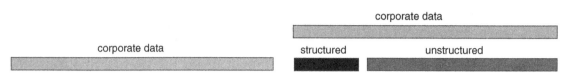

Figure 1.1.1

Figure 1.1.2

Dividing Unstructured Data

Unstructured data can further be divided into two basic forms of data – repetitive unstructured data and nonrepetitive unstructured data. As is the case with the division of corporate data, there are many ways to subdivide unstructured data. The method shown here is but one of many ways to subdivide unstructured data. This simple subdivision of unstructured data is shown in Figure 1.1.3.

Repetitive unstructured data is data that occurs many times, often in the same structure and even in the exact same embodiment. Typically, repetitive data occurs many, many times. The structure of repetitive data looks exactly the same or substantially the same as the previous record. There is no massive and elaborate infrastructure managing the content of repetitive unstructured data.

Nonrepetitive unstructured data is data where the records are substantially different from each other. In general each nonrepetitive record is markedly different from each other record.

The division of data types in the corporation has many different embodiments. Consider the data as shown in Figure 1.1.4.

Structured data is typically found as a by-product of transactions. Every time a sale is made, every time a bank account encounters a withdrawal, every time someone transacts an ATM activity, and every time a bill is sent a record of the transaction is made. The record of the transaction ends up as a structured record.

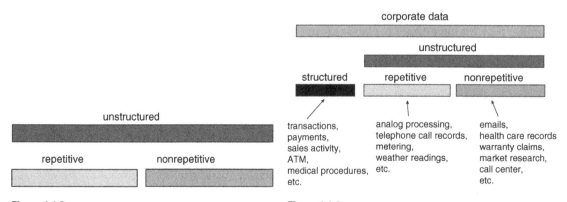

Figure 1.1.3

Figure 1.1.4

Unstructured repetitive data is quite different. Unstructured repetitive records are typically records of machine interactions, such as the analog verification of product coming off a manufacturing process or the metering of energy usage by a consumer. Consider metering. There is great repetition of records in both form and substance that are created when looking at metered readings.

Unstructured nonrepetitive information is fundamentally different than unstructured repetitive records. With unstructured nonrepetitive records there is little or no repetition of either form or content from one record to the next. Some examples of unstructured nonrepetitive information include email, call center conversations, and market research. When you look at one email, the odds are very good that the next email in the database will be different than the previous email. The same is true for call center information, warranty claims, market research, and so forth.

Business Relevancy

Unstructured repetitive data and unstructured nonrepetitive data have very different characteristics, in many different ways. One of the ways that these two types of data are different is in terms of business relevancy. In unstructured repetitive data, there often are very few records that are of real business interest. With unstructured nonrepetitive data, however, there is a very large percentage of business-relevant data.

This difference between the two types of data is shown in Figure 1.1.5.

As an example of a small percentage of repetitive unstructured data being business relevant, consider the millions of phone calls that are made each day. The government is only interested in a very few phone calls out of the millions that have been made. Or

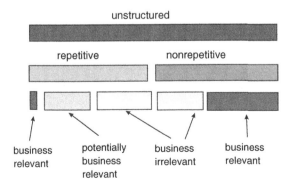

Figure 1.1.5

consider manufacturing control information. Nearly all manufacturing records are not of interest. Only a very few records – usually where the parameters being measured exceed a threshold – are of interest. Oftentimes with unstructured repetitive records, there are records that are not directly or immediately of interest but are *potentially* of interest in this category.

There are not too many records that are not of interest when it comes to unstructured nonrepetitive data. There is spam and there are stop words. But other than those two categories of information, nearly all unstructured nonrepetitive data is of interest.

Big Data

It is of interest to note that Big Data consists of the unstructured repetitive and the unstructured nonrepetitive data in the corporation, as seen in Figure 1.1.6.

The Great Divide

At first it may seem that the differences between the two types of unstructured data – unstructured repetitive and unstructured nonrepetitive data – are almost whimsical or trivial. In fact the differences between the two types of unstructured data are anything but trivial. Because of the profound differences between the two types of data, there is a great divide that separates the two types of unstructured data.

Figure 1.1.7 shows the great divide that separates the two types of unstructured data.

The great divide that separates the two types of unstructured data occurs because data on one side of the divide is handled one way and data on the other side of the divide is handled in an entirely different manner. For all practical purposes the data found on the different sides of the great divide might as well exist on different planets.

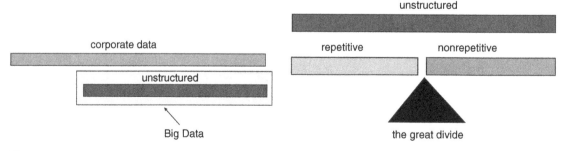

Figure 1.1.6

Figure 1.1.7

The division in the way that data is handled is such that unstructured repetitive data is almost entirely consumed with a fixation on managing Hadoop. For unstructured repetitive data the emphasis is entirely on accessing, monitoring, displaying, analyzing, and visualizing data residing on a Big Data manager such as Hadoop.

The emphasis on unstructured nonrepetitive data is almost entirely centered on textual disambiguation. The emphasis here is on the types of disambiguation, the reformatting of the output, the contextualization of the data, the standardization of the data, and so forth.

The remarkable thing about the great divide is that the disciplines surrounding the data are so diametrically different. Textual disambiguation is a very different subject than the access and analysis of data stored on Hadoop. It is because of the extreme differences between these two worlds that it is said that the two worlds live in different planets.

To use an analogy to illustrate just how different the worlds of managing Hadoop and the worlds of managing textual disambiguation are, consider this. The world of managing Hadoop is like biomedical science and the world of textual disambiguation is like the world of a rodeo bull rider. The worlds are so different that there is simply no comparison between the two. A person in biomedical science has no clue as to what it is like to ride a wild bull and a person expert at riding a wild bull is just not in tune with the procedures needed to produce a new medicine.

The differences between the two worlds are depicted in Figure 1.1.8.

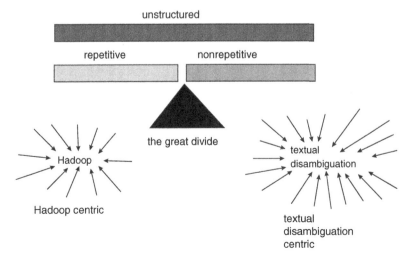

Figure 1.1.8

Figure 1.1.9

The Continental Divide

Another great divide that is analogically similar to the great divide of unstructured data is that of the Continental Divide of North America (Figure 1.1.9). In the Continental Divide, precipitation that falls on one side of the divide heads one direction – to the Atlantic Ocean – while precipitation that falls on the other side of the divide heads in an entirely different direction – to the Pacific Ocean.

The Complete Picture

The complete picture of what corporate data looks like is shown in Figure 1.1.10.

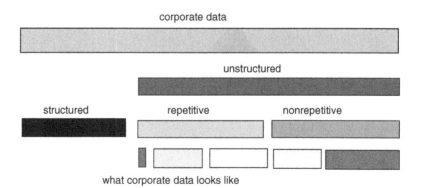

Figure 1.1.10

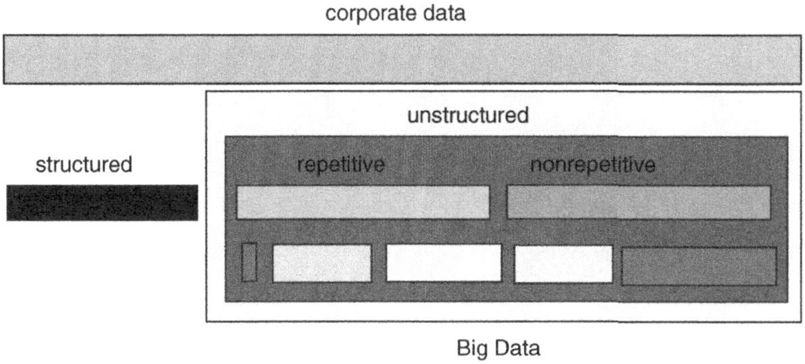

Figure 1.1.11

This figure is useful for depicting how different types of corporate data relate to each other. The figure is useful for showing the juxtaposition of different forms of data and how the different forms of data relate to each other. Each of the subdivisions of data has their own method of handling and management.

Another way of depicting corporate data, where Big Data is shown in its entirety, is seen in Figure 1.1.11.

THE DATA INFRASTRUCTURE

If there is any secret to data management and data architecture, it is understanding data in terms of its infrastructure. Stated differently, trying to understand the larger architecture under which data is managed and operates is almost impossible without understanding the underlying infrastructure that surrounds data. Therefore we shall spend some time understanding infrastructure.

Two Types of Repetitive Data

A good starting point for understanding infrastructure is to start with the observation that there are two types of repetitive data found in corporate data. In the structured side of corporate data is found repetitive data. In the unstructured Big Data side of corporate data is also found repetitive data. With structured repetitive data it is normal to have transactions as part of the repetitive data. There are sales transactions, stocking of sku transactions, inventory replenishment transactions, payment transactions, and so forth. In the structured world many of these transactions find their way into the repetitive structured world.

The other kind of repetitive data is the repetitive data found in the unstructured Big Data world. In the unstructured Big Data world we might have metering data, analog data, manufacturing data, clickstream data, and so forth.

We can ask if these types of repetitive data are the same. They certainly are repetitive. What is the difference then between these two types of repetitive data? Figure 1.2.1 shows (symbolically) these two types of repetitive data.

Repetitive Structured Data

In order to understand the differences between these two types of repetitive data, it is necessary to understand each type of data individually. Let's start with repetitive structured data. Figure 1.2.2 shows the repetitive structured data is broken into records and blocks.

Figure 1.2.1

Figure 1.2.2

The most basic unit of information in the repetitive structured environment is a block of data. Inside each block of data are records of data.

Figure 1.2.3 shows a simple record of data.

Normally, each record of data is representative of a transaction. For example, there are records of data representing the sale of a product. Each record is representative of a single sale.

Inside each record are keys, attributes, and indexes. Figure 1.2.4 shows the anatomy of a record.

If a record is representative of a sale, the attributes might be information about the date of the sale, the item sold, the cost of the item, any tax on the item, who bought the item, and so forth. The key of the record is one or more attributes that uniquely define the record. The key for a sale might be date of sale, item sold, and location of the sale.

The indexes that are attached to the record are on the attributes that are needed for quick access to the record.

The infrastructure that is attached to structured repetitive data managed under a database management system (DBMS) is seen in Figure 1.2.5.

Repetitive Big Data

The other type of repetitive data is repetitive data found in Big Data. Figure 1.2.6 depicts the repetitive data found in Big Data.

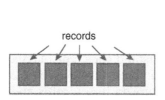

Figure 1.2.3

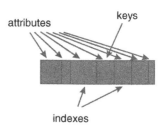

Figure 1.2.4

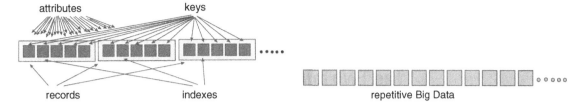

Figure 1.2.5   Figure 1.2.6

At first glance there are just a lot of repetitive records seen in Figure 1.2.6. But on closer examination, it is seen that all of those repetitive Big Data records are packed away into a string of data, and that string of data is stored inside a block of data, as seen in Figure 1.2.7.

The structured infrastructure seen in Figure 1.2.7 is typical of an infrastructure managed under one of several DBMSs such as Oracle, SQL Server, DB2, and so forth.

The infrastructure for Big Data is quite different than the infrastructure found in a standard DBMS. In the infrastructure for Big Data there is a block. And in the block are found many repetitive records. Each record is merely concatenated to each other record. Figure 1.2.8 is representative of a record that might be found in Big Data.

In Figure 1.2.8 it is seen that there is merely a long string of data, with records stacked one against the other. The system only sees the block and the long string of data. In order to find a record, the system needs to "parse" the string, as seen in Figure 1.2.9.

Suppose the system wants to find a given record "B." The system needs to sequentially read the string of data until it recognizes that there is a record. Then the system needs to go into the record and determine whether it is record "B." This is how a search is conducted in the most primitive state in Big Data.

It doesn't take much of an imagination to see that a lot of machine cycles are chewed up looking for data in Big Data. To this end the Big Data environment employees a means of processing referred to as the "Roman census" approach. More will be described about the Roman census approach in the chapter on Big Data.

block of data

Figure 1.2.7

recordArecordBrecordCrecordDrecordErecordFrecordg...

Figure 1.2.8

The Two Infrastructures

The two different infrastructures are contrasted in Figure 1.2.10.

Without much effort it is seen that the infrastructures surrounding Big Data and structured data are quite different. The infrastructure surrounding Big Data is quite simple and streamlined. The infrastructure surrounding structured DBMS data is elaborate and anything but streamlined.

There is then no argument as to the fact that there are significant differences between the infrastructure of repetitive structured data and repetitive Big Data.

What's being Optimized?

When looking at the two infrastructures, it is natural to ask the question: What is being optimized by the different infrastructures? In the case of Big Data the optimization of the infrastructure is on the ability of the system to manage almost unlimited amounts of data. Figure 1.2.11 shows that within the infrastructure of Big Data adding new data is an easy and a streamlined thing to do.

But the infrastructure behind a structured DBMS is optimized for something quite different than managing huge amounts of data. In the case of the structured DBMS environment, the optimization is on the ability to find any one given unit of data quickly and efficiently.

Figure 1.2.12 shows the optimization of the infrastructure of a standard structured DBMS.

Comparing the Two Infrastructures

Another way to think of the different infrastructures is in terms of the amount of data required to find a given unit of data. In order to find a given unit of data, the Big Data environment has to search

Figure 1.2.9

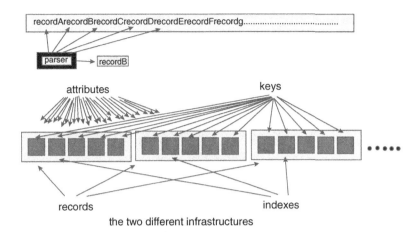

the two different infrastructures

Figure 1.2.10

through a whole host of data. Many input and output operations (I/Os) have got to be done to find a given item. To find that same item in a structured DBMS environment, only a few I/Os need to be done. So if you want to optimize on the speed of access of data, the standard structured DBMS is the way to go.

Conversely, in order to achieve the speed of access, an elaborate infrastructure for data is required by the standard structured DBMS. As data changes, infrastructure must be both built and maintained over time. A considerable amount of system resources are required for the building and maintenance of this infrastructure. But when it comes to Big Data, the infrastructure required to be built and maintained is nil because Big Data infrastructure is built and maintained very easily.

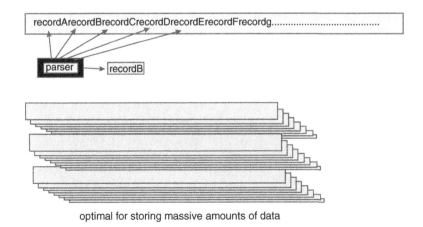

optimal for storing massive amounts of data

Figure 1.2.11

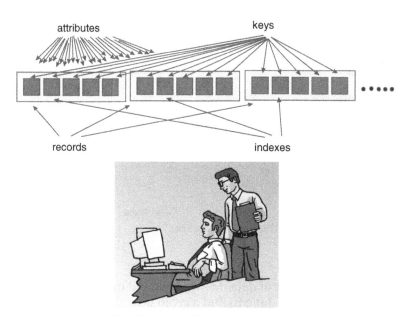

optimal for direct, online analysis of data

Figure 1.2.12

This chapter began with the proposition that repetitive data can be found in both the structured and Big Data environment. At first glance the repetitive data is the same, or is very similar. But when you look at the infrastructure and the mechanics implied in the infrastructure, it is seen that the repetitive data in each of the environments are indeed very different.

THE "GREAT DIVIDE"

Classifying Corporate Data

Corporate data can be classified in many different ways. One of the major classifications is by structured versus unstructured data. Unstructured data can be further broken into two categories: repetitive unstructured data and nonrepetitive unstructured data. This division of data is shown in Figure 1.3.1.

Repetitive unstructured data is data that occurs very often and whose records are almost identical in terms of structure and content. There are many examples of repetitive unstructured data, such as telephone call records, metered data, and analog data.

Nonrepetitive unstructured data is data that consists of records of data where the records are not similar, either in terms of structure or content. Examples of nonrepetitive unstructured data are emails, call center conversations, warranty claims, and so forth.

The "Great Divide"

Between the two types of unstructured data is what can be termed the "great divide."

The great divide is the demarcation of repetitive and nonrepetitive records, as seen in Figure 1.3.1. At first glance it does not appear that there should be a massive difference between repetitive unstructured records and nonrepetitive unstructured records of data. But such is not the case at all. There indeed is a huge difference between repetitive unstructured data and nonrepetitive unstructured data.

The primary distinction between the two types of unstructured data is that repetitive unstructured data focuses its attention on the management of data in the Hadoop environment whereas the attention of nonrepetitive unstructured data focuses its attention on textual disambiguation of data. And as shall be seen, this difference in focus makes a huge difference in how the data is perceived, how the data is used, and how the data is managed.

This difference, which is the great divide, is shown in Figure 1.3.2.

It is seen then that there is a very different focus between the two types of unstructured data.

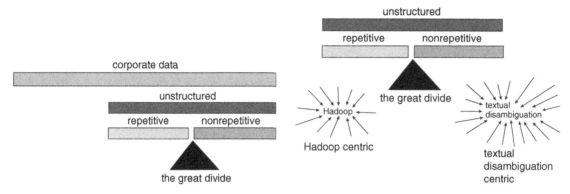

Figure 1.3.1   Figure 1.3.2

Repetitive Unstructured Data

The repetitive unstructured data is said to be "Hadoop centric." Being Hadoop centric means that processing of repetitive unstructured data revolves around processing and managing the Hadoop environment. The centricity of the repetitive unstructured data is seen in Figure 1.3.3.

The center of the Hadoop environment naturally enough is Hadoop. Hadoop is the technology by which very large amounts of data can be managed. Hadoop is at the center of what is known as Big Data. Hadoop is the primary storage mechanism for Big Data. The essential characteristics of Hadoop are:
– It is capable of managing very large volumes of data.
– It manages data on less expensive storage.
– It manages data by the "Roman census" method.
– It stores data in an unstructured manner.

Because of these operating characteristics of Hadoop, very large volumes of data can be managed. Hadoop is capable of managing volumes of data significantly larger than standard relational database management systems. The Big Data technology of Hadoop is depicted in the Figure 1.3.4.

But Hadoop is a raw technology. In order to be useful, Hadoop requires its own unique infrastructure.

The technologies that surround Hadoop serve to manage the data and to access and analyze the data found in Hadoop. The infrastructure services that surround Hadoop are seen in Figure 1.3.5.

The services that surround Hadoop are familiar to anyone that has ever used a standard DBMS. The difference is that in a standard DBMS the services are found in the DBMS itself, while in Hadoop many of the services have to be done externally. A second major difference is that throughout the Hadoop environment

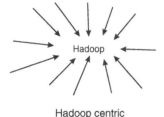

Figure 1.3.3

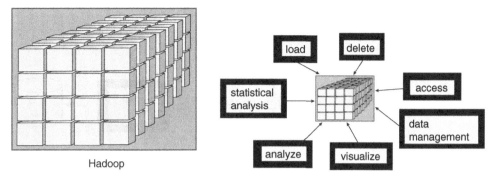

Figure 1.3.4   Figure 1.3.5

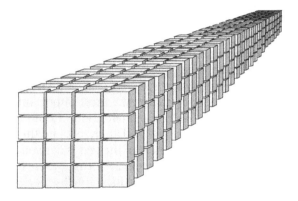

Figure 1.3.6

there is the need to service huge volumes of data. The developer in the Hadoop environment must be prepared to manage and handle extremely large volumes of data. This means that many infrastructure tasks can be handled only in the Hadoop environment itself.

Indeed, the Hadoop environment is permeated by the need to be able to handle extraordinarily large amounts of data. The need to handle nearly unlimited amounts of data is seen in Figure 1.3.6.

There is then an emphasis on doing the normal tasks of data management in the Hadoop environment where the process must be able to handle very large amounts of data.

Nonrepetitive Unstructured Data

The emphasis in the nonrepetitive unstructured environment is quite different than the emphasis on the management of the Hadoop Big Data technology. In the nonrepetitive unstructured

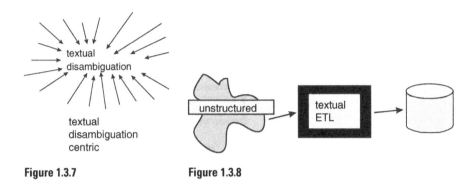

Figure 1.3.7   **Figure 1.3.8**

environment there is an emphasis on "textual disambiguation" (or on "textual extract/transform/load (ETL)"). This emphasis is shown in Figure 1.3.7.

Textual disambiguation is the process of taking nonrepetitive unstructured data and manipulating it into a format that can be analyzed by standard analytical software. There are many facets to textual disambiguation, but perhaps the most important functionality is one that can be called "contextualization." Contextualization is the process by which text is read and analyzed, and the context of the text is derived. Once the context of the text is derived, the text is then reformatted into a standard database format where the text can be read and analyzed by standard "business intelligence" software.

The process of textual disambiguation is shown in Figure 1.3.8.

There are many facets to textual disambiguation. Since textual disambiguation is completely free from the inadequacies of natural language processing (NLP), there is a multifaceted approach to derivation of context. Some of the techniques used to derive context include:

– The integration of external taxonomies and ontologies
– Proximity analysis
– Homographic resolution
– Subdocument processing
– Associative text resolution
– Acronym resolution
– Simple stop word processing
– Simple word stemming
– Inline pattern recognition

In truth there are many more facets to the process of textual disambiguation. Some of the more important facets of textual disambiguation are shown in Figure 1.3.9.

There is a concern regarding the volume of data that is managed by textual disambiguation. But the volume of data that can be

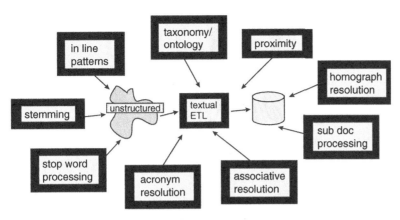

Figure 1.3.9

processed is secondary to the transformation of data that occurs during the transformation process. The fact that textual disambiguation is dominated by transformation is depicted in Figure 1.3.10.

There is then a completely different emphasis on the processing that occurs in the repetitive unstructured world versus the processing that occurs in the nonrepetitive unstructured world.

Different Worlds

This difference is seen in Figure 1.3.11.

Part of the reason for the difference between repetitive unstructured data and nonrepetitive unstructured data lies in the very data itself. With repetitive unstructured data, there is not much of a need to discover the context of the data. With repetitive unstructured data, data occurs so frequently and so repeatedly that the context of that data is fairly obvious or fairly easy to ascertain. In addition, there typically is not much contextual data to begin with when it comes to repetitive unstructured data.

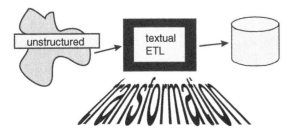

Figure 1.3.10

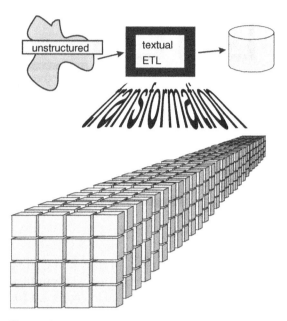

Figure 1.3.11

Therefore the emphasis is almost entirely on the need to manage volumes of data.

But with nonrepetitive unstructured data, there is a great need to derive the context of the data. Before the data can be used analytically, the data needs to be contextualized. And with nonrepetitive unstructured data, deriving the context of the data is a very complex thing to do. Truly there is a need to manage volumes of data when it comes to nonrepetitive unstructured data. But the primary need is the need to contextualize the data in the first place.

For these reasons, there is a great divide when it comes to managing and dealing with the different forms of unstructured data.

1.4

DEMOGRAPHICS OF CORPORATE DATA

It is one thing to understand that corporate data can be divided up into different categories. It is another thing to understand those categories in depth.

Figure 1.4.1 shows one way to divide corporate data.

Figure 1.4.1 shows that all data in Big Data is unstructured and that Big Data can be divided into two major categories, which are repetitive unstructured data and nonrepetitive unstructured data. The diagram in Figure 1.4.1 shows the major categorization of corporate data. But the diagram can be misleading. Some corporations have a tremendous amount of repetitive unstructured data and other corporations have no repetitive unstructured data at all.

A more realistic representation of the demographics of repetitive unstructured data is shown by Figure 1.4.2.

Figure 1.4.2 shows that there is a wide spectrum of ratios of repetitive data to other types of data. From a demographic standpoint, some corporations have a preponderance of repetitive unstructured data and other corporations have no repetitive unstructured whatsoever. And other corporations are somewhere between the two extremes.

The type of business has a great deal to do with exactly how much repetitive unstructured data there is (or is not). A typical scattering of repetitive ratios by type of business is shown in Figure 1.4.3.

In Figure 1.4.3 it is seen that certain industries have a lot of repetitive unstructured data. Weather services, manufacturing, and public utilities are at the top of the list. These types of corporations have activities that generate a huge amount of repetitive unstructured data. Conversely, small retailing organizations may have no repetitive unstructured data at all.

There is then a spectrum of ratios of repetitive unstructured data to other types of data depending on the business.

Another way to look at the same thing is to look at types of data. The spectrum of ratios is seen in Figure 1.4.4.

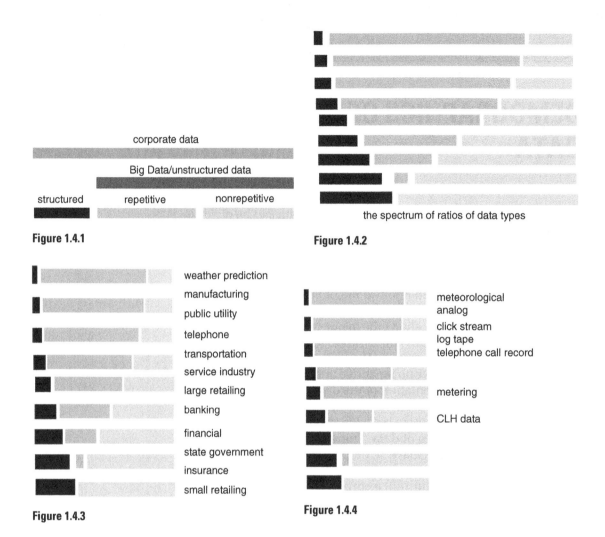

Figure 1.4.1

the spectrum of ratios of data types

Figure 1.4.2

Figure 1.4.3

Figure 1.4.4

Figure 1.4.4 shows that when it comes to repetitive unstructured data, there is a lot of meteorological data, a lot of analog data, and a lot of clickstream data for some corporations.

While the demographics of repetitive unstructured data is an interesting way to view corporate data, there are other interesting perspectives as well. Another interesting perspective is from the perspective of business relevancy. Business relevancy refers to the usefulness of data in the decision-making process. Some corporate data is highly business relevant and other corporate data is not relevant to the decision making in the corporation at all.

How business relevancy relates to corporate data is seen in Figure 1.4.5.

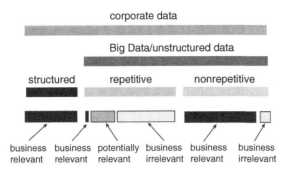

Figure 1.4.5

Figure 1.4.5 shows that there really are three classes of business relevancy – business relevant data, business irrelevant data, and potentially business relevant data.

Each of these categories of data deserves their own explanation.

The first category of data is that of structured data. Structured data is typically managed by a DBMS. Figure 1.4.6 shows that all structured data is (at least potentially) business relevant.

Much of structured data is available for online processing. And all elements of data in the structured environment are able to be located and accessed for processing. For this reason all structured data is categorized as business relevant data.

Consider an example. A customer walks into the bank and asks for a withdrawal of $500. The bank teller accesses the customer's account and sees that there is a sufficient balance in the account. The bank teller then authorizes the withdrawal for $500. The data regarding the customer's account has been used and is certainly business relevant. Now consider the data in the structured database of the bank that is not being accessed by a bank teller. Is this data still business relevant even though it is not being used? The answer is that the data is still business relevant even though it is not being used. It is still business relevant if it *might* be used.

That is why all structured data is considered to be business relevant. Its actual usage has little to do with its business value. The data still has business value and relevancy even if it is not being actively used.

Now consider the business relevancy of repetitive unstructured data. Figure 1.4.7 shows that only a tiny fraction of repetitive unstructured data is business relevant. A larger percentage of repetitive unstructured data is potentially business relevant. And a significant portion of repetitive unstructured data is not business relevant.

In order to understand the business relevancy of repetitive unstructured data, look at one of the many examples of repetitive

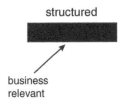

Figure 1.4.6

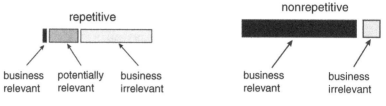

Figure 1.4.7   **Figure 1.4.8**

unstructured data. Consider log tapes. When looking at a log tape, nearly all the records on the log tape are meaningless. Most of the log records are just "marking time." Only a few important records on the log tape have direct business relevancy. The same phenomenon is true of clickstream data, analog data, metering data, and so forth. There do exist, however, records that are not directly business relevant but are *potentially* business relevant. These potentially business relevant records are records that are not immediately useful to the business but are potentially useful under other circumstances.

Now let's consider the business relevancy of nonrepetitive unstructured data. Nonrepetitive unstructured data is made up of records such as email, call center data, warranty data conversations, insurance claims, and so forth. Figure 1.4.8 depicts nonrepetitive unstructured data.

In nonrepetitive unstructured data there is data such as spam, blather, and stop words. These types of data are not business relevant. But much of the data found in the nonrepetitive unstructured category is business relevant (or is at least *potentially* business relevant).

Now let's stop and take a look at the demographics of business relevancy as it relates to unstructured data (Big Data). Figure 1.4.9 shows where business relevancy lies.

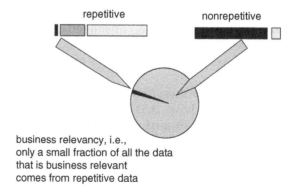

Figure 1.4.9

Figure 1.4.9 shows that the vast majority of the business relevancy of Big Data lies in the realm of nonrepetitive unstructured data. There simply is relatively little business relevancy found in repetitive unstructured data.

This graphic perhaps explains why the early proponents of Big Data that focused almost entirely on repetitive unstructured data had such a difficult time establishing business relevancy for Big Data.

CORPORATE DATA ANALYSIS

Data is fairly worthless unless it can be analyzed. So the data architect must always keep in mind that the ultimate purpose of data is to support analysis (which in turn supports business value).

The analysis of corporate data is pretty much like the analysis of other kinds of data with one exception. And that exception is that most of the time, corporate data comes from multiple sources and multiple types of data. The fact that the origins of corporate data are multifaceted colors all of the analysis of corporate data. Figure 1.5.1 depicts the need to analyze corporate data.

As is the case with all data analysis, the first consideration of analysis is whether the analysis will be a formal analysis or an informal analysis. A formal analysis is one with corporate or even legal consequences. Occasionally an organization has to do an analysis that is governed under rules of compliance. Typical governing bodies are those implementing the Sarbanes-Oxley Act or Health Insurance Portability and Accountability Act (HIPAA). And there are plenty other types of compliance, such as audit compliance. When a formal analysis is occurring, analysts have concern themselves with the validity and lineage of the data. If incorrect data is used for a formal analysis, the consequences can be dire. Therefore if a formal analysis is to occur, the veracity and the lineage of the data is very important. In the case of public corporations, an external public accounting firm must sign off on the quality and accuracy of the data.

The other type of analysis to be done is an informal analysis. An informal analysis is done quickly and can use any available numbers. While it is nice if the data used for an informal analysis is accurate, the consequences of using less than accurate information for an informal analysis are not severe.

When doing data analysis, constant awareness must be made as to whether the analysis is formal or informal.

The first step in doing corporate data analysis is physically gathering the data to be analyzed. Figure 1.5.2 shows there are usually many diverse sources of corporate data.

In many cases the sources of data are computerized, so physically gathering data is not much of a problem. But in some cases

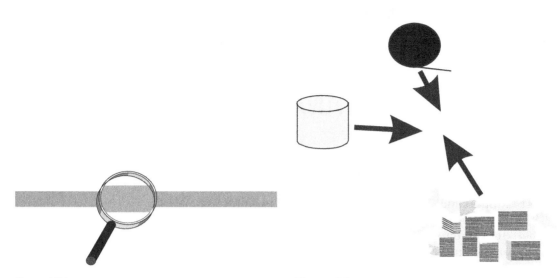

Figure 1.5.1

Figure 1.5.2

the data exists on a physical medium such as paper and the data must pass through technology such as optical character recognition (OCR) software. Or in other cases the data exists as conversations and must pass through voice recognition technology.

Usually gathering the data physically is the easiest part of doing analysis across the corporation. Much more challenging is the logical resolution problem. The logical resolution aspect of corporate data management addresses the issue of bringing together many disparate sources of data and reading and processing the data seamlessly. There are many problems with the logical resolution of corporate data. Some of the many problems are:

Resolving key structures in which a key in one part of the corporation is different from a similar key in another part of the corporation.

Resolving definitions in which data defined one way in the corporation is defined another way in a different part of the corporation.

Resolving calculations in which a calculation made one way in the corporation is made using a different formula in another part of the corporation

Resolving data structures in which data structured one way in the corporation is structured differently in another part of the corporation.

And the list goes on.

In many cases the difficulties of resolution are so difficult and so ingrained in the data that resolution cannot be satisfactorily done. In this case the corporation ends up having different analyses being done by different organizations in the corporation. The problem with different organizations doing their own separate analysis and calculation is that the result is parochial. No one at the corporate level is able to see what is going one at the highest level of the corporation.

The problem of resolution of data is magnified with corporate data when data crosses the boundary of structured data and Big Data. And even within Big Data, when data crosses the boundary between repetitive unstructured data and nonrepetitive unstructured data, there is a challenge.

There are then serious challenges when the corporation attempts to create a cohesive, holistic view of data across the entire corporation. If there is to be a true corporate foundation of data, it is necessary to integrate data, as seen in Figure 1.5.3.

Once data is integrated (or at least once as much data as can be integrated is in fact integrated), it is then reformatted into a normalized fashion. There is nothing particularly magical about a normalized structuring of data other than the following:
• Normalization is a logical way to organize data.
• Tools that do much of analytical processing operate best on normalized data.

Figure 1.5.4 shows that once data is normalized, it is easy to analyze.

The result of normalization is that data can be placed into flat file records. Once data is placed into normalized, flat file records, the data can be easily calculated, compared, and all the other aspects of normalization.

Normalization is an optimal state for data to be analyzed because in a normalized state, the data is at a very low point of granularity. Because the data is at a very low point of granularity,

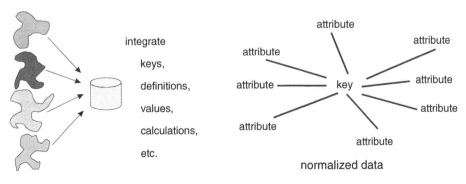

Figure 1.5.3   **Figure 1.5.4**

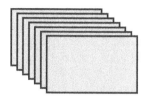

normalized
records
of data

Figure 1.5.5

it can be categorized and calculated in many different ways. From an analogical standpoint, data in a normalized state is similar to grains of silicon. Raw grains of silicon can be recombined and re-manufactured into many different forms, such as glass, computer chips, and body implants. By the same token, normalized data can be reworked into many different forms of analysis.

(As a side note, normalizing data does not necessarily mean that data will be placed into a relational structure. Most of the time the normalized data is placed into a relational structure. But it is entirely possible to place normalized data in a structure other than a relational structure if that makes sense.)

Whatever structuring of data is used, the result is that normalized data is placed into records of data that may or may not have a relational foundation, as seen in Figure 1.5.5.

Once the data is structured into a granular state, the data can then be analyzed in many different ways. In truth, once corporate data is integrated and placed into a granular state, the analysis of corporate data is not very different than the analysis of any other kind of data.

Typically the first step of analysis is categorization of data. Figure 1.5.6 suggests the categorization of data: Once data is categorized, many sorts of analysis can ensue. One of the typical forms of analysis is the identification of exceptional data. For example, the analyst may wish to find all customers who have spent more than $1,000 in the past year. Or the analyst may want to find days when production peaked more than 25 units a day. Or the analyst may want to find what products were painted red that weighed more than 50 pounds a day. Figure 1.5.7 depicts an exception analysis.

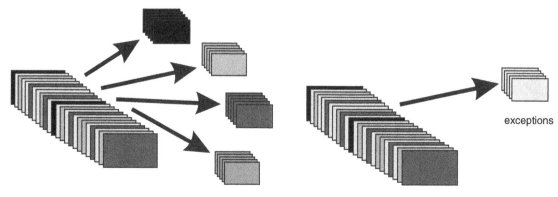

exceptions

Figure 1.5.6   **Figure 1.5.7**

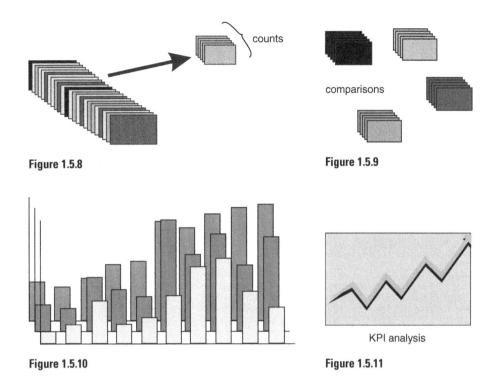

Figure 1.5.8

Figure 1.5.9

Figure 1.5.10

Figure 1.5.11

Another simple form of analysis is that of categorizing data and counting the data. Figure 1.5.8 shows a simple categorization and count.

And of course, once counts by category can be done, comparisons across categories can be done as well, as shown in Figure 1.5.9.

Another typical form of analysis is that of comparing information over time as shown in Figure 1.5.10.

And finally there are key performance indicators (KPIs). Figure 1.5.11 shows the calculation and tracking of a KPI over time.

THE LIFE CYCLE OF DATA – UNDERSTANDING DATA OVER TIME

Data in the corporation has a predictable life cycle. The life cycle applies to most data. There are, however, a few exceptions in that some data does not follow the life cycle that will be described. The life cycle of data looks like the diagram shown in Figure 1.6.1 and Figure 1.6.2.

The life cycle of data shows that raw data enters the corporate information systems. The entry of raw data can be made in many ways. The customer may do a transaction and the data is captured as a by-product of the transaction. An analog computer may make a reading and the data is entered as part of the analog processing. A customer may initiate an activity (such as make a phone call) and a computer captures that information. There are many ways that data can enter the information systems of the corporation.

After the raw detailed data has entered the system, the next step is that the raw detailed data passes through a capture/edit process. In the capture/edit process, the raw detailed data passes through a basic edit process. In the edit process, the raw detailed data can be adjusted (or even rejected). In general, the data that enters the information systems of the corporation is at the most detailed level.

After the raw detailed data has passed through the edit/capture process, the raw detailed data then goes through an organization process. The organization process can be as simple as simple indexing the data. Or the raw detailed data may be subjected to an elaborate filtering/calculation/merging process. At this point the raw detailed data is like putty that can be shaped many ways by the system designer.

Once the raw detailed data has passed through the organization process, the data is then fit to be stored. The data can be stored in a standard database management system (DBMS) or in Big Data (or in other forms of storage). After the data is stored and before the data is fit for analysis, it typically passes through an integration

⇨ entry ⇨ capture ⇨ organize ⇨ store ⇨   ⇨ integration ⇨ usefulness ⇨ archive ⇨ discard

life cycle of data (1)   life cycle of data (2)

Figure 1.6.1   **Figure 1.6.2**

process. The purpose of the integration process is to restructure the data so that it is fit to be combined with other types of data.

It is at this point that the data enters the cycle of usefulness. The cycle of usefulness will be discussed at length later. After the data has fulfilled its usefulness, the data can be either archived or discarded.

The life cycle of data that has been described is for raw detailed data. There is a slightly different life cycle of data for summarized or aggregated data. The life cycle of summarized or aggregated data is shown in Figure 1.6.3.

The life cycle for most summarized or aggregated data begins the same way that raw detailed data begins. Raw data is ingested into the corporation. But once that raw data becomes a part of the infrastructure, the raw data is accessed, categorized, and calculated. The calculation is then saved as part of the information infrastructure, as shown in Figure 1.6.3.

Once raw and summarized data become part of the information infrastructure, the data is then subject to the "curve of usefulness." The curve of usefulness states that the longer data remains in the infrastructure, the less likely it is that the data will be used in analysis.

Figure 1.6.4 illustrates that when looked at from the standpoint of age, the fresher data is, the greater the chances are that the data will be accessed. This phenomenon applies to most types of data found in the corporate information infrastructure.

As data ages in the corporate information infrastructure, the probability of access drops. The older data, for all practical purposes, becomes "dormant." The phenomenon of data becoming dormant is not quite as true for structured online data.

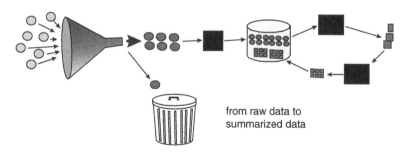

from raw data to
summarized data

Figure 1.6.3

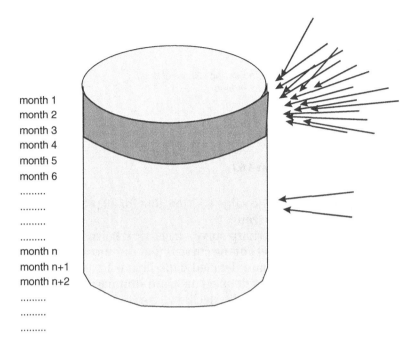

month 1
month 2
month 3
month 4
month 5
month 6
....
....
....
....
month n
month n+1
month n+2
....
....
....

Figure 1.6.4

There are certain types of businesses where the phenomenon of data aging does not hold true. One type of industry is the life insurance industry, where actuaries are regularly looking at data that is more than 100 years old. And in certain scientific and manufacturing research organizations, there may be great interest in results that were generated more than 50 years ago. But most organizations do not have an actuary or a scientific research facility. For those more ordinary organizations, the focus is almost always on the most current data.

The declining curve of usefulness can be expressed by a curve, as shown in Figure 1.6.5. The declining curve of usefulness states that over time, the value of data decreases, at least insofar as the probability of access is concerned. Note that the value never actually gets to zero. But after a while, the value *nearly* approaches zero.

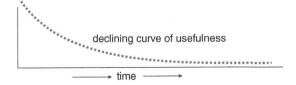

declining curve of usefulness

time

Figure 1.6.5

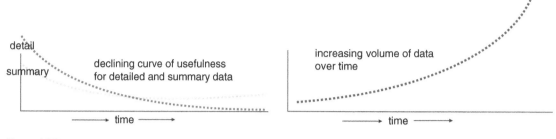

Figure 1.6.6

Figure 1.6.7

At some point in time, the value is so low that for all practical purposes it might as well be zero.

The curve is a rather sharp curve – a classical Poisson distribution. An interesting aspect of the curve is that the curve is actually different for summary and detailed data. Figure 1.6.6 shows the difference in the curve for detailed data and summary data.

Figure 1.6.6 shows that the declining curve of usefulness for data is much steeper for detailed data than it is for summary data. Furthermore, over time the usefulness of summary data goes flat but does not approach zero, whereas the curve for detailed data indeed, does approach zero. And in some cases the curve for summarized data over time starts to actually grow, although at a very incremental rate.

There is another way to look at the dormancy of data over time. Consider the curve that expresses the accumulation of data over time. This curve is shown in Figure 1.6.7, which shows that over time the volume of data that accumulates in the corporation accelerates. This phenomenon is pretty much true for every organization.

Another way to look at this accumulation curve is shown in Figure 1.6.8, which shows that as data accumulates over time in the corporation, that there are different and dynamic bands of usage of data. There is one band of data that shows that some data is heavily used over time. There is another band of data for lightly used data. And there is yet another band of data for data that is not used at all. As time passes these bands of data expand.

Usually the bands of data relate to the age of the data. The younger the data is, the more relevant the data is to the current business of the corporation. And the younger the data is, the more the data is accessed and analyzed.

When it comes to looking at data over time, there is another interesting phenomenon that occurs. Over long periods of time, the integrity of data degrades. Perhaps the term "degrades" is not appropriate because there is a pejorative sense to it. As used here the term has no such pejorative connotation. Instead, as used here,

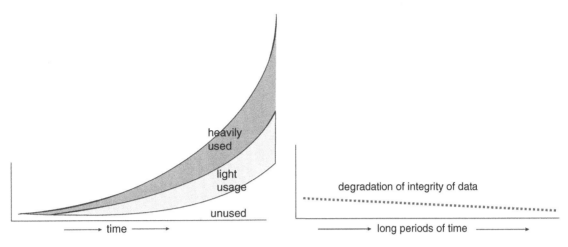

Figure 1.6.8

Figure 1.6.9

the term simply means that there is a natural and normal decay of meaning of data over time.

Figure 1.6.9 shows the degradation of integrity of data over time. To understand the degradation of integrity over time, let's look at some examples. Let's consider the price of meat – say hamburger – over time. In 1850 hamburger was $0.05 per pound. In 1950 the price of hamburger was $0.95 per pound. And in 2015 the price of hamburger is $2.75 per pound. Does this comparison of the price of hamburger over time make sense? The answer is *sort of*. The problem is not in the measurement of the price of hamburger. The problem is in the currency by which hamburger is measured. Even the meaning of what is a dollar is different in 1850 than what a dollar is in 2015.

Now let's consider another example. The stock price of one share of IBM was $35 in 1950 and the price of that same share of stock in 2015 is $200 a share. Is the comparison of a stock price over time a valid comparison? The answer is *sort of*. IBM in 2015 is not the same company as it was in 1950 in terms of products, customers and revenues, and in the value of the dollar. In a hundred ways, there simply is no comparison of IBM in 1950 and IBM in 2015. Over time the very definition of the data has changed. So while a comparison of IBM's stock price in 1950 versus the stock price in 2015 is an interesting number, it is a completely relative number, because the very meaning of the number has drastically changed.

Given enough time, the very definition of values and data changes. That is why degradation of the definition of data is simply a fact of life.

A BRIEF HISTORY OF DATA

No book on data architecture would be complete without a narrative regarding the advances made in the technology of data. In the beginning were wired boards. These hand-wired boards were "plug ins" to an early rendition of the computer. The hardwired connections directed the computer as to how data was to be treated.

Paper Tape and Punch Cards

But wired boards were clumsy and error prone and could handle only very small volumes of data. Soon an alternative was paper tape and punched cards. Paper tape and punched cards were able to handle larger volumes of data. And there was a greater range of functions that could be handled with punched cards and paper tape. But there were problems with paper tape and punched cards. When a programmer dropped a deck of cards it was a very laborious activity to reconstruct the sequence of the cards. And once a card was punched, it was next to impossible to make a change to the card (although in theory it could be done.) Another shortcoming was that a relatively small amount of data could be held in this media (Figure 1.7.1 depicts the media of cards and paper tape).

Magnetic Tapes

Quickly replacing paper tape and punched cards was the magnetic tape. The magnetic tape was an improvement over the paper tape and punched cards. A much larger volume of data could be stored with a magnetic tape. And the record size that could be stored on a magnetic tape was variable. (Previously, the record size stored on a punched card was fixed.) So there were some important improvements made by magnetic tape.

But there were limitations that came with magnetic tapes. One limitation was that the magnetic tape file had to be accessed sequentially. This meant that the analyst had to sequentially search through the entire file when looking for a single record. Another limitation of the magnetic tape file was that over time the oxide on

cards and paper tape

Figure 1.7.1

the tape stripped away. And once the oxide was gone, the data on the tape was irretrievable.

Despite the limitations of the magnetic tape file, the magnetic tape file was an improvement over punched cards and paper tape. Figure 1.7.2 shows a magnetic tape file.

Disk Storage

The limitations of the magnetic tape file were such that soon there was an alternative medium. That alternative medium was called disk storage (or *direct access storage*). Direct access storage held the great advantage that data could be accessed directly. No longer was it necessary to read an entire file in order to access just one record. With disk storage it was possible to go directly to a unit of data.

Figure 1.7.3 shows disk storage. At first disk storage was expensive and there wasn't all that much capacity that was available. But the hardware vendors quickly improved on the speed, capacity, and cost of disk storage. And the improvements have continued until today.

Database Management System

Along with the advent of disk storage came the appearance of the database management system (DBMS). DBMS controlled the placement, access, update, and deletion of data on disk storage. DBMS saved the programmer from doing repetitive and complex work.

With the appearance of the DBMS came the ability to tie processors to the database (and disk). Figure 1.7.4 shows the advent of the DBMS and the close coupling of the database with the computer.

magnetic tape

Figure 1.7.2

disk storage

Figure 1.7.3

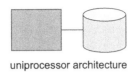

uniprocessor architecture

Figure 1.7.4

At first a simple uniprocessor architecture sufficed. In a uniprocessor architecture, there was an operating system, DBMS, and an application. The early computers managed all these components. But in short order, the capacity of the processor was stretched. It was at this point that the capacity considerations of storage switched from improvements on the storage technology to improvements on the management of the storage technology. Prior to this point in time, the great leaps forward in data had been made by improving the storage media. But after this, the great leaps forward were made architecturally, at the processor level.

Soon the uniprocessor simply ran out of capacity. The consumer could always buy a bigger faster processor, but soon the consumer was surpassing the capacity of the largest uniprocessor.

Coupled Processors

The next major advance was the tight coupling together of multiple processors, which is shown in Figure 1.7.5. By coupling together multiple processors, the processing capacity automatically increased. The ability to couple the processors together was made possible by the sharing of memory across the different processors.

Online Transaction Processing

With the advent of greater processing power and the control of DBMS, it was now possible to create a new kind of system. The new kind of system was called the "online real-time system." The processing done by this type of system was called "online transaction processing (OLTP)."

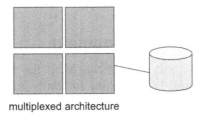

multiplexed architecture

Figure 1.7.5

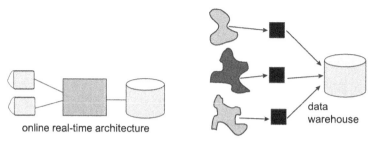

online real-time architecture

data warehouse

Figure 1.7.6   **Figure 1.7.7**

Figure 1.7.6 shows an online real-time system. With online real-time processing it was now possible to use the computer in a manner that had not before been possible. With the online real-time processing system, the computer could now be used interactively in a manner previously not possible. Suddenly there were airline reservation systems, bank teller systems, ATM systems, inventory management systems, car reservation systems, and many, many more systems. Once real-time online processing became a reality, the computer was used in business as never before.

And with the explosive growth in the usage of the computer there was an explosive growth in amount of data and types of data that were being created. With the flood of data came the desire to have *integrated* data. No longer was it sufficient to merely have data from an application. With the flood of data came the need to look at data in a cohesive manner.

Data Warehouse

Thus was born the data warehouse, as shown in Figure 1.7.7. With the data warehouse came what was called the "single version of the truth," or the "system of record." With the single version of the truth, the organization now had a foundation of data, which it could turn to with confidence.

The volumes of data continued to explode with the advent of the data warehouse. Prior to the data warehouse there was no convenient place to store historical data. But with the data warehouse, for the first time, there was a convenient and natural place for historical data.

Parallel Data Management

It is normal and natural that with the ability to store large amounts of data, the demand for data management products and technology skyrocketed. Soon there emerged an architectural approach called the "parallel" approach to data management, which is shown in Figure 1.7.8.

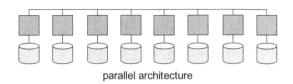

parallel architecture

Figure 1.7.8

With the parallel approach to data management, a huge amount of data could be accommodated. Far more data could be managed in parallel than was ever possible with nonparallel techniques. With the parallel approach, the limiting factor as to how much data could be managed was an economic limitation, not a technical limitation.

Data Vault

As data warehouses grew, it was realized that there needed to be flexibility in the design of the data warehouse and in the improvement in the integrity of data. Thus born was the "data vault," as shown in Figure 1.7.9. With the data vault, the data warehouse now enjoyed the ultimate in design and integrity.

Big Data

But volumes of data continued to increase. Soon there were systems that went beyond the capacity of even the largest parallel database. A new technology known as *Big Data* evolved in which the optimization of the data management software was on the volumes of data to be managed, not on the ability to access data in an online manner.

Figure 1.7.10 depicts the arrival of Big Data. With Big Data came the advent of the ability to capture and store an almost unlimited amount

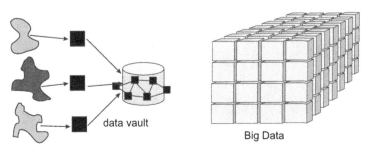

data vault

Big Data

Figure 1.7.9   **Figure 1.7.10**

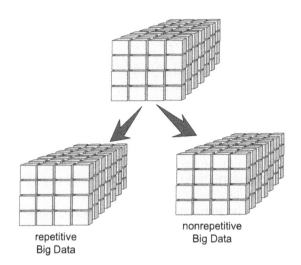

repetitive
Big Data

nonrepetitive
Big Data

Figure 1.7.11

of data. The arrival of the ability to handle massive amounts of data brought with it the need for a completely new infrastructure.

The Great Divide

And with the recognition of the need for a new infrastructure came the recognition that there were two distinctly different types of Big Data as previously discussed. There is repetitive Big Data and there is nonrepetitive Big Data. And both repetitive Big Data and nonrepetitive Big Data required dramatically different infrastructure.

Figure 1.7.11 shows the recognition of the difference between repetitive Big Data and nonrepetitive Big Data.

A BRIEF HISTORY OF BIG DATA

There are many ways to describe history. When it comes to describing parts of the history of computer science, one way to describe it is in terms of technology. Another way to describe it is in terms of organizations. The way that we will describe a brief history of Big Data is from a marketing standpoint.

An Analogy – Taking the High Ground

Using an analogy to describe the history of Big Data and how things came to be is useful. The analogy that will be used is the military tactic of taking the high ground.

Figure 2.1.1 shows that military tacticians have long known that taking the high ground was important in any military conflict. Figure 2.1.1 depicts an army cannon placed on top of a ridge, thus taking a position of command.

In many ways the maneuvering of database technology has been the moral equivalent of taking the high ground. Whatever company has the database management system (DBMS) that serves the largest amount of data is the company that enjoys a commanding advantage in the battlefield. In this case the battlefield is the database marketplace and the battle is over market share. How many customers have signed up for and are using the DBMS is the measurement of success in the battlefield.

There are other DBMS that do not use the volume of data that can be managed as their distinctive criteria. These DBMS have their own battlefield and their own criteria of success in the battlefield. The battlefield for Big Data, however, is a battlefield whose hallmark is the management of the largest amount of data.

Taking the High Ground

The progression of events that has led up to Big Data is seen in Figure 2.1.2.

In the early dawn of the computer industry there were many computer systems, many applications, and many operating systems. There were many vendors and choosing technology was a

Figure 2.1.1

A Brief Marketing History of Big Data

1. Early systems - chaos (pre-1960)
2. IBM system 360 - IMS database (1960–1970)
3. IBM online transaction processing (1970–1990)
4. Teradata - MPP parallel processing (1990–2010)
5. Hadoop - Big Data technology (2000–2005)
6. IBM/Hadoop Big Data marketing (2005–present)

Figure 2.1.2

risky and painful task. There were many problems with the early systems. One of the primary problems was that there was no standardization of languages, operating systems, or applications. Because there was no standardization of anything, everything had to be made on a customized basis. Furthermore all that custom code had to be maintained on a custom code basis. In short, in the early days there was chaos.

Standardization with the 360

Then IBM introduced the 360 line of processors. The IBM 360 was the first broadscale attempt at standardization. With the IBM 360 when you wrote code, that code could be upgraded to a larger processor in the 360 line of products with little or no alteration of the code. Today we take the interchangeability of software and systems for granted. But there once was a day when upgrading software and systems was a real headache.

Shortly after the IBM 360 was introduced, IBM introduced IMS, which was their DBMS. IMS ran on the IBM 360 line of products. IMS was not the first DBMS. But IMS was the first DBMS that could run on standardized software. In addition, IMS was able to manage a large amount of data. (Note that "large" is an entirely relative number. The amount of data that IMS could process in its early years is miniscule compared to what can be processed today. But the volume of data that IMS could handle was significant for the day and age.)

IBM had recognized and taken the high ground for large-scale, standardized database management with IMS. From a military standpoint, IBM enjoyed the high ground.

Online Transaction Processing

In short order it was discovered that things other than database management could be done with IMS. Not only could IMS manage databases, but when coupled with a data communications (DC) component, IMS could do what is termed "online transaction processing." This was a dramatic position for IBM.

Prior to online transaction processing, the computer was able to enhance many business processes. But with the advent of online transaction processing, the computer could be woven into the day-to-day operations of the corporation. Never before had the computer been an essential ingredient to the running of the business. With online transaction processing, the computer took on a role of importance never before envisioned and what had been impossible.

With online transaction processing, the organization was able to build reservation systems, such as airline car rental. With online transaction processing, there appeared online bank teller systems and ATMs. At this point IBM had a firm grip on the high ground of corporate processing.

Enter Teradata and Massively Parallel Processing

A company called Teradata entered the mix, introducing a new database technology called "massively parallel processing (MPP)." With MPP database technology, Teradata could process significantly more data than IBM. The architecture of MPP technology was such that IBM's IMS-based technology simply could not keep pace when it came to processing volumes of data. Suddenly Teradata took the high ground.

But Teradata's entrance into the marketplace was not an immediate and resounding success. IBM had very good account control and was able to resist Teradata's intrusion for a long time. Teradata persevered, and after much marketing, much sales effort, and much technology advancement, Teradata began to win over clients especially large clients. Now Teradata was beginning to capitalize on the holding of the high ground.

Then Came Hadoop and Big Data

Almost innocently into the fray came Hadoop technology. Hadoop was a response to the need to handle even more data than Teradata. In actuality, the limit to Teradata's management of data was an economic limitation more than a technological limitation. But Hadoop was addressing the problem of optimizing a DBMS on management of volumes of data, not on the ability to manage every field of data. There was a change in emphasis on the management of volumes of data from the management of units of data within the environment.

Hadoop is the heart of Big Data. With Hadoop's technology, Big Data went from a dream to a reality. Hadoop catered to just a few large-scale clients with specialized needs. Hadoop and its associated vendors were satisfied with being a niche player in the marketplace even though Hadoop had entered into even higher ground than Teradata.

IBM and Hadoop

After Hadoop proved that it was a viable commodity, IBM recognized that by partnering with Hadoop it could piggyback its way back to the higher ground. With the advent of Big Data, IBM once again achieved the high ground of large-scale DBMSs.

Holding the High Ground

The advantage of holding the high ground is of inestimable importance. So many opportunities appear when the vendor has the high ground. The vendor is free to exploit hardware, software, consulting opportunities, and more.

WHAT IS BIG DATA?

Although some people rely on the Gartner Group's definition of Big Data, which includes volume, velocity, and variety, these three characteristics could just as easily describe a load handled by a semitruck going down the highway or the cargo of an ocean liner. The *identifying* characteristics of Big Data are not disclosed.

Another Definition

In this book we want to define Big Data and list its identifying characteristics. Big Data is:

Data that is stored in very large volumes

Data that is stored on inexpensive storage

Data that is managed by the "Roman census" method

Data that is stored and managed in an unstructured format

These then are the defining characteristics of Big Data that will be used in this book. Each of these characteristics deserve a more elucidating explanation.

Large Volumes

Most organizations already have an adequate amount of data to run day-to-day business. But some organizations have an extraordinary amount of data. Some organizations have a need to look at such things as:

All the data on the Internet

Meteorological data sent down by a satellite

All of the emails in the world

Manufacturing data generated by an analog computer

Railroad cars as they traverse tracks

For some organizations there is a need to store and manage very large amounts of data and there is no good and inexpensive way to store and manage the data. Even if the data could be stored in a standard database management system (DBMS), the cost of storage would be exorbitantly high.

When facing the challenge of managing very large amounts of data, the issue of business value arises. "What business value is there in being able to look at massive volumes of data?" is a fundamental question that needs to be addressed. The old saw of "build it and they will come" does not apply to large amounts of data. Before the organization sets out to store massive amounts of data, there needs to be a good understanding of what business value of data lies in the data itself.

Inexpensive Storage

Even if Big Data were able to store and manage massive amounts of data, it would not be practical to create huge stores if the storage medium that was used was expensive. Stated another way, if Big Data stored data on only expensive high-performance storage, the cost of Big Data would be prohibitive. In order to be a practical and useful solution, Big Data, of necessity, must be able to use inexpensive storage.

The Roman Census Approach

One of the cornerstones of Big Data architecture is processing referred to as the "Roman census approach." By using the Roman census approach, a Big Data architecture can accommodate the processing of almost unlimited amounts of data.

When people first hear about the Roman census approach, it appears to be counterintuitive and unfamiliar. The reaction most people have is to ask what a Roman census approach is. Yet the approach, architecturally, is at the core of the functioning of Big Data. And surprisingly, it turns out that many people are much more familiar with the Roman census approach than they realized.

About 2000 years ago, the Romans decided that they wanted to tax everyone in the Roman Empire. But in order to tax the citizens of the Roman Empire, the Romans first had to have a census. The Romans quickly figured out that trying to get every person in the Roman Empire to march through the gates of Rome in order to be counted was an impossibility. There were Roman citizens across the known world of that time in North Africa, Spain, Germany, Greece, Persia, Israel, England, and so forth. Not only were there a lot of people in faraway places, trying to transport everyone on ships and carts and donkeys to and from the city of Rome was simply an impossibility.

So the Romans realized that creating a census where the processing (i.e., the counting, the taking of the census) was done centrally was not going to work. The Romans solved the problem by creating a body of census takers. The census takers were organized in Rome and then were sent all over the Roman Empire and on the appointed day a census was taken. Then, after taking the census, the census takers headed back to Rome where the results were tabulated centrally.

In such a fashion the work being done was sent to the data, rather than trying to send the data to a central location and doing the work in one place. By distributing the processing, the Romans solved the problem of creating a census over a large diverse population.

Many people don't realize that they are very familiar with the Roman census method. You see there is a story about two people, Mary and Joseph, who had to travel to the small city of Bethlehem for the taking of a Roman census. On the way there, Mary had a baby boy, named Jesus. The story goes on to say that the shepherds flocked to see this baby boy and the magi came and offered gifts. Thus was born the religion many people are familiar with – Christianity. The Roman census approach is intimately entwined with the birth of Christianity.

In the Roman census method, you don't centralize processing if you have a large amount of data to process. Instead you send the processing to the data. You distribute the processing. In doing so, you can service the processing over an effectively unlimited amount of data.

Unstructured Data

Another issue related to Big Data is that of whether Big Data is structured or unstructured. In many circles it is said that all Big Data is unstructured. In other circles it is said that Big Data is structured. So who is right? As we shall see, the answer lies entirely in how you define the terms "structured" and "unstructured."

One widely used definition of structured is that anything managed by a standard DBMS is structured. Figure 2.2.1 shows some data managed by a standard DBMS.

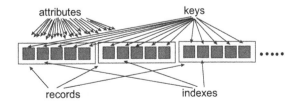

Figure 2.2.1

In order to load the data into the DBMS, there needs to be a careful definition of the logical and physical characteristics of the system. All data, including attributes, keys, and indexes, need to be defined before the data can be loaded into the system.

The notion of structure meaning "able to be managed under a standard DBMS" is widely used, has been around for a long time, and is widely understood by a large body of people.

Data in Big Data

Now consider what data looks like when it is stored in Big Data. There is none of the definitional infrastructure that is found in a standard DBMS. All sorts of data are stored in Big Data and they are stored with no notion of what the structure of the data looks like as shown in Figure 2.2.2.

If the definition of structured is taken to mean "managed by a standard DBMS," then the data stored in Big Data is definitely unstructured. However, there are different interpretations of what is meant by the term "structured." Consider the (very normal) circumstance of Big Data consisting of many repetitive records. Figure 2.2.3 shows that Big Data can contain blocks of data that are composed of many repetitive records. There are many instances where Big Data contains just this sort of information. Some are:

Clickstream data
Metered data
Telephone call record data
Analog data

When there are repetitive records, the same structure of data is repeated over and over, from one record to the next. And oftentimes the same value of data is repeated as well. When repetitive

Figure 2.2.2

Figure 2.2.3

records are found in Big Data, there is no index facility as there is in a standard DBMS. But there still is indicative data in Big Data even if it is not managed by an index.

Context in Repetitive Data

Figure 2.2.4 shows that inside the repetitive record inside Big Data there is information that can be used to identify the record. Sometimes this information is known as "context." In order to find this information in the record, the record must be *parsed* to determine its value. But the fact remains that the information is there, inside the record. And when you look at all of the repetitive records inside the Big Data storage blocks, the same type of data is in each record, in precisely the same format. Figure 2.2.5 shows that the repetitive records have the same identifying information in exactly the same structure. From the standpoint of repetitiveness and predictability, Big Data indeed has very structured data inside it.

So in answer to the question of whether Big Data has a structure, if you look at the question from the standpoint of structure meaning a structured DBMS infrastructure, then Big Data does not contain structured data. But if you look at Big Data from the standpoint of containing repetitive data with predictable context, then Big Data can be said to be structured. The answer to the question then, is neither yes nor no. The answer to the question depends entirely on the definition of what is meant by structured and unstructured.

Nonrepetitive Data

Even if Big Data can contain structured data, Big Data can also contain what is called "nonrepetitive" data. Nonrepetitive records of data are records where the structure and content of the records are entirely independent of each other. Where there is nonrepetitive data, it is entirely an accident if any two records resemble each other, either in content or structure.

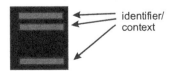
identifier/
context

Figure 2.2.4

Figure 2.2.5

There are many examples of nonrepetitive data. Some examples of nonrepetitive data include:

Emails

Call center information

Health care records

Insurance claim information

Warranty claim information

Nonrepetitive information contains indicative information. But the indicative information found in nonrepetitive records is erose. There simply is no pattern to the contextual information found in nonrepetitive data.

Context in Nonrepetitive Data

Figure 2.2.6 shows that the blocks of data found in the Big Data environment that are nonrepetitive are irregular in shape, size, and structure. There is contextual data found in the nonrepetitive records of data. But the contextual data must be extracted in a customized manner as shown in Figure 2.2.7.

Context is found in nonrepetitive data. However context is not found in the same manner and in the same way that it is found in using repetitive data or classical structured data found in a standard DBMS. In later chapters the subject of textual disambiguation will be addressed. It is through textual disambiguation that context in nonrepetitive data is achieved.

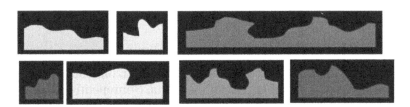

Figure 2.2.6

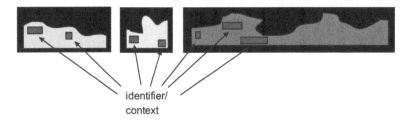

identifier/
context

Figure 2.2.7

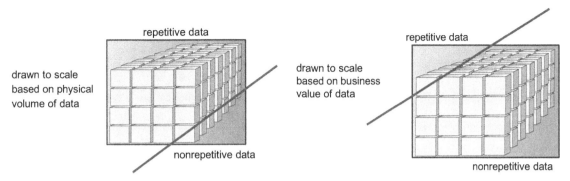

Figure 2.2.8   **Figure 2.2.9**

There is another way to look at the repetitive and the nonrepetitive data found in Big Data. As shown in Figure 2.2.8, the vast majority of the volume of data found in Big Data is typically repetitive data. Figure 2.2.8 shows that nonrepetitive data composes only a fraction of the data found in Big Data, when examined from the perspective of volume of data.

However, Figure 2.2.9 shows a very different perspective. From the perspective of business value, the vast majority of value found in Big Data lies in nonrepetitive data.

There is then a real mismatch between the volume of data and the business value of data. For people who are examining repetitive data and hoping to find massive business value there, there is most likely disappointment in their future. But for people looking for business value in nonrepetitive data, there is a lot to look forward to.

When you compare looking for business value in repetitive and nonrepetitive data, there is an old adage that applies here: "90% of the fishermen fish where there are 10% of the fish." The converse of the adage is that "10% of the fishermen fish where 90% of the fish are."

PARALLEL PROCESSING

The essence of Big Data is the ability to handle very large volumes of data as shown in Figure 2.3.1. There is so much data that needs to be handled by Big Data that trying to load, access, and manipulate the data is a real challenge. It is safe to say that no one computer is capable of handling all the data that can be accumulated in the Big Data environment. The only possible strategy is to use multiple processors to handle the volume of data found in Big Data. To understand why it is mandatory to use multiple processors, consider the old story about the farmer that drives his crop to the marketplace in a wagon. When the farmer is first starting out he doesn't have much of a crop. He uses a donkey to pull the wagon. But as the years pass by, the farmer raises bigger crops. Soon he needs a bigger wagon. And he needs a horse to pull the wagon. Then one day the crop that is put in the wagon becomes immense and the farmer doesn't just need a horse. The farmer needs a large Clydesdale horse. Time passes and the farmer prospers even more and the crop continues to grow. One day even a Clydesdale horse is not large enough to pull the wagon. The day comes where multiple horses are required to pull the wagon. Now the farmer has a whole new set of problems. A new rigging is required. A trained driver is required to coordinate the team of horses that pull the wagon and so forth.

The same phenomenon occurs where there is lots of data. Multiple processors are required to load and manipulate the volumes of data found in Big Data.

In a previous chapter there was a discussion of the "Roman census" method. The Roman census method is one of the ways in which parallelization of processing for the management of large amounts of data can occur. Figure 2.3.2 depicts the parallelization that occurs in the Roman census approach. The figure shows that multiple processors are linked together to operate in a coordinated manner. Each processor controls and manages its own data. Collectively, the data that is managed constitutes the volumes of data known as "Big Data."

Note that the network is irregular in terms of its shape. Note that new nodes can be easily added to the network. Also note that

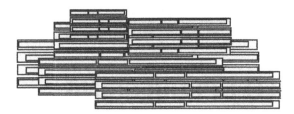

Figure 2.3.1

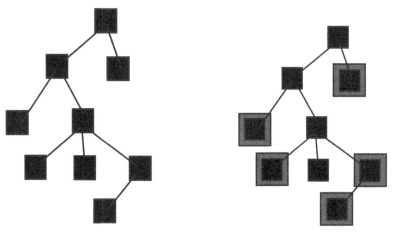

Figure 2.3.2   Figure 2.3.3

the processing that occurs in one node is entirely independent of the processing that occurs in another node. Figure 2.3.3 shows that several nodes can be processing at the same time as other nodes.

An interesting thing about parallelization is that the total number of machine cycles required to process Big Data is not reduced by parallelization. In fact the total number of machines cycles required is actually increased by parallelization because coordination of processing across different nodes is now required. Instead, the total elapsed time is reduced by introducing parallelization. The more parallelization there is, the less elapsed time there is to manage the data found in Big Data.

There are different forms of parallelization. The Roman census method is not the only form of parallelization. Another classical form of parallelization is that seen in Figure 2.3.4. The form of parallelization seen in Figure 2.3.4 is called massively parallel processing (MPP). In the MPP form of parallelization, each processor controls its own data (as is the case where the Roman census approach is used.) But in the MPP approach, there is a tight coordination of

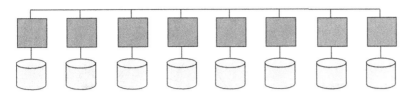

Figure 2.3.4

processing across the nodes. The tight control of the nodes can be accomplished by the fact that before the data is loaded, it is parsed and defined to fit the MPP data structure. Figure 2.3.5 shows the parsing and fitting of the data to the MPP structure.

Figure 2.3.5 shows that in the MPP architecture, the parsing of the data greatly affects the placement of the data. One record is placed on one node. Another record is placed on another node.

The great benefit of parsing the data and using the parsing information as the basis for the placement of data is that the data is efficient to locate. When an analyst wishes to locate a unit of data, the analyst specifies the value of data that is of interest to the system. The system uses the algorithm that was used to place the data into the database (typically a hashing algorithm) and the system locates the data very efficiently.

In the Roman census approach to parallelization, the sequence of events is different from the MPP approach. In the Roman census approach, a query is sent to the system to search for some data. The data managed by a node is searched and then parsed. On parsing, the system knows it has found the data that was being sought. Figure 2.3.6 shows the parsing that occurs.

Figure 2.3.6 shows that to find a single instance of data quite a bit of work has to be done by the system. But, given that there are lots of processors, the elapsed time to do the search can be cut

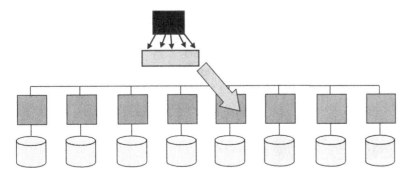

Figure 2.3.5

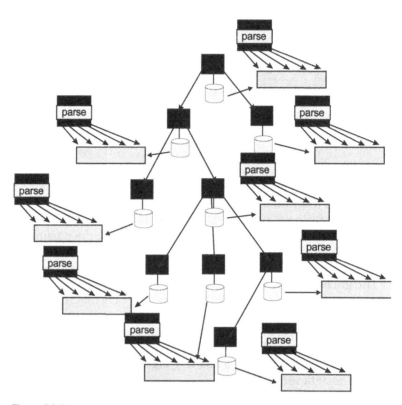

Figure 2.3.6

into a reasonable amount of time. If it were not for parallelism, the amount of time to do a search would be abhorrent.

There is, however, some good news. The good news is that parsing repetitive data is a fairly straightforward exercise. Figure 2.3.7 shows the parsing of repetitive data. In the case of repetitive data in Big Data, the parsing algorithm is fairly straightforward. Relative to other data found in the repetitive record, there is very little contextual information, and where there is contextual information, it is found easily. This means that the work done by the parser is

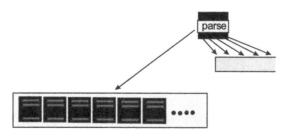

Figure 2.3.7

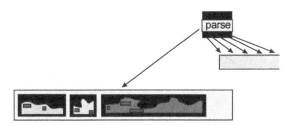

Figure 2.3.8

fairly simple work. (Note: the term "simple" here is entirely relative to the work that must be done by the parser elsewhere.)

Compare the parsing of repetitive data versus the parsing of nonrepetitive data. Figure 2.3.8 shows the parsing of nonrepetitive data. The parsing of nonrepetitive is an entirely different matter than the parsing of repetitive data. In fact, parsing of nonrepetitive data is often referred to as "textual disambiguation." There is much more to the reading of nonrepetitive data than merely parsing it. However it is done, nonrepetitive data is read and turned into a form that can be managed by a DBMS.

There is a very good reason why nonrepetitive data requires something well beyond a parsing algorithm. The reason is that context in nonrepetitive data hides in many and complex forms. For that reason, textual disambiguation is usually done external to the nonrepetitive data in Big Data. In other words, because of the inherent complexity of nonrepetitive data, textual disambiguation is done outside of the database system that manages Big Data.

A related issue to parallel processing in the Big Data environment is that of the efficiency of queries. As shown in Figure 2.3.6, when a simple query is done against Big Data, the parsing of the entire set of data contained in Big Data must be parsed. Even though the data is managed in parallel, such a full database scan of data causes many machine resources to be used.

An alternate approach is to scan the data once and create a separate index. This approach works only for repetitive data, not nonrepetitive data. Once the index for the repetitive data is created, it can be scanned much more efficiently than doing a full table scan. Once the index is created, there no longer is a need to do a full table scan every time Big Data needs to be searched.

Of course the index must be maintained. Every time data is added to the Big Data collection, an update to the index is required. In addition, the designer must know what contextual information is available at the moment of the building of the index. Figure 2.3.9 shows the building on an index from the contextual data found on repetitive data.

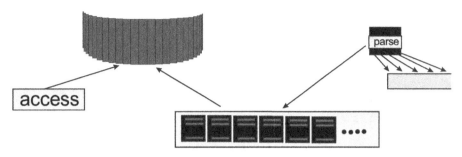

Figure 2.3.9

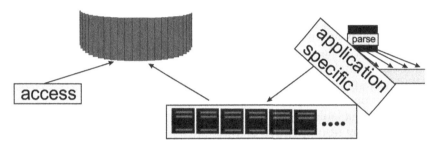

Figure 2.3.10

One of the issues of creating a separate index on data found in repetitive data is that the index that is created is application specific. The designer must know what data to look for before the index is built. Figure 2.3.10 displays the application specific nature of building an index for repetitive data in Big Data.

2.4

UNSTRUCTURED DATA

It is estimated that more than 80% of the data in the corporation is unstructured information. There are many different forms of unstructured information: video, audio, images. But far and away the most interesting and useful unstructured data is textual information.

Textual Information Everywhere

Textual information is found everywhere in the corporation. Text is found in contracts, email, reports, memorandum, human resource evaluations, and so forth. In a word, textual information makes up the fabric of corporate life, and that is true for every corporation.

Unstructured information can be broken into two major categories – repetitive unstructured data and nonrepetitive unstructured data. Figure 2.4.1 shows the categories that describe all corporate data.

Decisions Based on Structured Data

For a variety of reasons, the vast majority of corporate decisions are made based on structured data. There are several reasons for this. The primary reason is that structured information is easy to automate. Structured data fits naturally and normally on standard database technology. And once on database technology, the data can easily be analyzed inside the corporation. It is easy to read and analyze 100,000 records of structured information. There are plenty of analytical tools that can handle the analysis of standard database records.

Figure 2.4.2 shows that most corporate decisions are made based on structured data. Despite the fact that most corporate decisions are made on the basis of structured information, there is a wealth of untapped potential in the unstructured information of the corporation. The challenge then is unlocking that potential.

63

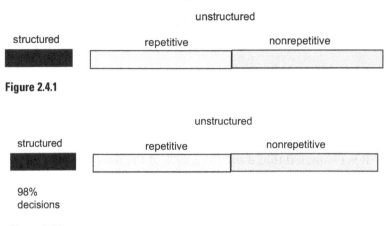

Figure 2.4.1

unstructured

98%
decisions

Figure 2.4.2

The Business Value Proposition

Figure 2.4.3 shows that there is a different business value proposition for the different types of unstructured data. Repetitive unstructured data has business value. But the business value in repetitive unstructured data is hard to find and hard to unlock. And in many cases, there simply is no business value whatsoever in repetitive unstructured data.

It is in nonrepetitive unstructured data, however, where there is huge business value. There are many, many cases where the business value in nonrepetitive unstructured data is very high. Some of the more obvious cases where there is business value in nonrepetitive unstructured data include:

Emails, where customers express their opinions

Call center information, where customers have a direct line to the corporation

Corporate contracts, where corporate obligations are disclosed

Warranty claims, where the manufacturer can find out where the weak points of the manufacturing process are

Insurance claims, where the insurance company can assess where profitable business lies

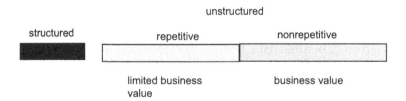

Figure 2.4.3

Marketing analysis companies, where direct customer feedback can be analyzed

These cases represent merely the most obvious tip of the iceberg
for finding and using nonrepetitive unstructured information.

Repetitive and Nonrepetitive Unstructured Information

Figure 2.4.4 illustrates the visceral differences between the
repetitive and the nonrepetitive unstructured environments. As
has been discussed in conversations on the "great divide," there
are many differences between the repetitive and the nonrepetitive environments. But perhaps the most poignant, most relevant
difference between the two environments is that of the ease with
which analytical processing can be done. Figure 2.4.5 shows that
analytical processing is quite easy to do when it comes to working with repetitive unstructured data. But when it comes to doing
analysis on nonrepetitive unstructured data, it is awkward and
difficult to do.

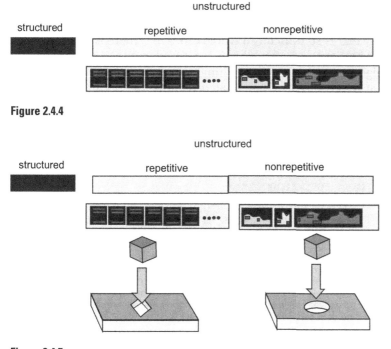

Figure 2.4.4

Figure 2.4.5

Ease of Analysis

Figure 2.4.5 shows that analysis in the repetitive unstructured environment is as easy as putting a square peg in a square hole whereas analysis in the nonrepetitive unstructured environment is as awkward and as difficult as placing a square peg in a round hole. There are lots of reasons for this major difference between repetitive and nonrepetitive unstructured data. Repetitive unstructured data is easy to analyze because:

The records are uniform in shape.

The records are usually small and compact.

The records are easy to parse because the contextual information in the record is easy to find.

Pretty much the opposite is true of the nonrepetitive unstructured records. Nonrepetitive unstructured records are:

Very nonuniform in shape

Sometimes small, sometimes large, sometimes very large

The records are quite difficult to parse because the records are composed of text and text requires an entirely different approach than simple parsing.

There are probably more differences between these two types of data. But these differences alone warrant the recognition of the great divide between the types of unstructured data.

So what is so difficult about going in and working with text? Figure 2.4.6 shows some typical text. There are many reasons why text is so difficult to work with. First, there is the discussion of whether text is actually unstructured at all. An English teacher might argue that text is anything but unstructured. There are rules that govern the structure of all text. Some of the rules include:

Spelling

Punctuation

Grammar

Proper sentence construction

"Account 123 is questionable. The payment for last month was late. How revenue recognition can be done is debatable, especially in light of the promise to deliver, which has not been fulfilled. The expense to shipment is another issue as well. The next account for review is the Inmon account. In this case there has been adequate revenue but no growth. Growth has been promised, but so far we have seen nothing. The expenses have stabilized and there have been no promises to deliver. However, all revenue has gone into salaries with no debt service...."

Figure 2.4.6

It cannot be argued that there are not rules that govern the creation of proper text. But those rules are so complex that the rules are not obvious and apparent to the computer. From the computer's perspective, text is unstructured simply because the computer cannot understand all the rules of proper textual construction.

Contextualization

There are many parts of text that must be managed if text is to be turned into a form that is useful to the computer. But easily the most important and the most complex aspect of text that must be mastered is that of finding and determining the context of text. Stated differently, if you do not understand the context of text, you cannot use text for any form of useful decision making.

Contextualization of text then is the single largest challenge facing the analyst who wishes to use nonrepetitive unstructured text in the decision-making process. Figure 2.4.7 shows an example of the importance of understanding context.

Two gentlemen are standing on a corner and one gentleman says to the next as a young woman passes by, "She's hot." Now what is being said here?

One interpretation is that the gentleman finds the young woman to be attractive and he would like to have a date with her. Another interpretation is that it is Houston, Texas, on a July day and it is 98 degrees and 100% humidity. The woman is wet from pouring sweat. She's hot. Another interpretation is that the two gentlemen are in a hospital and they are doctors. One doctor has just taken the woman's temperature and she has a temperature of 104 degrees. She is burning up with fever and she's hot.

She's hot.

Figure 2.4.7

finding context

Figure 2.4.8

These then are three very different meanings of the words, "She's hot." Trying to use and interpret these words without understanding the context could lead to disaster and embarrassment.

The need to find and understand context is hardly limited to the words in the preceding example. The need to find and understand context is true for *all* words. The largest challenge facing the analyst who wishes to make sense of nonrepetitive unstructured data then is that of understanding how to *contextualize* text. Figure 2.4.8 shows that finding context in nonrepetitive unstructured data is a major challenge.

It is noteworthy that there are other challenges as well. As important as contextualization is, it is hardly the only challenge when it comes to doing analysis.

Some Approaches to Contextualization

The notion that finding context in nonrepetitive unstructured data is a challenge is not a new idea. Indeed people have been attempting to contextualize text for a long time. The earliest attempt to trying to contextualize text is a technology called "natural language processing" (sometimes called "natural language programming"; NLP)

NLP has been around a long time and has met with modest success. However, there are several inherent limitations to NLP. The first limitation is that NLP makes the assumption that context of text can be derived from text itself. The problem is that only a small amount of context comes from text itself. In the case of the preceding example with the two gentlemen, the vast majority of the context comes from external sources, not textual sources. Is the woman young and attractive? Is it Houston, Texas, in the summertime? Is the conversation taking place in a hospital? All of these circumstances that provide context are external to the words that are being spoken.

The second limitation of NLP is that NLP does not account for emphasis. Suppose the words, "I love you" are spoken. How are these words to be interpreted?

If you say "I love you" where the emphasis is on "I," the meaning is that it is me and not someone else who loves you. If the emphasis is on the word "love," the meaning is that the emotion I feel is strong, one of love. I don't merely like you, I actually love you. If the emphasis is on the word "you," the meaning is that it is you, and not someone else that I love.

So the same words can have very different meaning based on the way the words are said.

But there is a very different reason why NLP has had a hard time showing concrete results. That reason is that NLP, in order to be implemented effectively, must understand the logic behind words. The problem is that the English language has evolved over many years and many circumstances, and at the end of the day, the logic behind the English language is very complex. Trying to map out the logic of the English language is no only difficult, but tortuous.

For these reasons (and probably more) NLP processing has met with modest success. A much more practical approach is that of textual disambiguation. Figure 2.4.9 shows the two approaches toward contextualization of text. In later chapters much more will be said about textual disambiguation.

MapReduce

Another approach to contextualization that is found in Big Data is that of a technology called MapReduce. Figure 2.4.10 shows MapReduce, which is a language for the technician that can be used to do all sorts of useful things in Big Data. However, the number of lines of code that must be written and maintained and the sheer complexity of contextualizing nonrepetitive unstructured data limits the usefulness of MapReduce for the purpose of contextualizing nonrepetitive unstructured data.

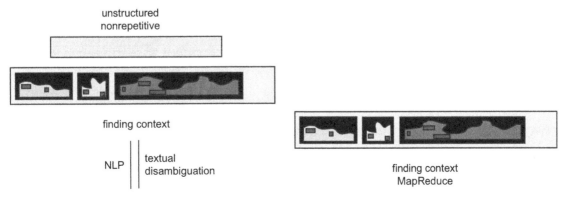

unstructured
nonrepetitive

finding context

NLP | textual disambiguation

finding context
MapReduce

Figure 2.4.9   **Figure 2.4.10**

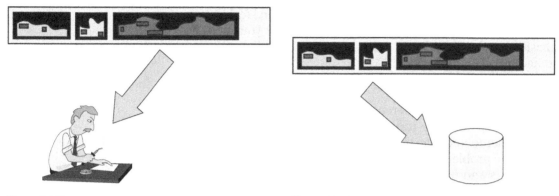

Figure 2.4.11   **Figure 2.4.12**

Manual Analysis

There is one other time-honored approach to analyzing non-repetitive unstructured data. That approach is to do things manually. Figure 2.4.11 shows that nonrepetitive unstructured data can be analyzed manually.

The great appeal of doing analysis manually is that no infrastructure is required. The only thing that is required is a human being who is capable of reading and analyzing information. So a person can start right away doing analysis of nonrepetitive unstructured information. The great drawback of doing analysis manually is that the human brain can only absorb so much information. There is no contest between the amount of information a computer can absorb and digest versus what a human can absorb and digest. Figure 2.4.12 shows that when it comes to reading and storing information in a database, a computer far outstrips even the brightest of human beings. Einstein was a simpleton compared to a modern computer when it comes to capacity. It simply is no contest.

CONTEXTUALIZING REPETITIVE UNSTRUCTURED DATA

To be used for analysis, all unstructured data needs to be contextualized. This is as true for repetitive unstructured data as it is for nonrepetitive unstructured data. But there is a big difference between contextualizing repetitive unstructured data and nonrepetitive unstructured data. That difference is that contextualizing repetitive unstructured data is easy and straightforward to do whereas contextualizing nonrepetitive unstructured data is anything but easy to do.

Parsing Repetitive Unstructured Data

In the case of repetitive unstructured data the data is read, usually in Hadoop. After the block of data is read, the data is then parsed. Given the repetitive nature of the data, parsing the data is straightforward. The record is small and the context of the record is easy to find. The process of parsing and contextualizing the data found in Big Data can be done with a commercial utility or can be a custom written program.

Once the parsing takes place, the output can be placed in any one of many formats. One format the output data can be placed in is in the form of selected records. If the selection criteria is met during the parsing, the data, one record at a time, is gathered. A variation of the record selection process occurs when only the context is selected, not the entire record. Yet another variation occurs when the record, once selected, is merged on output with another record. There are undoubtedly many other variations other than the ones that are suggested here. Figure 2.5.1 shows the possibilities that have been discussed.

Recasting the Output Data

Once the parse and selection process has been completed, the next step is to physically recast the data. There are many factors that determine how the output data is to be physically recast. One

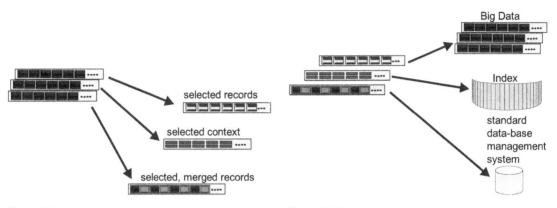

Figure 2.5.1   **Figure 2.5.2**

of the factors is how much output data is there. Another factor is what the data will be used for. And there are undoubtedly many other factors as well.

Some of the possibilities for that recasting of the output data include placing the output data back into Big Data. Another possibility is to place the output data into an index. Yet another possibility is to send the output data to a standard database management system. Figure 2.5.2 shows the output recasting possibilities.

In the final analysis, even though repetitive unstructured data has to be contextualized, the process of contextualizing repetitive unstructured data is a straightforward process.

TEXTUAL DISAMBIGUATION

The process of contextualizing nonrepetitive unstructured data is accomplished by technology known as "textual disambiguation" (or "textual ETL"). The process of textual disambiguation has an analogous process in structured processing known as "ETL," which stands for "extract/transform/load." The difference between ETL and textual ETL is that classical ETL transforms old legacy systems data and modern textual ETL transforms text. At a very high level they are analogous, but in terms of the actual details of processing they are very different.

From Narrative into an Analytical Database

The purpose of textual disambiguation is to read raw text – narrative – and to turn that text into an analytical database. Figure 2.6.1 shows the general flow of data in textual disambiguation.

Once raw text is transformed, it arrives in the analytical database in a normalized form. The analytical database looks like any other analytical database. Typically the analytical data is "normalized," where there is a unique key with dependent elements of data. The analytical database can be joined with other analytical databases to achieve the effect of being able to analyze structured data and unstructured data in the same query.

Each element in the analytical database can be tied back directly to the originating source document. This feature is needed if there ever is any question to the accuracy of the processing that has occurred in textual disambiguation. In addition, if there ever is any question as to the context of the data found in the analytical database, it can be easily and quickly verified. Note that the originating source document is not touched or altered in any way. Figure 2.6.2 shows that each element of data in the analytical database can be tied back to originating source.

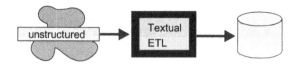

Figure 2.6.1

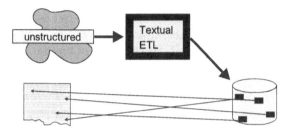

Figure 2.6.2

Input into Textual Disambiguation

The input into textual disambiguation comes from many different places. The most obvious source of input is the electronic-based text that represents the document that is to be disambiguated. Another important source of data are taxonomies. Taxonomies are essential to the process of disambiguation. There will be an entire chapter on taxonomies. And there are many other types of parameters based on the document being disambiguated.

Figure 2.6.3 shows some of the typical input into the process of textual disambiguation.

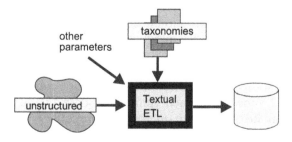

Figure 2.6.3

Mapping

To execute textual disambiguation, it is necessary to "map" a document to the appropriate parameters that can be specified inside textual disambiguation. The mapping directs textual disambiguation as to how the document needs to be interpreted. The mapping process is akin to the process of designing how a system will operate. Each document has its own mapping process.

The mapping parameters are specified and on completion of the mapping process, a document can then be executed. All documents of the same type can be served by the same mapping. For example, there may be one mapping for oil and gas contracts, another mapping for human resource resume management, another mapping for call center analysis, and so forth. Figure 2.6.4 shows the mapping process.

In almost every case the mapping process is done in an iterative manner. The first mapping of a document is created. A few documents are processed and the analyst sees the results. The analyst decides to make a few changes and reruns the document though textual disambiguation with the new mapping specifications. The process of gradually refining the mapping continues until the analyst is satisfied.

The iterative approach to the creation of a mapping is used because documents are notoriously complex and there are many nuances to a document that are not immediately apparent. For even an experienced analyst, the creation of the mapping is an iterative process.

Because of the iterative nature of the creation of the mapping, it *never* makes sense to create a mapping and then process thousands of documents using the initial mapping. Such a practice is wasteful because it is almost guaranteed that the initial mapping will need to be refined.

Figure 2.6.5 shows the iterative nature of the mapping process.

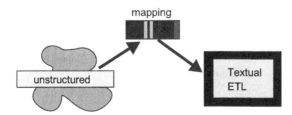

Figure 2.6.4

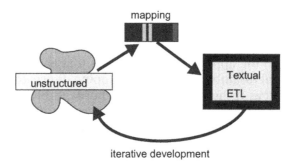

Figure 2.6.5

Input/Output

The input to the process of textual disambiguation is electronic text. There are *many* forms of electronic text. Indeed electronic text can come from almost anywhere. The electronic text can be in the form of proper language, slang, shorthand, comments, database entries, and many other forms. Textual disambiguation needs to be able to handle all the forms of electronic text. In addition electronic text can be in different languages.

Textual disambiguation can handle nonelectronic text after the nonelectronic text passes through an automated capture mechanism such as optical character recognition (OCR) processing.

The output of textual disambiguation can take many forms. The output of textual disambiguation is output that is created in a "flat file format." As such, the output can be sent to any standard database management system (DBMS) or to Hadoop. Figure 2.6.6 shows the types of output that can be created from textual disambiguation.

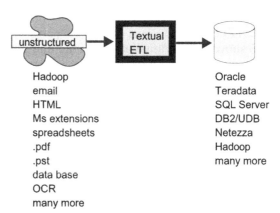

Figure 2.6.6

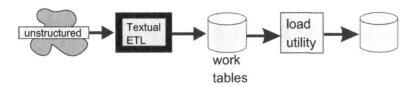

Figure 2.6.7

The output from textual disambiguation is placed into a work table area. From the work table area, the data can be loaded into a standard DBMS using the load utility of the DBMS. Figure 2.6.7 shows that data is loaded into the DBMS load utility from the work area created and managed by textual disambiguation.

Document Fracturing/Named Value Processing

There are many features to the actual processing done by textual disambiguation. But there are two primary paths of processing a document. These paths are called "document fracturing" and "named value processing."

Document fracturing is the process by which a document is processed word by word, such as stop word processing, alternate spelling and acronym resolution, homographic resolution, and the like. The effect of document fracturing is that on processing, the document still has a recognizable shape, albeit in a modified form. For all practical purposes it appears as if the document has been fractured.

The second major type of processing that occurs is named value processing. Named value processing occurs when inline contextualization needs to be done. Inline contextualization is done where the text is repetitive, as sometimes occurs. When text is repetitive it can be processed by looking for unique beginning delimiters and ending delimiters.

There are other types of processing that can be done by textual disambiguation, but document fracturing and named value processing are the two primary analytical processing paths.

Figure 2.6.8 depicts the two primary forms of processing that occur in textual disambiguation.

Preprocessing a Document

On occasion it is necessary to preprocess a document because the text of a document cannot be processed in a standard fashion by textual disambiguation. In these circumstances, it is necessary to pass the text through a preprocessor. In the preprocessor, the text can be edited to alter the text to the point that the text can be processed in a normal manner by textual disambiguation.

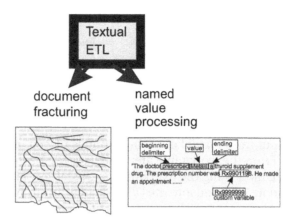

Figure 2.6.8

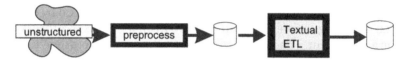

Figure 2.6.9

As a rule you don't want to preprocess text unless you absolutely have to. The reason why you don't want to have to preprocess text is that by preprocessing text you automatically double the machine cycles that are required to process the text. Figure 2.6.9 shows that if necessary, electronic text can be preprocessed.

Emails – A Special Case

Emails are a special case of nonrepetitive unstructured data. Emails are special because everybody has them and because there are so many of them. Another reason why emails are special is that emails carry with them an enormous amount of system overhead that is useful to the system and no one else. Also, emails carry a lot of valuable information when it comes to customer's attitudes and activities.

It is possible to simply send emails into textual disambiguation. But such an exercise is fruitless because of the spam and blather that is found in emails. Spam is the nonbusiness-relevant information that is generated outside the corporation. Blather is the internally generated correspondence that is nonbusiness related. For example, blather contains the jokes that are sent throughout the corporation.

In order to use textual disambiguation effectively, the spam, blather, and system information needs to be filtered out. Otherwise the system

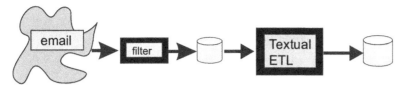

Figure 2.6.10

becomes overwhelmed meaningless information. Figure 2.6.10 shows a filter to remove unnecessary information from the stream of emails before the emails are processed by textual disambiguation.

Spreadsheets

Another special case is the case of spreadsheets. Spreadsheets are ubiquitous. Sometimes the information on the spreadsheet is purely numerical. But on other occasions there is character-based information on a spreadsheet. As a rule, textual disambiguation does not process numerical information from a spreadsheet. That is because there is no metadata to accurately describe numeric values on a spreadsheet. (Note: there is formulaic information for the numbers found on a spreadsheet, but the spreadsheet formulae are almost worthless as metadata descriptions of the meaning of the numbers.) For this reason the only data that is found on the spreadsheet that makes its way into textual ETL is the character-based descriptive data.

To this end, there is an interface that allows the data on the spreadsheet that is useful to be formatted from the spreadsheet into a working database. From the working database, the data is then sent into textual disambiguation, as shown in Figure 2.6.11.

Report Decompilation

Most textual information is found in the form of a document. And when text is on a document it is processed linearly by textual disambiguation. Figure 2.6.12 shows that textual disambiguation operates in a linear fashion.

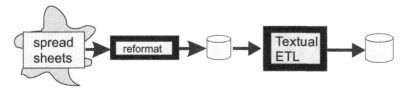

Figure 2.6.11

linear processing of text

Figure 2.6.12

But text on a document is not the only form of nonrepetitive unstructured data. Another common form of nonrepetitive unstructured data is that of a table. Tables are found everywhere including bank statements, research papers, and corporate invoices.

On some occasions it is necessary to read the table in as input, just as text is read in on a document. To this end a specialized form of textual disambiguation is required. This form of textual disambiguation is called "report decomposition."

In report decomposition the contents of the report are handled very differently than the contents of text. The reason why reports are handled differently from text is that in a report, the information cannot be handled in a linear format. Figure 2.6.13 shows that there are different elements of a report that must be brought together in a normalized format. The problem is that those elements appear

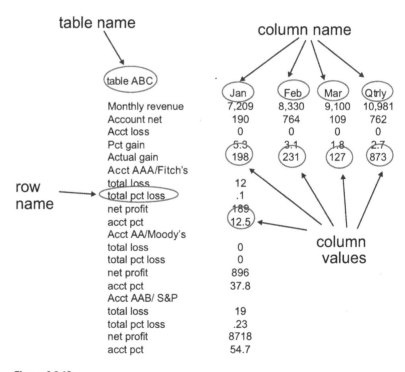

Figure 2.6.13

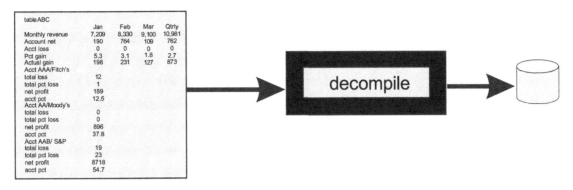

table ABC				
	Jan	Feb	Mar	Qtrly
Monthly revenue	7,209	8,330	9,100	10,981
Account net	190	764	109	762
Acct loss	0	0	0	0
Pct gain	5.3	3.1	1.8	2.7
Actual gain	198	231	127	873
Acct AAA/Fitch's				
total loss	12			
total pct loss	1			
net profit	189			
acct pct	12.5			
Acct AA/Moody's				
total loss	0			
total pct loss	0			
net profit	896			
acct pct	37.8			
Acct AAB/ S&P				
total loss	19			
total pct loss	23			
net profit	8718			
acct pct	54.7			

Figure 2.6.14

is a decidedly nonlinear format. Therefore an entirely different form of textual disambiguation is required.

Figure 2.6.14 shows that reports can be sent to report decompilation for reduction to a normalized format. The end result of report decompilation is exactly the same as the end result of textual disambiguation. But the processing and the logic that arrive at the end result are very different in content and substance.

TAXONOMIES

Taxonomies are classifications of information. Taxonomies play a large and important role in the disambiguation of narrative information. Figure 2.7.1 shows that taxonomies are to unstructured data what the data model is to structured data.

Data Models and Taxonomies

The data model classically has played the role of serving as a map – an intellectual guideline – to the understanding and management of data in the structured environment. The taxonomy plays the same role in the unstructured environment. While not perfectly equivalent to each other, the taxonomy serves much the same purpose as the data model.

There is one anomaly in the world of unstructured data that must be explained. The classification of information that has been developed in this book has one very confusing anomaly. Unfortunately that anomaly is important in understanding the role and function of taxonomies.

Consider the classification of data shown in Figure 2.7.2. The figure shows that there is unstructured data with a subclassification of unstructured data that is repetitive and nonrepetitive unstructured data. Then beneath nonrepetitive data there is a lower classification of repetitive and nonrepetitive data. Using this classification scheme, there is repetitive nonrepetitive data. And this is confusing, but it is not a mistake.

In order to explain this anomaly and explain why it is important, consider the following real example. In general, unstructured data can be considered to be repetitive and nonrepetitive. Repetitive unstructured data is unstructured data whose content and structure is highly repetitive. Into this classification of data falls clickstream data, analog data, metering data, and so forth. Into the other classification of data falls all data that is written. There are emails, call center data, contracts, and a whole host of written narrative data.

Now consider that in the classification of narrative data there appears a further subclassification of data. For all written data,

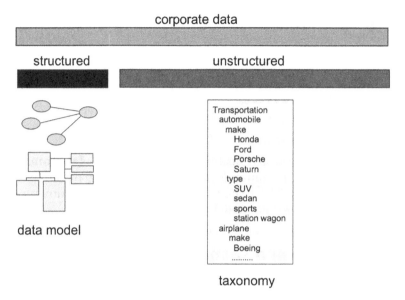

Figure 2.7.1

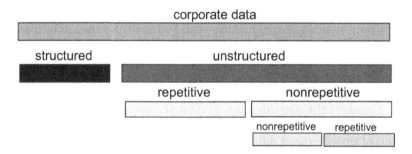

Figure 2.7.2

there can be nonrepetitive written data and repetitive written data. For example, lawyers who write contracts use what is called a "boilerplate." A boilerplate contract is a contract where the primary body of the contract is predetermined. The lawyer only fills in a few details into the contract such as the name, address, and social security number of the recipient of the contract. There may be a few other terms that are negotiated, but at the end of the day, the boilerplate contracts are very similar. This then is an example of a repetitive nonrepetitive occurrence of data. The contract is nonrepetitive because it is in narrative form. But it is repetitive because it is boilerplate contracts.

The reason why we are making the distinction between non-repetitive nonrepetitive text and nonrepetitive repetitive text is that taxonomies apply to nonrepetitive nonrepetitive text. Some examples are needed here.

Applicability of Taxonomies

Taxonomies are most applicable to text such as emails, call center information, conversations, and other free form narrative text. Taxonomies are less applicable to boilerplate contracts and other places where there is repetitive narrative text. Hopefully, the examples make the preceding discussion clear.

What is a Taxonomy?

So what is a taxonomy? In its simplest form, a taxonomy is simply a related list of words. Figure 2.7.3 shows some simple taxonomies. The figure shows that a car can be a Honda, Porsche, Volkswagen, and so forth. Or a German product may be sausage, beer, a Porsche, software, and so forth.

Of course there are many other ways to classify these items. A car may be a sedan, an SUV, a sports car, and so forth. Or American products may be a hamburger, software, movies, corn, wheat, and so forth.

There are indeed almost an infinite number of taxonomies. Taxonomies are applied to nonrepetitive unstructured data on the basis of applicability. For example, an automaker may use taxonomies relating to engineering and manufacturing. Or an accounting firm may choose taxonomies that apply to taxes and to the rules of accounting. Or a retailer may choose taxonomies that relate to products and sales. Conversely, it would be very unusual

Figure 2.7.3

```
Transportation
  automobile
    make
      Honda
      Ford
      Porsche
      Saturn
    type
      SUV
      sedan
      sports
      station wagon
  airplane
    make
      Boeing
      ..........
```

Figure 2.7.4

to have an engineering firm use a taxonomy relating to religion or law making.

Related to a taxonomy is an ontology. Figure 2.7.4 depicts an ontology. A simple definition of an ontology is that it is a taxonomy where there are interrelationships of the elements within the taxonomy.

As a rule either taxonomies or ontologies (or both) can be used when creating the foundation for textual disambiguation of non-repetitive unstructured data.

Taxonomies in Multiple Languages

One of the issues relating to taxonomies is that taxonomies can exist in multiple languages. Figure 2.7.5 shows that taxonomies can exist in multiple languages.

A related issue is whether to use commercially created taxonomies or to use individually created taxonomies. One of the major advantages of a commercially created taxonomy is that the commercially created taxonomy can be easily and automatically translated into different languages. One of the features of commercially created taxonomies is that the taxonomy is created in multiple languages. With a commercially created taxonomy, you can read

car   English
    Honda   Spanish
    Porsche   Dutch
    Volkswagen   German
    Ferrari   French
    Ford   Russian
    Toyota   Portuguese
    Kia   Mandarin
    Subaru   Cantonese
    Yugo   Kanji
                             Italian
                             ....

Figure 2.7.5

a document in one language and create the associated analytical database in a different language.

But the largest advantage of using a commercially created taxonomy is that the commercially created taxonomy does not require a large investment in the creation of the taxonomy. If an organization decides to manually create their own taxonomies, the organization is inviting a disaster because of its inability to estimate how much effort is required to actually build and maintain the taxonomies that it needs.

Dynamics of Taxonomies and Textual Disambiguation

The dynamics of how a taxonomy interacts with textual disambiguation is illustrated in the simple example seen in Figure 2.7.6, which shows raw text. The raw text is passed against the taxonomies for a car and another taxonomy for a motor thoroughfare. The output shows that where the word "Porsche" is encountered, it is recognized to be part of the taxonomy for car. The word "Porsche" is changed to the expression "Porsche/car" in the output. The same processing occurs for "Volkswagen" and "Honda."

raw text -
"she drove her Porsche past the Volkswagen on the highway.
 And soon they both passed a Honda on the right-hand side."

processes text -
"she drove her <u>Porsche/car</u> past the <u>Volkswagen/car</u> on the <u>highway/road</u>.
And soon they passed a <u>Honda/car</u> on the right-hand side."

Figure 2.7.6

Using the taxonomy for thoroughfare, the term "highway" is seen to be a form of "road." The output for "highway" is written out as "highway/road."

The example in the figure is very simple, but it serves to illustrate the dynamics of how the taxonomy is used to interact with raw text inside the textual disambiguation process. In reality the actual uses of taxonomies are usually much more sophisticated and elaborate than this simple example.

Note that on output the analyst can now create a query on "car" and find all mentions of any type of car. Also note that the term "car" appears nowhere in the raw text.

The ability to classify data externally is extremely useful when disambiguating nonrepetitive unstructured data.

Taxonomies and Textual Disambiguation – Separate Technologies

Taxonomies – the gathering, classification, and maintenance of the taxonomy – require their own care and handling. Usually it makes sense to build and manage the taxonomy external to the technology for textual disambiguation. Figure 2.7.7 shows that arrangement.

There are many reasons for the logic behind separating the building and management of the taxonomies from textual disambiguation. But the primary reason is that textual disambiguation is complex enough without adding the further complexity of the building and management of taxonomies to the process.

Another way to explain the differences between the two processes is to look at the representation of taxonomies in the different technologies. In the world of taxonomy management, taxonomies require a robust and complex representation. But in the

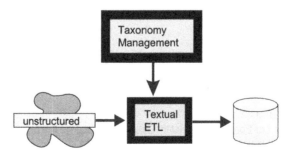

Figure 2.7.7

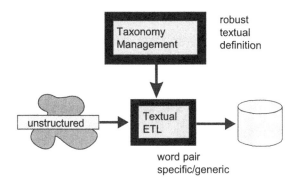

Figure 2.7.8

world of textual disambiguation, taxonomies are represented as a series of word pairs.

Figure 2.7.8 shows this distinct difference between the two technologies.

Different Types of Taxonomies

An interesting point about taxonomies is that taxonomies themselves can be classified many ways. Stated differently, there are many different ways to create the lists that make up taxonomies. Some taxonomies are composed of words that are synonyms. Other taxonomies are simply a list of words that happen to be gathered together. Other taxonomies are categories of words, and so forth. Figure 2.7.9 shows that there are many different kinds of taxonomies.

Taxonomies – Maintenance Over Time

A final observation about taxonomies is that over time, taxonomies require maintenance. Taxonomies require maintenance because language is constantly changing. For example, in 2000 if

> taxonomies –
>   synonyms
>   lists
>   categories
>   preferred
>   many more

Figure 2.7.9

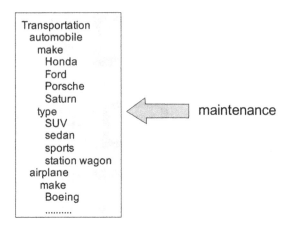

Figure 2.7.10

you referred to a "blog," no one would have known what you were talking about. But 10 years later the term "blog" is a commonly used term.

Over time language and terms change. And as language and terms change, the taxonomies which track those changes must be brought up to date. Figure 2.7.10 shows that over time taxonomies require periodic maintenance.

A BRIEF HISTORY OF DATA WAREHOUSE

The original concept of a database was as a single source of data for all purposes. This notion of what a database was grew from the magnetic tape file systems where there were master files.

Early Applications

Soon the magnetic tape files were replaced by disk storage as the predominant storage media. And with the advent of magnetic tapes files, where data could be accessed directly, applications grew. Figure 3.1.1 depicts the advent of the early applications where disk storage began to be used.

With disk storage came technology called database management systems (DBMSs). And in short order, online systems appeared.

Online Applications

With online systems it was possible to integrate the computer into places in the business that was not previously possible. Soon there were bank teller systems, airline reservation systems, manufacturing control systems, and the like. The use of the computer in online systems heralded the great dawn of the age of computation as depicted in Figure 3.1.2.

As computer systems began to multiply, it was noticed that there were two basic components of the systems – processing and data. At the same time a problem appeared: There began to be requests to use data from a single system for other purposes. There were some basic reasons for the need to share data across systems. The requirements for the building of the systems were very narrowly defined because the requirements used to shape the systems focused almost entirely on the immediate user of the system or even the clerical help that needed to operate the system. After the system was up and running it was discovered that there were other people who needed to look at and use the data found in the

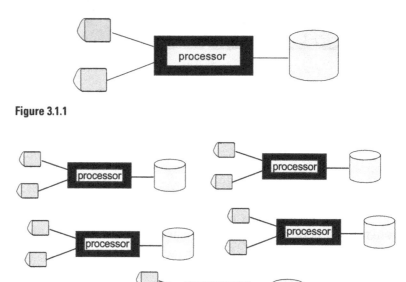

Figure 3.1.1

Figure 3.1.2

system. People from accounting needed to look at the data. People from marketing needed to look at the data. People from sales and finance needed to look at the data found in the early systems. The problem was that the requirements from these communities had never been considered when the systems were being built.

Extract Programs

Thus the simple "extract" program was born. The extract program was a simple program that read data that had been collected in one system and moved that data to another system. Figure 3.1.3 shows the advent of the innocent looking extract program.

For a while the extract program appeared to satisfy the needs of the organization. But soon end users discovered that they needed information that was not readily available. There was an attitude among the end user community that "the data is in there somewhere if we could just lay our hands on it."

4GL Technology

Into this fray came technology known as "fourth-generation programming language" (4GL) technology as shown in Figure 3.1.4. With 4GL technology the end user was able to take data and do his

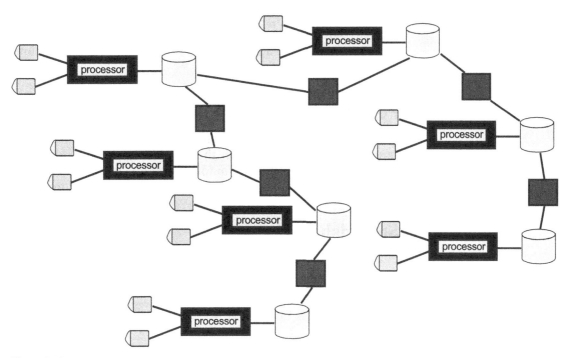

Figure 3.1.3

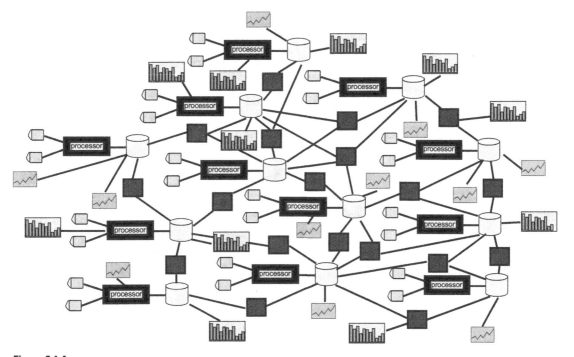

Figure 3.1.4

or her own processing. 4GL technology was the first step that was made to free data from the control of the information technology (IT) department and it gave the end user community the illusion of control of their own destiny.

Personal Computers

Shortly after 4GL technology began to be popularized, the personal computer arrived. With the personal computer came the opportunity for even greater autonomy of the end user and even more freedom from the IT department as depicted in Figure 3.1.5.

Spreadsheets

Figure 3.1.6 shows the arrival of the spreadsheet, which gave personal computer users even more autonomy. Another tie had been broken between the end user and the IT department.

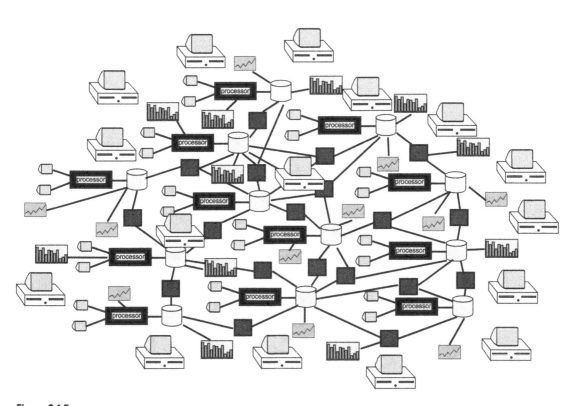

Figure 3.1.5

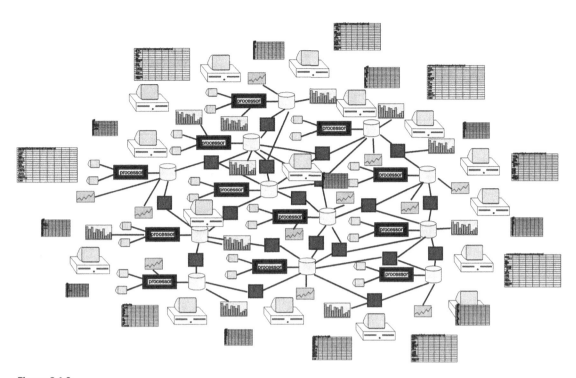

Figure 3.1.6

Integrity of Data

But the end user still wasn't happy. Along the way it was noticed that there was no integrity of data in the environment that had been created. In the thirst for data, the end user had not taken care to find, access, and capture the *right* data. Instead end users had been content to lay their hands on *any* data. The result was that no one had believable data. The same data element existed in many places in the organization and no one had the slightest idea what the *correct* value of the data was, which is depicted in Figure 3.1.7.

Spider-Web Systems

There are several names for the architecture that evolved. One name is "spider-web system." When one looks at the general structure of the systems, it is easy to see where the name spider web came from. Figure 3.1.8 shows the diagram of a real spider-web environment.

Another name for the architecture that evolved is called the "silo system" environment. The silo system environment stems

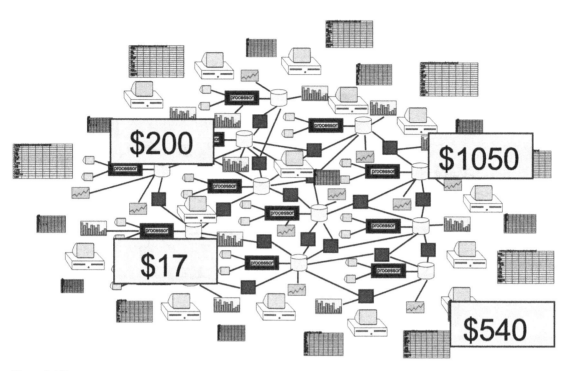

Figure 3.1.7

from the fact that throughout the architecture data tended to exist entirely in the "silo" of an application. There simply was no integration of information outside the silo system environment.

The Maintenance Backlog

One of the biggest and most understood aspects of the spider-web environment was that of the maintenance backlog. For many years, as the number of systems grew, a "maintenance backlog" also grew. The maintenance backlog was the requests being made for changes in the requirements to the systems. The problem was not that the requirements were not being done properly but that there were a whole new class of requests for information. Eventually these requests for information completely overwhelmed the organization and end users began to take their destiny into their own hands and the move away from IT as the controller of the information destiny of the corporation.

At the same time, the notion was born that there was a difference between getting any data to look at versus getting the *right* data to look at. Another observation that became apparent was

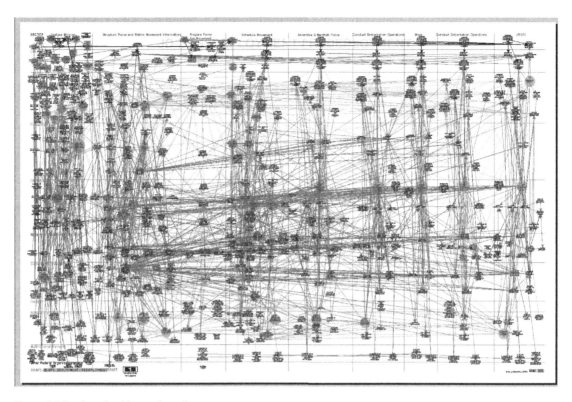

Figure 3.1.8   A real spider-web environment.

that throwing more technology or more money at the problems of the spider-web environment was a waste and added fuel to the flames. Nothing short of a change in architecture was ever going to cure the problems of the spider-web environment.

The Data Warehouse

It was into this environment that the notion that there should be a data warehouse was born. The idea of a data warehouse suggested that there should be a different types of databases. There should be one type of database for operational systems and another type of database for decision support systems (DSSs).

The notion that there should be two types of databases was heresy to the database theoreticians of the day. The database theoreticians still clung to the theory that there should be one database for all purposes. The advent and popularity of data warehouses shook the academic database theoreticians to their core.

A database was a subject-oriented, integrated, nonvolatile, and time-variant collection of data in support of management's decisions.

This notion of a data warehouse has stood the definition of time and has been accepted as the definition of what a data warehouse is.

Another term for the data warehouse was the "single version of the truth." The data warehouse formed the basis for *believable* corporate data. Data across the corporation, not application data, was represented by the data warehouse.

To an Architected Environment

Figure 3.1.9 shows the movement away from spider-web systems to an architected environment where there are operational databases and data warehouses.

As interesting and as important as the architectural evolution away from spider-web systems to data warehousing was, it was merely the start of an evolution.

To the CIF

Soon it was discovered that there was a lot more to the data warehouse than just a place to store and retrieve data. Indeed a whole infrastructure was required. There was ETL software (extract/transform/load) technology and operational systems.

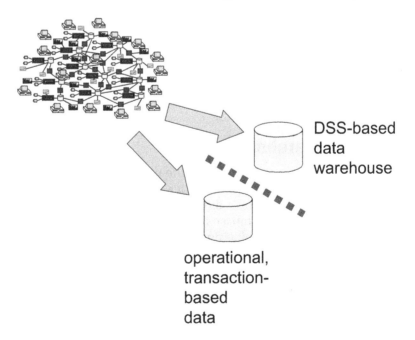

DSS-based data warehouse

operational, transaction-based data

Figure 3.1.9

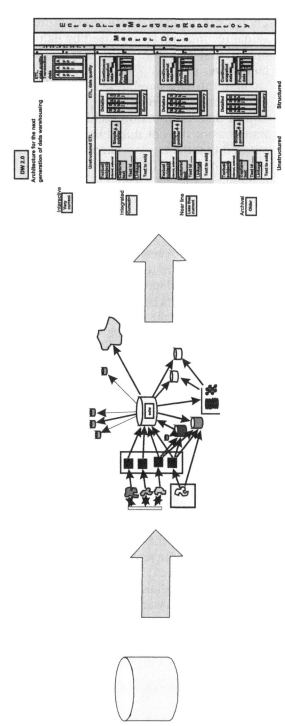

Figure 3.1.10

There were data marts, whose structure was centered on dimensional technology, as espoused by Ralph Kimball. There was the operational data store (ODS) that was an essential part of the architecture.

Soon the data warehouse evolved into the corporate information factory (CIF). For many organizations, CIF became the definition of their information architecture. But the evolution of data warehousing did not stop there. After a period of time it was recognized that there was an architecture beyond CIF. The next step in the evolution of information architecture centered on the data warehouse was DW 2.0 architecture.

DW 2.0

With DW 2.0, several important aspects of the data warehouse environment were recognized. One of these was the life cycle of data within the data warehouse environment. It was simply true that over time data began to live out its own life cycle once entered into a data warehouse.

Another important point of DW 2.0 was that unstructured data was an important and essential aspect of the world of data warehousing. Prior to DW 2.0 the only data found in data warehousing was operational structured information. But with DW 2.0, there was the recognition that unstructured data also belonged in the data warehouse.

Yet another revelation of DW 2.0 was the recognition that metadata was an integral part of the infrastructure. DW 2.0 recognized that enterprise metadata was as important as local metadata. And finally, at about the time that DW 2.0 was being discussed, it was recognized that the design of data warehouses was greatly enhanced by the advances made by the Data Vault.

But perhaps the greatest advance made by DW 2.0 was the recognition that another form of bulk storage was necessary. DW 2.0 speaks to near line storage. In fact near line storage was a predecessor to Big Data.

Figure 3.1.10 shows the evolution of information architecture surrounding data warehouse.

INTEGRATED CORPORATE DATA

In the beginning were applications. The focus and concern when applications were being built was on automation – the very creation of the application. At the end of the building of the application, if the application could store data and produce reports, the application development was considered to be a success. And soon one application begat another application. In short order applications began to appear all over the corporation as shown in Figure 3.2.1.

Many Applications

When any one application was being built there was little or no attention paid to the other applications that had already been built. Each application had its own requirements and its own specific and unique solution. There was no attempt to have any uniformity of data across the applications. And each application designer did his or her own thing as shown in Figure 3.2.2.

In particular, there was no uniformity of:
- Naming conventions for the same data
- Physical attributions for the same data
- Physical structuring of attributions for the same data
- Encoding of values for the same data

The development of many distinct and unique applications continued and the hallmark of success was whether or not data could be stored and whether reports could be generated.

Looking Across the Corporation

Then one day something interesting happened. Someone looked across the corporation and asked, "*For the corporation, what data values do we have?*" The analyst was not looking at any one application. Instead the analyst wished to look at all data across the corporation. Perhaps the analyst wanted to look at customers across the corporation or revenues across the corporation. Or perhaps the analyst wished to measure product activity across the corporation.

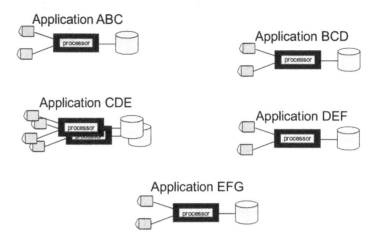

Figure 3.2.1

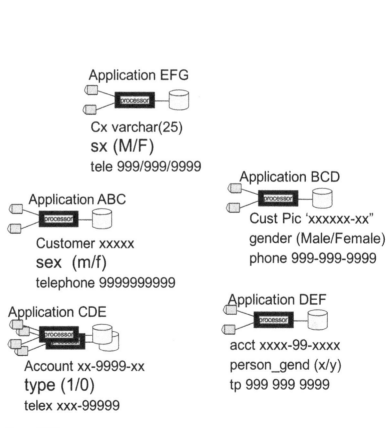

Figure 3.2.2

But once the question was cast in the form of "*For the corporation, …*" problems arose. The analyst could answer questions cast in the form of "*For the application, …*" easily enough. But when it came to looking at data across the corporation, there was a problem because there was no common understanding of data across the corporation.

Figure 3.2.3 shows the analyst struggling to look at data across the corporation. The struggling analyst had several bad choices. The analyst could selectively select data from the applications and hope that he or she had picked the data properly. Or the analyst could roll up his or her sleeves, dig, and try to integrate the data.

In any case, trying to create a corporate understanding of data from a foundation of applications was a very difficult thing to do (as the analyst found out).

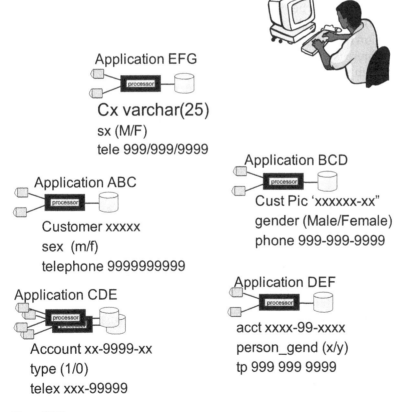

Application EFG

Cx varchar(25)
sx (M/F)
tele 999/999/9999

Application BCD

Cust Pic 'xxxxxx-xx"
gender (Male/Female)
phone 999-999-9999

Application ABC

Customer xxxxx
sex (m/f)
telephone 9999999999

Application DEF

acct xxxx-99-xxxx
person_gend (x/y)
tp 999 999 9999

Application CDE

Account xx-9999-xx
type (1/0)
telex xxx-99999

Figure 3.2.3

More Than One Analyst

But the problem did not stop when one analyst wished to look across the corporation. The problem became exacerbated when more than one analyst tried to look across the corporation. When there is more than one analyst trying to look across the corporation, the following occurs:

- No two analysts select the same data in the same way. When analysts compare results, they are at odds with each other. Each analyst is convinced that he or she has the right data.
- One day an analyst wishes to recreate a report. The problem is that the analyst cannot remember exactly how the first report was created. So the analyst creates the report again, but creates it in a different fashion.
- Management becomes frustrated with the conflicting reports given by different analysts. Management tells the analysts to reconcile the data. The problem is that the analysts cannot reconcile their data.
- Every time management wants a new analysis, some analyst from somewhere must start from scratch.
- When an analyst goes through the pain of integrating application data, no one is able to reuse the work the analyst has done. There is no reusability of integration.

Figure 3.2.4 shows the problems with multiple analysts trying to operate on the basis of application data.

The problems of trying to do corporate analysis based on application data are such that at some point the corporation simply gives up and faces the problem squarely. Instead of looking at the problem as an analytical problem, the organization recognizes that it has an integration problem.

ETL Technology

It is at this point that the organization decides to build an integrated corporate store of data. Another name for the integrated store of corporate data is a data warehouse. The means by which the organization goes about building the data warehouse is through ETL (which stands for extract/transform/load) technology. With ETL technology the many different forms of application data are integrated into a single form of data. The single form of data becomes "integrated corporate data." The net result of transformation is that there is a single definition of usable data for the corporation. The transformation of data includes:

- Standardizing naming conventions
- Standardizing physical attribution of data

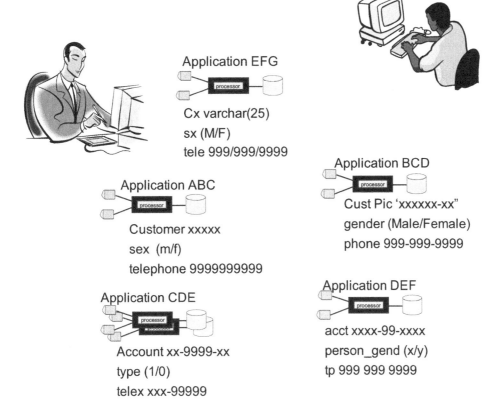

Application EFG

Cx varchar(25)
sx (M/F)
tele 999/999/9999

Application BCD

Cust Pic 'xxxxxx-xx"
gender (Male/Female)
phone 999-999-9999

Application ABC

Customer xxxxx
sex (m/f)
telephone 9999999999

Application DEF

acct xxxx-99-xxxx
person_gend (x/y)
tp 999 999 9999

Application CDE

Account xx-9999-xx
type (1/0)
telex xxx-99999

Figure 3.2.4

- Standardizing encoded values of data
- Standardizing calculations of data
- Standardizing classifications of data

Figure 3.2.5 shows the effects of the creation of the integrated store of corporate data.

The Challenges of Integration

There is no argument that the process of standardizing the older legacy data is a complex and tedious job. It is especially difficult because:

- Many older systems were never documented properly.
- Many older systems had data in very different structures.
- Many older systems had data that was never designed to be integrated with other data.

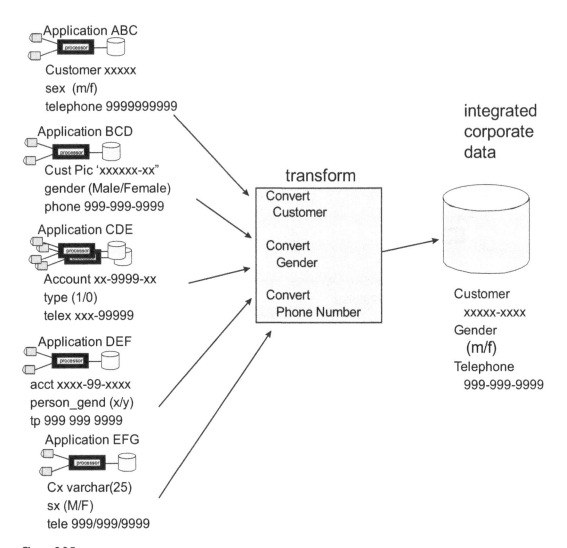

Figure 3.2.5

- Many older systems were in very diverse and older technologies.
- Some older systems had a very large amount of data.
- Many older systems had data on unreliable storage mechanisms.
  Although there were many other challenges to the integration of application data into integrated corporate data, the good news was that there is technology that can automate the process of integration of corporate data. ETL technology is shown in Figure 3.2.6.
  ETL technology is designed to read as input old legacy data. ETL processing is similar in concept to textual disambiguation. But the difference between ETL technology and textual disambiguation

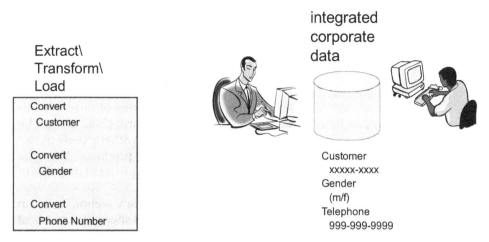

Extract\
Transform\
Load

Convert
  Customer

Convert
  Gender

Convert
  Phone Number

integrated
corporate
data

Customer
xxxxx-xxxx
Gender
  (m/f)
Telephone
  999-999-9999

Figure 3.2.6   **Figure 3.2.7**

is that ETL is designed to operate on older legacy data as input whereas textual disambiguation is designed to operate on raw text as input. From a high conceptual standpoint, textual disambiguation and ETL look very similar. But from the standpoint of mechanics of operation, textual disambiguation and ETL are very different.

One of the remarkable aspects of ETL is the diversity of function that it has. Any one activity of ETL is not terribly difficult. But taken together, all of the functions of ETL are really difficult.

The Benefits of a Data Warehouse

Once the organization has made the investment to create integrated corporate data, there are many benefits (see Figure 3.2.7). Some of the many benefits of having a data warehouse include:

- Data is immediately available to the analyst. The data exists in a data warehouse and awaits analysis. There is no integration work required in order to begin analysis.
- Data is integrated consistently for all analysts. One analyst does not integrate data one way and another analyst does not integrate data another way.
- Data reconciliation is a real possibility. If there is a discrepancy in the results achieved by any two analysts, it is a simple matter to do a reconciliation.
- If an entirely new analysis needs to be built, there is a foundation of data on which to build.
- If it becomes necessary to do compliance or an audit, there is a believable foundation that stands ready for analysis.

The Granular Perspective

There is another way to look at integrated corporate data, or a data warehouse. The other perspective is that a data warehouse is like a bucketful of grains of sand. The sand can be reshaped in many ways.

Consider silicon. Silicon is like a lot of grains of sand. But silicon can be reshaped into many different forms. Silicon can be used to make computer chips, soda bottles, synthetic body parts, children's toys, jewelry, and many more products. The data found in the data warehouse is analogically equivalent to grains of silicon. Figure 3.2.8 shows the equivalency.

Once the organization has created its data warehouse, it can then be used for many purposes. Figure 3.2.9 shows the grains of sand in the data warehouse.

Of the many uses of the granular data found in the data warehouse, one of the most useful is that the grains of silicon can be recast into many different forms. Marketing can look at the data one way. Accounting can look at the same data another way. And finance can look at the same data yet another way. And through it all there is a single foundation that can be used for reconcilability, if needed. Figure 3.2.10 shows the versatility of the granular data found in the data warehouse.

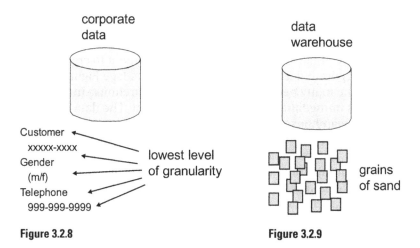

Figure 3.2.8

Figure 3.2.9

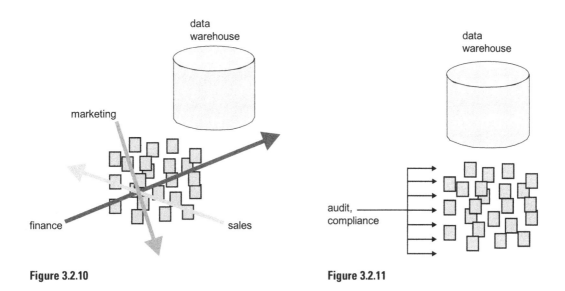

Figure 3.2.10   **Figure 3.2.11**

Not every organization is concerned with compliance. But in a world where there is Basel II, the Sarbanes-Oxley Act, and the Health Insurance Portability and Accountability Act (HIPAA) (and others), most large organizations have some need for compliance. Where there is a need for compliance, a data warehouse serves as an ideal foundation, as shown in Figure 3.2.11.

3.3

HISTORICAL DATA

Keeping data over time has always been problematic. For a variety of reasons keeping a historical record of data has had its problems. Figure 3.3.1 shows that storing historical data has always been a challenge.

The first challenge of storing historical data was that of the cost of storage. In the early days of computing, the cost of storage was a significant factor. The good news was that in the early days of computing, there really wasn't all that much historical data.

Figure 3.3.2 shows that storing a lot of historical data in the early days of computing was an issue because of the cost of storage. But the cost of storage rapidly fell and the capacity of storage grew, to the point that keeping a volume of historical data was no longer a great issue.

But almost as soon as there was disk storage and a database management system (DBMS), there began to be online real-time processing. With online processing came the issue of transaction performance. Prior to online transaction processing, transaction performance was a nonissue. But the minute that there was high-performance transaction processing, the amount of historical data that was kept by the system became a real issue.

System tuners found out that the less historical data they kept, the faster online transaction processing became. Therefore, in the face of online transaction processing systems, it was desirable to keep the minimum of historical data in the system as shown in Figure 3.3.3.

After online transaction processing had been around for a while, it was discovered that there was a need for integrated corporate data. And with this recognition, data warehouse soon appeared.

For the first time, with the data warehouse, there was a place for historical data. Storage was cheap enough and there was no need to accommodate high-performance transaction processing. So historical data had a natural place in the information systems of the organization, which is shown in Figure 3.3.4.

But there was another interesting reason why historical data fit well with data warehousing. It became popular to start to do

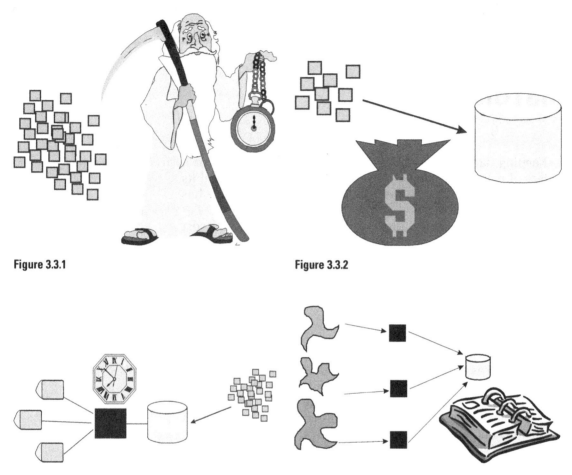

Figure 3.3.1

Figure 3.3.2

Figure 3.3.3

Figure 3.3.4

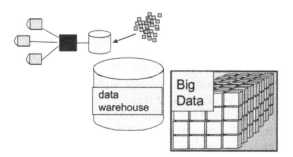

Figure 3.3.5

deeply analytical processing on data, especially customer data. And it was discovered that historical data was a natural fit with analyzing the likes and dislikes of a customer. Customers are creatures of habit. The patterns formed early in a customer's life stick with the customer for a long time. Therefore, having historical data was quite useful when it came to understanding customers. But the evolution did not end there. One day there was Big Data. With the advent of Big Data, it became natural to have a cheap place to store historical data. Figure 3.3.5 shows the hierarchy of processing and storage and how with Big Data, there now was an easy fit with historical data.

DATA MARTS

The essence of the data warehouse is granular data. The granular data found in the data warehouse forms the foundation for business intelligence (BI) and many other forms of analysis.

Granular Data

Figure 3.4.1 shows the granular data that is at the heart of the data warehouse. From a database design perspective, the granular data at the heart of the data warehouse is best shaped around database design that is relational. The relational model is ideal for the data warehouse because when data is shaped around the data model it is:
- Nonredundant
- Organized around the major subject areas of the corporation
- Organized in a manner where many different business relationships can be realized

In addition, in the relational model for the data warehouse there is no summarized or aggregated data.

Relational Database Design

When the granular data is designed using the relational data model, the data warehouse is prepared to serve many different perspectives of data as depicted in Figure 3.4.2.

From a practical standpoint, the granular data found in the data warehouse serves many purposes. But many users want the granular data to be summarized or otherwise aggregated in order to do their analysis. While the data warehouse serves as a foundation of data, in order to serve the different needs of the users, it is more convenient for end users to look at their data in a less granular manner. Furthermore different users have different perspectives. Marketing wants to look at their data one way. Accounting wants to look at their data another way. Sales has yet a different understanding of data. And finance has their own unique understanding of data.

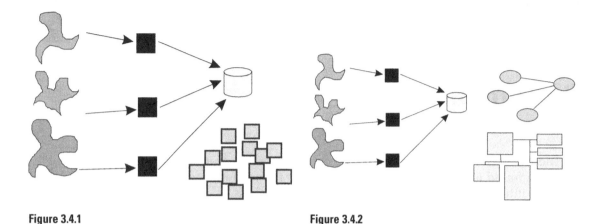

Figure 3.4.1   Figure 3.4.2

The Data Mart

In order to service the different needs for unique views of summarized and aggregated data, a different data structure is used – the data mart. Figure 3.4.3 shows that data marts emanate from the data warehouse.

Figure 3.4.3 shows that each different organization has its own perspective of data. All data begins with the granular data found in the data warehouse. But the different interpretation of data is created for each different department from that granular data. Note that while each department has its own interpretation of data, *all* data is still reconcilable to the common data warehouse. Also note that if it is desired to build a new data mart, the data in the data warehouse is available for the immediate construction of a new perspective of data.

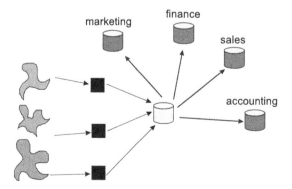

Figure 3.4.3

Key Performance Indicators

It is a normal practice for data marts to contain what are called "key performance indicators" (KPIs). Every organization has several KPIs. KPIs often track such important measurements as revenue, profitability, production, growth in customer base, and new product acceptance.

Usually a KPI is measured over time, typically monthly. By looking at KPIs over time, an organization can start to track progress (or lack thereof). Each department will typically have a different set of KPIs for the department.

An interesting aspect of KPIs are that they change over time. At one moment in time the organization is interested in profitability. There will be one set of KPIs that measure profitability. At another moment in time the organization is interested in market share. There will be another set of KPIs that measure market share. As the focus of the corporation changes over time, so do the KPIs that measure that focus.

The Dimensional Model

The database design for the data mart that is optimal is the dimensional model. Figure 3.4.4 shows that there is a different and unique dimensional model for each data mart.

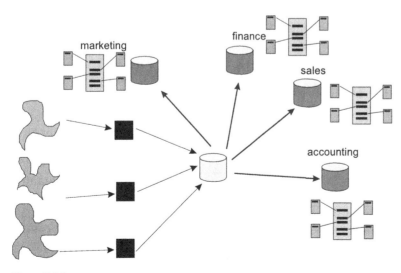

Figure 3.4.4

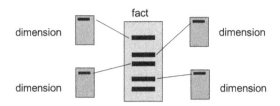

Figure 3.4.5

The dimensional model is unique for each different department. The source of all data for the dimensional model is the data warehouse.

The dimensional model is sometimes called the "star join" or sometimes called the "snowflake" model. The dimensional model consists of a fact table and dimensions. Figure 3.4.5 shows a typical dimensional model.

Usually the fact table consists of a table that occurs many times. The dimension describes some aspect of the fact table, such as time, or product description, or customer name.

The main value of the dimensional model is that it is easy to construct and easy to analyze. Data found in the dimensional model is so easy to construct that oftentimes when changes need to be made to the dimensional model it is easier to construct a new model than it is to do maintenance on an older model that it out of date.

Note that the dimensional model does not have changes made to the data found in the model. If changes to data need to be made to the data in the dimensional model, the data is "refreshed." In a refreshment, whole new rows of data are added to the dimensional model.

Combining the Data Warehouse and Data Marts

The data warehouse combines with the dimensional model to form an analytic environment that is suitable for servicing the analytical needs of the organization. A typical arrangement is seen in Figure 3.4.6.

Figure 3.4.6 shows that the data warehouse holds the granular data of the corporation that serves as the single version of the truth. All data marts are fed from the data warehouse. As such, the data marts are called "dependent data marts" because the only data found in the data marts is data that comes from the data warehouse. It is possible to create "independent data marts" where the source of data is something other than the data warehouse.

There are, however, many problems with independent data marts. Independent data marts:
- Do not have data that can be reconciled with other data marts
- Require their own independent integration of raw data
- Do not provide a foundation that can be built on whenever there are future analytical needs

Note that Figure 3.4.6 shows that the majority of analytical processing is done at the data mart. Only rarely does an analyst have to go against the data found in the data warehouse.

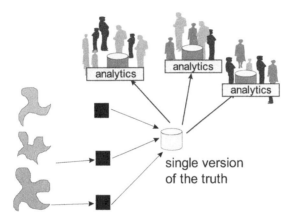

Figure 3.4.6

THE OPERATIONAL DATA STORE

In most organizations the operational environment and the data warehouse environment constitute the backbone of the day-to-day processing and decision making. In addition there are usually data marts that emanate from the data warehouse. Figure 3.5.1 shows this standard architecture

Online Transaction Processing on Integrated Data

There are, however, circumstances where other kinds of processing than operational processing and data warehouse processing are warranted. Not every organization has these needs. But some organizations find themselves in a different set of circumstances.

In order to understand the need for a different kind of data structure, consider the classical environment, as shown in Figure 3.5.2. Figure 3.5.2 shows that there is a convenient place for online transaction processing and there is a convenient place for housing integrated, historical data. Once the integrated historical data – the "system of record" or "the single version of the truth" – is created, there is a foundation for analytical processing.

Occasionally organizations find they have a need for online transaction processing for integrated data. Looking at Figure 3.5.2 we see that there is no place for online transaction processing of integrated historical data.

The Operational Data Store

When there is a need for online transaction processing of integrated data, a different type of data structure is needed. An operational data store (ODS) is needed.

There are many reasons why an organization needs an ODS. One reason is because their operational systems are unintegrated and intractable. For a variety of reasons organizations sometimes arrive at the point where they have unintegrated operational systems and the operational systems cannot be rewritten or reshaped.

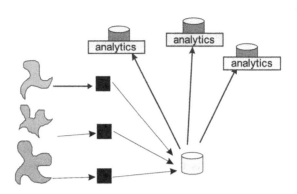

Figure 3.5.1

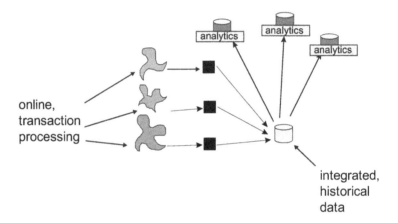

Figure 3.5.2

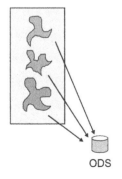

ODS

Figure 3.5.3

When an organization needs integrated data and cannot modify or alter their existing systems environment they need an ODS, as shown in Figure 3.5.3.

But there may be other reasons why an organization needs an ODS. Another motivation for an ODS stems from the fact that occasionally an organization needs to do online updating to integrated data. Since online updating is *never* done in a data warehouse, for *any* purpose the place to do online updating is the ODS. (Figure 3.5.4 shows that online update is never done in a data warehouse.)

There may be other motivations for an ODS as well. But for whatever reason an organization awakes one day and discovers that it needs an ODS. Figure 3.5.5 shows that an ODS has been added to the standard operating environment of an organization.

Figure 3.5.5 shows that operational applications can send their transaction data to the ODS. The data may be sent directly

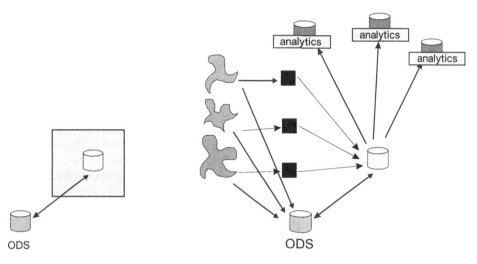

Figure 3.5.4   Figure 3.5.5

to the ODS or the data may pass through the ETL interface. After the data settles in the ODS, there may be an interface to the data warehouse as well.

Once the data has been loaded into the ODS, online transactions can occur there. The ODS environment is built so that it can support high-performance online transaction processing. In addition, data in the ODS is integrated.

ODS and the Data Warehouse

At first glance the ODS appears to be very much like the data warehouse. Indeed the ODS and the data warehouse do have some common characteristics. But they also have some distinct differences. Figure 3.5.6 shows how a data warehouse and an ODS compare to each other.

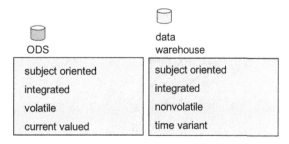

Figure 3.5.6

Both the ODS and a data warehouse contain subject-oriented, integrated information. In that regard they are similar. But an ODS contains data that can be individually updated, deleted, or added. And a data warehouse contains nonvolatile data. A data warehouse contains snapshots of data. Once the snapshot is taken, the data in the data warehouse does not change. So when it comes to volatility, a data warehouse and an ODS are very different.

Another major difference between the ODS and the data warehouse is in terms of the timeliness of data found in the different environments. A data warehouse contains data over a lengthy period of time. It is normal for a data warehouse to contain 5 to 10 years' worth of data. An ODS, however, rarely contains more than 30 days' worth of data. So there is a major difference in the amount of historical data held in a data warehouse and an ODS.

ODS Classes

ODS can be divided into three classes. There is a class I ODS, a class II ODS, and a class III ODS. The class an ODS belongs in depends entirely on the speed with which data comes from the operational environment and goes into the ODS. Figure 3.5.7 shows that there are different classes of ODS.

A class I ODS is one where the speed coming from the operational environment to the ODS is measured in milliseconds. In a class I ODS, data is updated into the operational environment at 10:56:15 in the morning and the same data enters the ODS environment at 10:56:16. The transfer of data occurs so quickly that the end user does not even know that there has been an instant of time where the two environment were not in synch with each other.

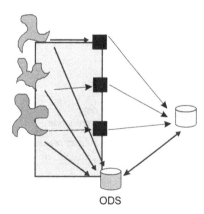

ODS

Figure 3.5.7

In a class II ODS, the synchronization of data from the operational environment to the ODS is a matter of hours. In a class II ODS, an update occurs to the operational environment at 10:56:15 in the morning and the ODS is updated by 3:00 that same afternoon.

In a class III ODS, operational data is updated at 10:56:15 in the morning and the movement of data to the ODS does not occur until the next day.

All three classes of ODS are valid and have their place. A class I ODS optimizes the speed of movement throughout the system. The technology to accomplish a class I ODS is expensive and complex. In addition there is hardly any time at all to alter the data as it enters the ODS. In truth there are not may class I ODS.

A class II ODS is much more common. The technology to create a class II ODS environment is common and not terribly expensive or complex. And there is plenty of time to alter the data as it goes from the operational environment to the ODS environment.

A class III ODS is very common. The technology required to implement a class III ODS is very straightforward and there is plenty of time to make any alterations of data necessary to the data as it passes into the ODS.

The only circumstance that warrants a class I ODS is where there are pressing business reasons why data has to be treated in such a hurry. There are many business circumstances where a class II or a class III ODS provides the business function that is needed.

External Updates into the ODS

A related issue is that on occasion data needs to be placed into the ODS from a source other than the legacy systems environment. Figure 3.5.8 shows that there may be sources of data

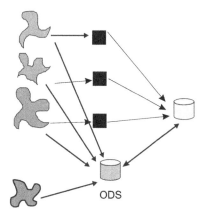

ODS

Figure 3.5.8

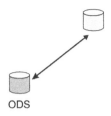

ODS

Figure 3.5.9

other than the legacy systems environment for data entering the ODS.

Data can be updated directly or indirectly when it comes from external sources.

The ODS/Data Warehouse Interface

There is one other peculiarity when it comes to the ODS and the environment in which it operates. That peculiarity is that the interface between the ODS and the data warehouse is a two-way exchange of data.

Figure 3.5.9 shows that the interface goes two ways.

The movement of data from the ODS to the data warehouse is normal and natural. After all, legacy systems pour their data into the data warehouse. But it is possible for there to be a backward flow of data from the data warehouse to the ODS. This backward flow of data occurs when a calculation is made using data warehouse data that affects the processing done in the ODS. For example, a bank may decide to raise its rates based on information found in the data warehouse. Once the bank decides to raise its rates, the rate is passed back to the ODS for doing whatever processing that needs to be done.

There are many other cases where there is a "*backflow*" of data from the data warehouse to the ODS.

WHAT A DATA WAREHOUSE IS NOT

The advent of the data warehouse led to the ability of corporations to:
- Look at data from a corporate perspective
- Look at data from an integrated perspective
- Look at data cross vistas of time
- Have a single foundation that served many communities in the organization.

A Simple Data Warehouse Architecture

As such, data warehousing marked an important event in the maturing of the information environment in the corporation. Figure 3.6.1 depicts a simple data warehouse architecture.

But the advent of the data warehouse also led to some amount of confusion in some environments. There were some instances where people tried to use a data warehouse for something that the data warehouse could not or should not be used for. Over time the errors in judgment as to what as data warehouse was and was not corrected themselves. Over time, the pain and the cost of trying to use a data warehouse for something that it was not intended for caused the organization to go back and use a data warehouse properly.

Online High-Performance Transaction Processing in the Data Warehouse

One of the mistaken thoughts about a data warehouse was that a data warehouse was a foundation for online transaction processing. The thought was that there was data that was being managed by a big, powerful computer. Why not use the data warehouse as a basis for holding data that supported online transaction processing?

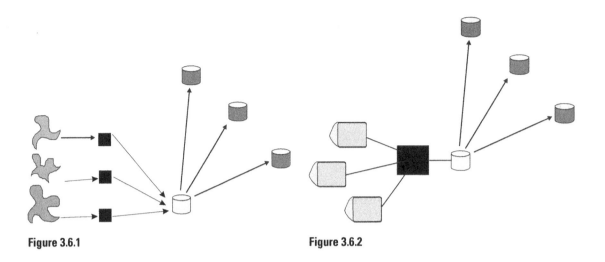

Figure 3.6.1   Figure 3.6.2

Figure 3.6.2 shows that online transaction processing is being done on a data warehouse. So what is wrong with this picture? It turns out that there is plenty that is wrong.

Integrity of Data

The first problem with trying to do online transaction processing against the data in a data warehouse is that the integrity of the data is destroyed. A data warehouse consists of a series of snapshots of data. Each snapshot of data has a moment in time associated with it. As long as the snapshot has been taken properly, going back and changing the data on the snapshot ruins the integrity of the data.

As an example of the loss of integrity of data in the data warehouse, suppose a report is made on data in the data warehouse as of 11:52 a.m. The report is made against the bank balances of people as of that moment in time.

Now at 1:13 p.m. John Jones goes in and withdraws $500 from his account in the data warehouse. Then at 3:34 p.m. someone goes in and runs the exact same report against the data that was run at 11:52 a.m. The report at 3:34 p.m. shows a different result because the data on which the report has been run has changed. Figure 3.6.3 shows these two reports. By allowing online transaction processing to occur against the data in the data warehouse, the integrity of the data is lost.

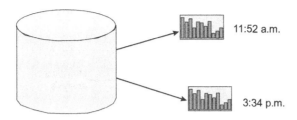

Figure 3.6.3

The Data Warehouse Workload

As important as integrity of data is, it is not the only reason why online transaction processing should not be done against the data in a data warehouse. Another reason is the workload that runs against the data warehouse.

Consider the workload that is suggested by Figure 3.6.4, which shows that there is a mixed workload running against the data warehouse. Some queries are short and fast and other queries are large and bulky. The workload suggested by Figure 3.6.4 is similar to the traffic on a highway. There are speedy Porsches and BMWs on the highway. Then there are large semitrucks on the highway as well – Kenworths and Mack trucks. The workload is a general purpose workload such as you might see on any interstate.

Now consider the workload suggested in Figure 3.6.5. In Figure 3.6.5 the workload is fast and homogenous. It is as if only Porsches and Ferraris were allowed on the track – sort of like the Indianapolis speedway or the Daytona 500. Semitrucks are not allowed to drive on this road.

The homogenous workload is typical for an online high-performance system. In order to get the good consistent response time that is a hallmark of an online high-performance system, the work load must be fast and homogenous.

Stated differently, the types of queries done against a data warehouse prevent the data warehouse from being used by high-performance transaction processing. This then is a second good reason why data warehousing should not be used for high-performance transaction processing.

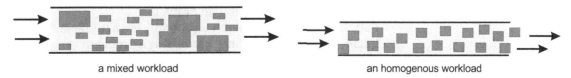

a mixed workload   an homogenous workload

Figure 3.6.4   **Figure 3.6.5**

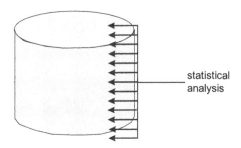

statistical
analysis

Figure 3.6.6

Statistical Processing from the Data Warehouse

Another misuse of the data warehouse experienced by some organizations was using the data warehouse for heavy amounts of statistical processing. Figure 3.6.6 shows that it is a temptation to use the data warehouse as a basis for heavy statistical processing.

A statistical process is normally quite different from a standard query. The difference is in terms of the amount of data accessed by the statistical query. A normal query may access from 10 to 1000 records of data. A normal statistical process may access from 100,000 to 10,000,000 records or more. The amount of resources used by a statistical process is orders of magnitude larger than the resources used by a standard query process.

There is an old saying: "When you run a statistical process, the lights go out." The implication is that the processing done by the statistical query uses so many resources that it sucks up all available electricity.

The Frequency of Statistical Processing

In truth, most modern processors *can* do statistical processing. It is just that they cannot do statistical processing very often without damaging the regular users of the data warehouse. It is more a matter of how often can a statistical process be done than a matter of can it be done at all.

A typical pattern of usage looks like this:
1 statistical process a year = no problem
1 statistical process a quarter = probably not a problem
1 statistical process a month = probably a problem
1 statistical process a week = problem
1 statistical process a day = no way
1 statistical process an hour = forget it

The Exploration Warehouse

So what does an organization do if it needs to run regular statistical processing (as some organizations need to do)? In the eventuality that there is a need to run regular statistical processing against data, there is a need to build a specialized structure called an *"exploration warehouse."* Figure 3.6.7 shows an exploration warehouse.

An exploration warehouse has many similarities to a data warehouse. But there are some distinct differences. Some of the differences between a data warehouse and an exploration warehouse are:

- The data warehouse is a persistent structure, whereas the exploration warehouse is built on a project or as-needed basis.
- The data warehouse is built to accommodate business intelligence (BI) software, whereas the exploration warehouse is built to accommodate statistical analysis software.
- The data warehouse contains data that is highly normalized, whereas the exploration warehouse often contains data that is edited (sometimes called *"convenience fields"*), in anticipation of the statistical analysis that will be done.
- The data warehouse contains data from the legacy environment, whereas the exploration warehouse contains data from the legacy environment and external. In truth, the data warehouse normally does not contain much (if any) external data, whereas the exploration warehouse contains a lot of external data.

But other than these differences, there is considerable overlap between the data warehouse and the exploration warehouse and there are lots of advantages to the exploration warehouse. But the primary advantage is that when it comes time to do statistical analysis, statisticians can do anything they wish to do with the exploration warehouse and create no effect whatsoever on the data

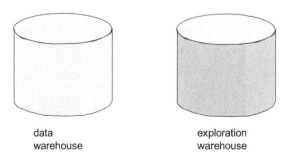

data
warehouse

exploration
warehouse

Figure 3.6.7

warehouse. The existence of the exploration warehouse insulates the environment from the ravages of resources used in exploration processing.

Figure 3.6.8 shows the data warehouse and the exploration warehouse in a complementary juxtaposition to each other.

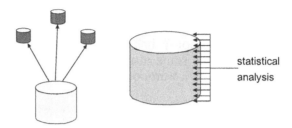

statistical
analysis

Figure 3.6.8

4.1

INTRODUCTION TO DATA VAULT

Data Vault 2.0 (DV2) is a system of business intelligence that includes: modeling, methodology, architecture, and implementation best practices. The components, also known as the *pillars* of DV2 are identified as follows:

- DV2 Modeling (changes to the model for performance and scalability)
- DV2 Methodology (following Scrum and agile best practices)
- DV2 Architecture (including NoSQL systems and Big Data systems)
- DV2 Implementation (pattern-based, automation, generation Capability Maturity Model Integration [CMMI] level 5)

The term "Data Vault" is merely a marketing term chosen in 2001 to represent the system to the market. The true name for the Data Vault System of business intelligence (BI) is "common foundational warehouse architecture." The system includes several aspects that relate to the business of designing, implementing, and managing a data warehouse as shown in Figure 4.1.1.

There are many special aspects of Data Vault, including the modeling style for the enterprise data warehouse. The methodology takes commonsense lessons from software development best practices such as CMMI, Six Sigma, total quality management (TQM), Lean initiatives, and cycle-time reduction and applies these notions for repeatability, consistency, automation, and error reduction.

Each of these components plays a key role in the overall success of an enterprise data warehousing project. These components are combined with industry-known and time-tested best practices ranging from CMMI to Six Sigma, TQM (total quality management) to Project Management Professional (PMP).

Data Vault 1.0 is highly focused on just the data modeling section, while DV2 encompasses the effort of business intelligence. The evolution of Data Vault extends beyond the data model and enables teams to execute in parallel while leveraging Scrum agile best practices. DV2 architecture is designed to include NoSQL (think: Big Data, unstructured, multistructured, and structured data sets). Seamless integration points in the model and

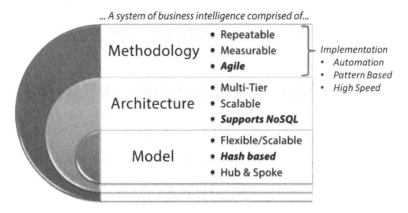

Figure 4.1.1

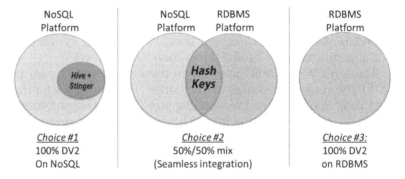

Figure 4.1.2

well-defined standards for implementation offer guidance to the project teams. They can shift the responsibilities to any of the set-ups shown in Figure 4.1.2.

Data Vault 2.0 Modeling

DV2 Modeling is focused on providing flexible, scalable patterns that work together to integrate *raw* data by business key for the enterprise data warehouse. DV2 modeling includes minor changes to ensure the modeling paradigms can work within the constructs of Big Data, unstructured data, multistructured data, and NoSQL. Data Vault Modeling changes the sequence numbers for hash keys. The hash keys provide stability, parallel loading methods, and decoupled computing of parent key values for records.

Data Vault 2.0 Methodology Defined

DV2 Methodology focuses on two- to three-week sprint cycles with adaptations and optimizations for repeatable data warehousing tasks. The idea of DV2 Methodology is to enable the team with agile data warehousing and business intelligence best practices. DV2 encompasses methodology as a pillar or key component in order to achieve the next level of maturity in the data warehousing platform.

Data Vault 2.0 Architecture

We need DV2 Architecture because it includes NoSQL, real-time feeds, and Big Data systems for unstructured data handling and Big Data integration. The architecture also provides a basis for defining what components fit where, and how they should integrate. In addition, the architecture provides a guideline for incorporating aspects such as managed self-service BI, business write back, natural language processing (NLP) result set integration, and direction for where to handle unstructured and multistructured data sets.

Data Vault 2.0 Implementation

DV2 Implementation fits in by focusing on automation and generation patterns for timesavings, error reduction, and rapid productivity of the data warehousing team. The DV2 implementation standards provide rules and working guidelines for high-speed reliable build-out with little to no errors in the process. The DV2 implementation standards dictate where and how specific business rules execute in the process chain, indicating how to decouple the business changes or data provisioning from data acquisition.

Business Benefits of Data Vault 2.0

There are hundreds of benefits, far too many to list, all of which are drawn from the existing best practices of CMMI, Six Sigma, TQM, PMP, Scrum agile, automation, and so on. However, the reason for DV2 BI systems can be nicely summed up in one word: *maturity.*

Maturity of the BI and data warehousing systems require the following key elements:
- Repeatable patterns
- Redundant architecture and fault-tolerant systems

- High scalability
- Extreme flexibility
- Managed consistent costs for absorbing changes
- Measurable key process areas (KPAs)
- Gap analysis (for the business of building data warehouses)
- Incorporation of Big Data and unstructured data

From a business perspective, DV2 addresses the needs of Big Data, unstructured data, multistructured data, NoSQL, and managed self-service BI. DV2 really is targeted at the evolution of the *system of data warehousing (enterprise data warehouse(EDW)) and BI.* DV2's goal is to mature the processes of building BI systems for the enterprise in a repeatable, consistent, and scalable fashion while providing seamless integration with new technologies (i.e., NoSQL environments).

The resulting business benefits include (but are not limited to) the following:

- Lowering total cost of ownership (TCO) for EDW/BI programs
- Increasing agility of the entire team (including delivery)
- Increasing transparency across the program

The resulting business benefits can be found in the following categories:

Data Vault 2.0 Agile Methodology Benefits	Data Vault 2.0 Model Benefits
– Drives agile deliveries (2–3 weeks)	– Follows scale-free architecture
– Includes CMM, Six Sigma, TQM	– Based on hub and spoke design
– Manages risk, governance, versioning	– Backed by set logic and massively parallel processing (MPP) math
– Defines automation, generation	– Includes seamless integration of NoSQL data sets
– Designs repeatable optimized processes	
– Combines best practices for BI	– Enables 100% parallel heterogeneous loading environments
	– Limits impacts of changes to localized areas

Data Vault 2.0 Architecture Benefits	Data Vault 2.0 Methodology Benefits
– Enhances decoupling	– Enhances automation
– Ensures low-impact changes	– Ensures scalability
– Provides managed self-service BI	– Provides consistency
– Includes seamless NoSQL platforms	– Includes fault-tolerance
– Enables team agility	– Provides proven standards

Data Vault 1.0

Data Vault 1.0 is highly focused on the Data Vault Modeling components (to be introduced shortly). A Data Vault 1.0 model attaches surrogate sequence keys as its primary key selection for each of the entity types. Unfortunately surrogate sequences exhibit the following problems:

- Introduce dependencies on the ETL/ELT loading paradigm
- Contain an upper bound/upper limit; when reached can cause issues
- Are meaningless numbers (mean absolutely nothing to the business)
- Cause performance problems (due to dependencies) on load of Big Data sets
- Reduce parallelism (again due to dependencies) of loading processes
- Cannot be used as MPP partition keys for data placement, to do so would potentially cause hot spots in the MPP platform
- Cannot be reliably rebuilt or reassigned (reattached to their old values) during recovery loads

Data Vault 1.0 *does not* meet the needs of Big Data, unstructured data, semistructured data, or very large relational data sets.

INTRODUCTION TO DATA VAULT MODELING

A Data Vault Model Concept

From a conceptual level, the Data Vault model is a hub-and-spoke–based model, designed to focus its integration patterns around business keys. These business keys are the keys to the information stored across multiple systems (hopefully the master keys), used to locate and uniquely identify records or data. From a conceptual level, these business keys stand alone, meaning they don't rely on other information in order to exist.

The concepts are derived from business context (or business ontologies), which are elements that make sense to the business from a master data perspective, such as customer, product, service, and so on. These concepts are business drivers at the lowest level of grain. The Data Vault model *does not* subscribe to the notion of supertype and subtype unless that is the way the source systems are providing the data.

Data Vault Model Defined

A Data Vault model is a detail-oriented, historical tracking, and uniquely linked set of normalized tables that support one or more functional areas of business. In Data Vault 2.0, the model entities are keyed by hashes, where in Data Vault 1.0 the model entities are keyed by sequences.

The modeling style is a hybrid of third normal form techniques and dimensional modeling techniques, uniquely combined to meet the needs of the enterprise. The Data Vault model is also based on patterns found in hub-and-spoke type diagramming, otherwise known as "scale-free network" design.

Figure 4.2.1 is an example of a Data Vault model.

These design patterns enable the Data Vault model to inherit scale-free attributes, meaning there is no known inherent limitation on the size of the model or the size of data that the model can represent, other than those limitations imposed by the infrastructure.

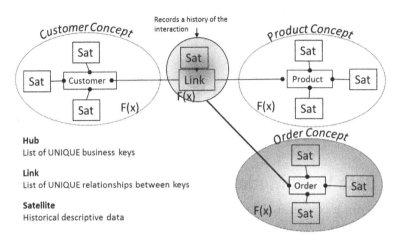

Figure 4.2.1 Data Vault Conceptual model

Components of a Data Vault Model

There are three basic entities or structures in a Data Vault model: hub, link, and satellite. In business terms, the hubs represent the actual business keys or master key sets that exist across the enterprise in a horizontal fashion. The links represent the relationships and associations that exist across the business keys in the enterprise. The real *data warehousing* components are the satellites, which store nonvolatile data over time.

The Data Vault model is based on normalization and separation of classes of data. In this particular case, the business keys (hubs) are considered a different class than the relationships (links). Both of these types are separated by *context* or descriptive information (satellites), which has a tendency to change over time.

Business keys

Business keys are the drivers in business and this is what makes them so interesting. They tie the data set to the business processes and the business processes to the business requirements. Without business keys, the data set has no value. Business keys are the sole source of tracking of the data through the business processes, across lines of business.

Figure 4.2.2 represents several concepts, starting with a full-scale enterprise. The blue boxes represent hundreds of individual business processes that occur within the business. The blue boxes are tied together through a business process life cycle. The

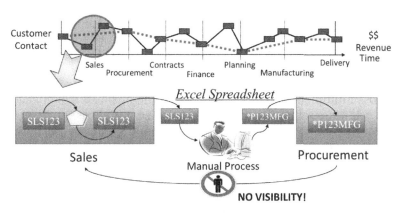

Figure 4.2.2 Business Keys across Lines of Business

objective of this organization is to identify the critical path (as they are engaged in cycle time reduction and lean initiatives). The critical path of the business processes is labeled with a dotted line.

> *Note: The critical path is an important part to overhead cost reduction, time to market delivery, and quality improvements. By identifying the critical path in the organization, the company can achieve "better, faster, and cheaper" throughout the enterprise. Identifying and tracking the data through the business processes is necessary in order to trace the critical path through company's business processes.*

Within each of the business processes, the business keys are identified. This is how the source systems and the individuals in the organization track and manage the data and contracts underneath. The business keys (in this example, SLS123) originate in the sales systems. When these keys cross the process boundaries from sales to procurement, a manual process takes place. The result of the manual process is to change the business key from *SLS123* to **P123MFG*. Unfortunately, the manual change to the business keys (in this example) is not recorded anywhere except in an external Excel spreadsheet.

Data Vault and Data Warehousing

As stated earlier, the objective is to lower total cost of ownership (TCO) in the organization. This means reducing overhead costs, increasing quality of the deliverable, and decreasing the amount of time to deliver the product or service. A properly designed and implemented Data Vault data warehouse can help with these tasks, including the discovery and tracing activities needed to identify critical path.

The ability to track and trace the data set across multiple lines of business is part of creating value or treating data as an asset on the books. Without traceability back to the business processes, data becomes nearly valueless.

Critical path analysis in the business and establishing the trace across multiple lines of business means the business can engage in cycle-time reduction (or Lean enterprise initiatives) and gives them the ability to identify critical path and eliminate business processes that add no value and only lend themselves to slowing down the production and delivery of the product or service. Understanding the path of the data (identified by business keys) across the multiple lines of business can actually show the critical path and the long-standing business processes that need to be addressed in cycle-time reduction efforts.

By tracking the business processes to the data through business keys, it is easier to not only assign value, but understand the gaps in the business perception (i.e., requirements they provide to the enterprise data warehouse (EDW) team) and the reality of what multiple source systems are capturing and executing on.

One of the end results from this process is to help (hopefully) understand where the business may be hemorrhaging money. When they close the gap through total quality management (TQM) best practices, they stop the money loss and potentially increase revenue and quality of the product or service at the same time.

Translating to Data Vault Modeling

The Data Vault model, more specifically the hub table, shows how many different keys there are across the entire business. The hub table tracks when each key is inserted to the warehouse and from what source application it arrived in. The hub table does not track anything else. In order to understand the "changing of the business keys" from one line of business to another, the data warehouse needs another table structure and another source feed.

The next table structure that the Data Vault uses is called a "link." The link structure houses the feed from the manual process, for example, FROM SLS123 TO *P123MFG, otherwise known as a same-as link structure.

An example Data Vault 2.0 model for this case is shown in Figure 4.2.3. The Hub Customer represents the two keys found in the business process. The Link Same-As shows their connection, with the record source being "Joes Excel," meaning the Data Vault loads processed an Excel spreadsheet based on the manual process. The Link Satellite Effectivity provides the timeline for when the relationship starts and stops. Satellites are where the descriptive data lives and breathes.

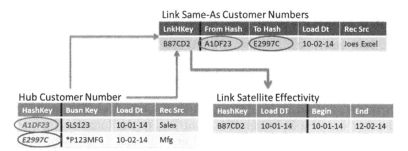

Figure 4.2.3 Data Vault 2.0 Data model

Satellites carry more than just effectivity. In the case of customers (not shown here), the satellite may carry additional descriptive details such as their names, addresses, and phone numbers. Other examples of satellites and satellite data are provided further on in this section.

The link in this case carries the key matches (from and to). This type of link structure can be used to connect master key selections or to explain the mapping and changing of keys from one source system to another. It can also be used to represent multilevel hierarchies (not shown here).

> *Note: The importing of the Excel spreadsheet shows the first step toward managed self-service business intelligence (SSBI). Managed SSBI is the next step in the evolution of data warehousing, allowing the business users to interact with the raw data sets in the warehouse and affect their own information marts by changing the data.*

The Data Vault model not only provides immediate business value but is capable of tracking all relationships over time. It also demonstrates the different hierarchies of data (even though this is highly focused on two particular business keys at the moment) that are possible for loading into the warehouse.

By tracking the changes to business keys, the relationship across and between business keys, the business can then begin to ask and answer the following questions:

- How *long* does my customer account stay in sales before it is passed to procurement?
- Can I compare an AS-SOLD image with an AS-CONTRACTED, and an AS-MANUFACTURED image with an AS-FINANCED image?
- How many actual customers do I really have?
- How long does it take for a customer, product, or service to make it from "initial sale" to "final delivery" in my business?

Many of these questions cannot be answered without a consistent business key that spans the different lines of business.

Data Restructure

Data restructuring from the staging area allows integration across multiple systems into a single place in the target data warehouse without changing the data set itself (i.e., no conformity). This is called "passive integration." It is considered integrated by business key, but passively (again because there is no change to the raw data). It is integrated according to the location (i.e., all individual customer account numbers will exist in the same hub, while all corporate customer account numbers exist in a different hub).

Basic Rules of Data Vault Modeling

There are some fundamental rules in Data Vault Modeling that must be followed, or the model itself no longer qualifies to be a Data Vault model. These rules are documented in a classroom environment in full. However, some of the rules are as follows:

1. Business keys are separated by grain and semantic meaning. That means the keys customer corporation and customer individual must exist or be recorded in two separate hub structures.
2. Relationships, events, and intersections across two or more business keys are placed into link structures.
3. Link structures have no begin or end dates; they are merely an expression of the relationship at the time the data arrived in the warehouse.
4. Satellites are separated by type of data and classification and rate of change. Type of data is typically a single source system.

Raw Data Vault Modeling does not allow nor provide for the concepts or notions such as conformity, nor does it deal with supertypes. Those responsibilities fall into the business vault models (another form of Data Vault Modeling that is used as an information delivery layer).

Why We Need Many-to-Many Link Structures

Many-to-many link structures allow the Data Vault model to be future proof extensible. The relationships expressed in source systems are often a reflection of business rules or business execution *today*. The relationship definition has changed over time and will continue to change. To represent history, as well as future data (without reengineering the model and the load routines), many-to-many relationship tables are necessary.

It is in this fashion that the Data Vault 2.0 data warehouse can expose the patterns of relationship changes over time. This means we can ask where the gap is between "current requirements" and "relationships" in history. Because of the many-to-many table (link), the raw Data Vault provides metrics around what percentage of data is "broken" and when it breaks the relationship requirement.

For example, in the past, for a sample customer, it was common to have one portfolio manager. Today, the company might have three or more portfolio managers. If the data warehouse model enforces the "past" relationship (many customers to one portfolio manager) then, in order to support today's relationship, the data model and the ELT/ETL loading routines would have to be reengineered.

Reengineering costs money, an ever-increasing amount (as the data set grows and the model grows), the time and complexity and cost also grow. Eventually this increase in cost and time to maintain outgrows the business ability to pay.

The *only* way to represent both relationships over time is to place the data in a many-to-many link table, then based on requirements to query (and provide data marts downstream), the warehouse can tell the business users exactly what they have and when it "breaks" the current rule.

Hash keys Instead of Sequence Numbers

Hash keys are important to Data Vault 2.0 because of the efforts to connect heterogeneous data environments such as Hadoop. Another reason is to remove the dependency on "loading" the Data Vault 2.0 structures. When dealing with high ingestion rates (i.e., velocity) or big data (variety and volume), the last thing the load routines need is a dependency, forcing the loads to be strung together in a sequential fashion. The loading components and reasoning behind this choice is discussed in another section of this chapter.

In fact, in Big Data systems it is near impossible to scale properly if there are such load dependencies in place. Sequences in Data Vault 1.0 force the hubs to be loaded, then the links, then the satellites, because the child tables, like links, depend on the hub sequences, and the hub satellites depend on the hub sequences, and the link satellites depend on the link sequences, which depend on the hub sequences.

This type of dependency not only slows the loading process down, it kills any potential for parallelism, even with referential integrity shut off. Furthermore it places a dependency into the loading stream in heterogeneous environments; for example, if you are loading satellite data into Hadoop (perhaps a JSON document), you would have to look up the sequence number from a hub in a relational database. This dependency alone defeats the entire purpose of having a system like Hadoop in the first place.

All that said, hash keys are critical to the success of Data Vault 2.0 in a Big Data and NoSQL world. The hash function that has been chosen is MD5 (message digest 5), a 128-bit precomputed number based on the business keys that arrive in the staging areas. All lookup dependencies are hence removed, and the entire system can load in parallel across heterogeneous environments.

The hashing function that is selected for Data Vault 2.0 models is MD5. MD5 produces a precomputed 128-bit 99.8% unique number based on the business key value and business key combinations (for link structures). The data set in the model now can actually be spread across massively parallel processing (MPP) environments by selecting the hash value as the distribution key. This allows for better, mostly random, mostly even distribution across the MPP nodes.

To reach a 50% chance of creating a "collision" (i.e., same hash key for two different business key values), 6 billion new business keys per second per hub would need to be inserted. Chances of getting a collision are extremely rare by using this technique.

Sequence numbers are "old" technology and introduce unwanted dependencies in the relational world. They also (if chosen as the distribution key in MPP) can cause hot spots. Furthermore, sequences have an upper limit to the number of records they can represent, 128-bit hashes increase that limit drastically.

From a modeling perspective, it does mean increasing the storage; the model changes the 128-bit hash to a CHAR(32) length field, turning the column join (previously on numeric) to a character-length 32 join. The join operates just a bit slower, however, having the hash in place more than makes up for this loss in performance on load and cross-system or heterogeneous support.

This is just for the Data Vault 2.0 model, which acts as the enterprise warehouse. It is still possible (and even advisable) to use or leverage sequence numbers in persisted information marts (data marts) downstream in order to engage fastest possible joins within a homogeneous environment.

The largest benefit isn't from the modeling side of the house, it's from the loading and querying perspectives. For loading, it releases the dependencies and allows loads to Hadoop and other NoSQL environments in parallel with loads to relational database management systems (RDBMSs). For querying, it allows "late-join" or run-time binding of data across JDBC and open database connectivity (ODBC) between Hadoop, NoSQL, and RDBMS engines on demand. It is not suggested that it will be fast, but rather that it can be easily accomplished.

Deeper analysis of this subject is covered in Data Vault 2.0 Boot Camp training courses and in Data Vault 2.0 published materials. It is beyond the scope of this book to dive deeper into this subject.

INTRODUCTION TO DATA VAULT ARCHITECTURE

Data Vault 2.0 Architecture

Data Vault 2.0 Architecture is based on three-tier data warehouse architecture. The tiers are commonly identified as staging or landing zone, data warehouse, and information delivery layer (or data marts). Figure 4.3.1 shows an overview of Data Vault 2.0 Architecture.

The multiple tiers allow implementers and designers to decouple the enterprise data warehouse from both sourcing and acquisition functions and information delivery and data provisioning functions. In turn, the team becomes more nimble and the architecture is more resilient to failure and more flexible in responding to changes.

The sections are: staging, enterprise data warehouse (EDW), and information marts or information delivery layer. Regardless of platforms and technology used for implementation, these layers will continue to exist. However, as the system nears full real-time enablement, the need and dependency on the staging area will decline. True real-time data will feed directly into the EDW layer.

In addition to the three tiers, the architecture of Data Vault 2.0 dictates several different components:
1. Hadoop or NoSQL handles Big Data.
2. Real-time information flows both *in* and *out* of the business intelligence (BI) ecosystem; in turn, over time this also evolves the EDW into an operational data warehouse.
3. Managed self-service business intelligence (SSBI) through write-back and master data capabilities is used, enabling total quality management (TQM).
4. Hard and soft business rules are split, making the enterprise data warehouse a *system of record* for raw facts that are loaded over time.

How NoSQL Fits into the Architecture

NoSQL platform implementations will vary. Some will contain SQL-like interfaces; some will contain relational database management system (RDBMS) technology integrated with nonrelational

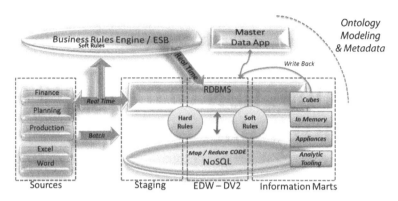

Figure 4.3.1 Data Vault 2.0 Architecture Overview

technology. The line between the two (RDBMS and NoSQL) will continue to be blurred. Eventually, it will be a "data management system" capable of housing both relational and nonrelational data simply by design.

The NoSQL platform today, in most cases, is based on Hadoop at its core, which is comprised of the Hadoop file system (HDFS) or metadata management for files in the different directories. Various implementations of SQL access layers and in-memory technology will sit on top of the HDFS.

Once ACID, which stands for atomicity, consistency, isolation, and durability, compliance is achieved (which is available today with some NoSQL vendors), the differentiation between RDBMS and NoSQL will fade. Note that not all Hadoop or NoSQL platforms offer ACID compliance today, and not all NoSQL platforms offer *update* of records in place making it impossible to completely supplant the RDBMS technology. This is changing quickly. Even as this section is written, the technology continues to advance. Eventually the technology will be seamless and what is purchased from the vendors in this space will be hybrid based.

Current positioning of a platform such as Hadoop is to use it or leverage it as an ingestion area and a staging area for any and all data that might proceed to the warehouse. This includes structured data sets (delimited files, fixed width columnar files), multistructured data sets, such as XML and JSON files, and unstructured data such as Microsoft Word documents, Excel spreadsheets, video, audio, and images. This is because it is quite simple to ingest a file into Hadoop: Copy the file into a directory that is managed by Hadoop. It is from that point that Hadoop splits the file across the multiple nodes or machines that it has registered as part of its cluster.

The second purpose for Hadoop (or best practice today) is to leverage it as a place to perform data mining, using SAS, R, or textual mining. The results of the mining efforts often are structured data sets that can and should be copied into relational database engines, making them available for ad hoc querying.

Data Vault 2.0 Architecture Objectives

There are several objectives of the architecture of Data Vault 2.0:

1. To seamlessly connect existing RDBMSs with new NoSQL platforms
2. To engage business users and provide space for managed SSBI (write back and direct control over data in the data warehouse)
3. To provide for real-time arrival direct to the data warehouse environment without forcing a landing in the staging tables
4. To enable agile development by decoupling the always changing business rules from the static data alignment rules

The architecture plays a key role in separation of responsibilities, isolating data acquisition from data provisioning. By separating responsibilities and pushing ever-changing business rules closer to the business user, agility by the implementation teams is enabled.

Data Vault 2.0 Modeling Objective

The objective of Data Vault 2.0 Modeling is to provide seamless platform integration, or at least make it available and possible via design. The design that is leveraged includes several basic elements. The first is the use of the hash keys (to replace the surrogates as primary keys). The hash keys allow the implementation of parallel decoupled loading practices across heterogeneous platforms. The hash keys and loading process are introduced and discussed in the Implementation and Modeling sections of this chapter.

That said, the hash keys provide the *connection* between the two environments, allowing cross-system joins to occur where possible. Performance of the cross-system join will vary depending on the NoSQL platform chosen and the hardware infrastructure underneath. Figure 4.3.2 shows an example data model that provides a *logical* foreign key between RDBMS and Hadoop-stored satellite.

In other words, the idea is to allow the business to *augment* their current infrastructure by adding a NoSQL platform to the mix, while retaining the value and use of their currently existing

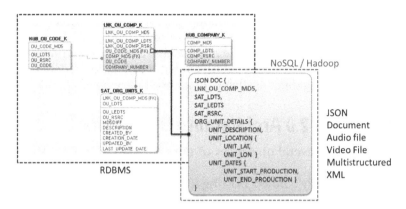

Figure 4.3.2 Hadoop Based Satellite

RDBMS engines, not to mention all the historical data they already contain.

Hard and Soft Business Rules

Business rules are the requirements translated into code. The code manipulates the data and in some cases turns data into information. Part of the Data Vault 2.0 BI system is to enable agility (which will be covered a bit more in the Methodology section of this chapter). Agility is enabled by first splitting the business rules into two distinct groups: hard rules and soft rules as shown in Figure 4.3.3.

The idea is to separate data interpretation from data storage and alignment rules. By decoupling these rules, the team can be increasingly agile. Also, the business users can be empowered and the BI solution can be moved toward managed SSBI.

Beyond that, Data Vault 2.0–based data warehouse carries *raw* data, in a nonconformed state. That data is aligned with the

- **_Hard Rules:_**
  - Any rule that does **not** change content of individual fields **or** grain

- For example:
  - Data type alignment
  - Normalization / Denormalization
  - Tagging (adding system fields)
  - De-duplication
  - Splitting by record structure

- **_Soft Rules:_**
  - Any rule that **changes** or **interprets** data or changes grain of the data
  - (turning data in to information)

- For example:
  - Concatenating name fields
  - Standardizing addresses
  - Computing monthly sales
  - Coalescing
  - Consolidation

Figure 4.3.3 Hard and Soft Business Rules

business constructs known as "business keys" (which is defined in the Data Vault Modeling section of this chapter).

The raw data, integrated by business keys, serve as a foundation for passing audits. Especially since the data set is *not* in conformed format. The idea of the Data Vault 2.0 model is to provide for data warehousing–based storage of raw data, so that if necessary (due to an audit or other needs), the team can reconstruct or reassemble the source system data.

This in turn makes the Data Vault 2.0–based data warehouse a system of record. Mostly because after warehousing the data from the source systems, those systems are either shut down or replaced by newer sources. In other words, the Data Vault 2.0 data warehouse becomes the only place where one can find the raw history integrated by business key.

Managed SSBI and the Architecture

First, understand that "self-service business intelligence" in and of itself is a misnomer. It emerged in the market in the 1990s as "federated query" engines, also known as "enterprise information integration." While it is a grand goal, it never truly was able to overcome technical challenges that vendors touted it would. In the end, a data warehouse and business intelligence ecosystem is still needed in order to make accurate decisions. Hence, "managed SSBI" is feasible, and the term is readily applicable to the solution space discussed in this book.

That said, Data Vault 2.0 Architecture provides for the managed SSBI capabilities with the injection of write-back data (reabsorbing data on multiple levels) from either direct applications (sitting on top of the data warehouse) or from external applications such as SAS, Tableau, QlikView, and Excel, where the data sets are physically "exported" from the tools after having been altered and fed back into the warehouse as another source.

The difference then is that the aggregations and the rest of the soft business rules rely on the new data in order to assemble the proper output for the business. The soft business rules (i.e., code layers) are managed by information technology while the processes are data driven, and the business manages the data. An example of this can be found in the simple example of allowing businesses direct access to managing their own hierarchies.

INTRODUCTION TO DATA VAULT METHODOLOGY

Data Vault 2.0 Methodology Overview

The Data Vault 2.0 standard provides a best practice for project execution, which is called "Data Vault 2.0 Methodology." It is derived from core software engineering standards and adapts them for use in data warehousing. Figure 4.4.1 shows the standards that have influenced the methodology of Data Vault 2.0.

The methodology for Data Vault projects is based on best practices pulled from disciplined agile delivery (DAD), automation and optimization principles (Capability Maturity Model Integration [CMMI], key process areas [KPAs], and key performance indicators [KPIs]), Six Sigma error tracking and reduction principles, Lean enterprise initiatives, and cycle-time reduction principles.

In addition, Data Vault Methodology takes into account a notion known as "managed self-service business intelligence (BI)." The notion of managed self-service BI is introduced in the Data Vault 2.0 Architecture section of this chapter.

The idea of the methodology is to provide teams with current working practices and a well-designed information technology (IT) process for building data warehouse systems (BI systems) in repeatable fashion, reliably and rapidly.

CMMI and Data Vault 2.0 Methodology

CMMI, developed by Carnegie Mellon University, contains the foundations of management, measurement, and optimization. These components are applied to the methodology at the levels of KPAs and KPIs. These pieces are necessary in order to understand and define what the business processes are and should be around the implementation and life cycle of the BI build-out.

The business of building BI solutions needs to mature. To accomplish these goals, the implementation team must first accept that a BI system is a software product. As such, system development life cycle (SDLC) components, along with best practices of managing, identifying, measuring, and optimizing must be

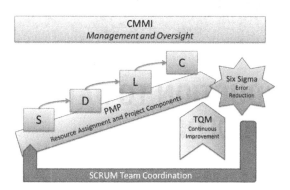

Figure 4.4.1 Data Vault 2.0 Methodology Overview

applied, particularly if the team is to become and remain agile going forward. Figure 4.4.2 demonstrates how CMMI levels map to Data Vault 2.0 Methodology. It is not a complete map, just a representative portion of the entire piece.

The end goal of CMMI is optimization. Optimization cannot be achieved without metrics (quantitative measurements) or KPIs. These KPIs cannot be achieved without the KPAs or definitions of key areas to be measured, which of course cannot be achieved without first managing the project.

The road to agility is paved with metrics and well-defined and well-understood business processes. Data Vault 2.0 Methodology relies on the necessary components of CMMI in order to establish a solid foundation on which to build and automate enterprise BI systems.

Taking a step back, here is a simplified definition of what CMMI focuses on:

	Data Vault 2.0 Methodology
Level 1 – initial chaos	N/A
Level 2 - Managed	Pre-Defined Document Templates Implementation Standards Pattern Based Architecture
Level 3 - Defined	Defined Project Process
Level 4 - Quantitatively Managed	Estimates and Actuals Captured Measured Lead Times Measured Complexity Measured Defects
Level 5 - Optimizing	Automation Tools Rapid Delivery Reduced Cost Parallel Teams

Figure 4.4.2 CMMI Mapped to Data Vault 2.0

In CMMI, process management is the central theme. It represents learning and honesty as demonstrated through work according to a process. Process also enables transparency by communicating how work should be done. Such transparency is within the project, among projects, and being clear about expectations. Also, measurement is part of process and product management and provides the information needed to make decisions that guide product development.*

CMMI brings consistency to the processes, it also brings manageability, documentation, and cost control. CMMI helps the people assigned to the project execute with a specific quality metric in mind. It also assists with the measurements of those metrics by identifying common processes that must happen in every BI system.

CMMI provides the *framework* to operate within. Teams implementing Data Vault 2.0 Methodology inherit the best parts of CMMI level 5 specifications and can successfully hit the ground running. Why? Because Data Vault 2.0 Methodology provides the transparency, defines many of the KPAs and KPIs, and also enriches the project process by allocating template-based predefined deliverables used during the implementation phases.

Transparency is implemented in the Data Vault 2.0 projects in different manners. The first recommendation for teams is to set up an in-company wiki, one that can reach any and all employees (including executives) in the firm. All meetings, all models, all templates, designs, metadata, and documentation should be recorded in the wiki.

The wiki should be updated at least once a day (if not more) by different members of the team. There will be more updates at the start or kickoff of new projects than at any other time during the life cycle. This should indicate a level of communication, which is stressed in Scrum agile development, with the business users.

The second component is the recording of business requirements meetings. The time allotted for all business requirements meetings can be shortened; the quality of the requirements increases when the meetings themselves are recorded using an MP3 recorder. The audio files should be submitted to the wiki so that team members can retroactively attend or review when necessary.

This leads to a more agile business requirements meeting. When meetings are recorded, noisemakers tend to be quiet until

---

* Glazer H., Dalton, J., Anderson, D., Konrad, M., Shrum, S. (2008). CMMI or agile: Why not embrace both! (Technical Note CMU/SEI-2008-TN-003). Retrieved from Carnegie Mellon University, Software Engineering Institute: http://resources.sei.cmu.edu/asset_files/TechnicalNote/2008_004_001_14924.pdf, p.17.

or unless they have a significant contribution to make that would impact the outcome of the project goals. Please note that the rest of the explanation of how and why this works is beyond the scope of this book and is available in Data Vault 2.0 Boot Camp training classes and online at http://LearnDataVault.com.

CMMI Versus Agility

Scrum agility development or DAD is still necessary to manage the individual sprint cycles or miniprojects that need to occur. CMMI manages the overall enterprise goals and provides a baseline consistency to the enterprise wide efforts so everyone in IT is on the same page (at least those involved with the BI project).

> *An agile implementation should be tailored to match an organization's actual maturity level; however, implementing agile when an organization is at CMMI level three can result in less rework and improve the overall CMMI initiative while providing the significant benefits of agile. Implementing a CMMI compliant software development process that is also agile will bring the repeatability and predictability offered by CMMI. Agile, by design, is highly adaptable and therefore can be molded into a CMMI-compliant software development process without altering the primary objectives set forth by the Agile Manifesto.[†]*

Please keep in mind that teams don't wake up one day and just decide to be agile right there on the spot. It's an evolutionary process; the team must undergo training both in agile and in Data Vault 2.0 Methodology to achieve the desired goals. Most teams that undertake training with Data Vault 2.0 start with seven-week sprint cycles (if they have had zero exposure to CMMI and agile previously).

Usually the second sprint cycle reduces seven weeks to six weeks. The third, if the team is working in earnest, measuring their productivity, and following the agile and Scrum review process, can see sprint cycles drop to about four weeks. From there, it simply improves to two weeks as the team gets better at it. Currently there is a team implementing Data Vault 2.0 Methodology and attempting to achieve one-week sprint cycles. There doesn't seem to be a bottleneck to optimizing the processes.

But as a reminder, the optimization of these processes comes from CMMI in direct correlation to the KPAs and KPIs of building

---

[†] Shelton, C. (2008). Agile and CMMI: Better together. Scrum Alliance, July 9. Retrieved from https://www.scrumalliance.org/community/articles/2008/july/agile-and-cmmi-better-together

a data warehouse. It is tied as well to repeatable designs, pattern-based data integration, pattern-based models, and pattern-based BI build cycles. The value of Data Vault 2.0 Methodology is it provides the patterns out of the gate, to get the teams kick-started in the right direction.

Project Management Practices and SDLC Versus CMMI and Agile

That said, CMMI doesn't describe *how* to achieve these goals, it just describes *what* should be in place. Agile doesn't describe *what* you need, but rather *how* to manage the people and the life cycle. Projects and SDLC components are necessary for the next step, which is pattern-based development and delivery. The next pieces of the puzzle come from project management practices (PMPs) and SDLC. PMP lays the project foundation for the common project best practices.

While the team strives to be agile in the end, at some level, waterfall project practices must be adhered to. Otherwise, a project cannot progress through its life cycle to completion. According to the *Guide to the Project Management Body of Knowledge* (*PMBok Guide*), the project management framework embodies a project life cycle and five major project management process groups:
1. Initiating
2. Planning
3. Executing
4. Monitoring and Controlling
5. Closing[‡]

The difference is this "life cycle" is now assigned to a two-week sprint, with DAD overseeing the process.

There are several components to how this fits in with the Data Vault 2.0 Methodology. First, there is the master project, which is the overall enterprise wide vision. This generally consists of a multiyear, large-scale effort (for large enterprises). These projects are then often broken into subprojects (as they should be), with outlined goals and objectives within 6-month time frames.

Then, the subprojects should be broken into two-week sprint cycles (to meet agile requirements). The idea is to not have the project levels become top heavy and full of planning, but rather to act as an overall guide or map from start to finish in terms of what the enterprise BI solution needs to provide.

At the end of the day, project managers should have a firm grasp on what they are managing (CMMI), how they will manage

[‡] http://encyclopedia.thefreedictionary.com/Project+Management+Professional

the people (agile, Scrum, DAD), how the sprints have to be lined up in order to accomplish the goals and objectives of the enterprise, and how to measure the success or failure of particular parts of the process. Otherwise, without hindsight or measurement, then there will be no room for improvement or optimization.

Six Sigma and Data Vault 2.0 Methodology

Six Sigma is defined to be:

Six Sigma seeks to improve the quality of process outputs by identifying and removing the causes of defects (errors) and minimizing variability in manufacturing and business processes. It uses a set of quality management methods, including statistical methods, and creates a special infrastructure of people within the organization ("Champions," "Black Belts," "Green Belts," "Yellow Belts," etc.) who are experts in these methods.[§]

To paraphrase for enterprise BI projects: Six Sigma is all about measuring and eliminating *defects* that plague the enterprise warehouse build process. Data Vault 2.0 Methodology attaches Six Sigma school of thought to the metrics that are captured in the life cycle of each sprint (i.e., the KPIs and the Scrum review process – what's broken, why, how do we fix it?).

In order to *reach full optimization* (or *full maturity*) for the enterprise BI initiatives, all miniprojects or minisprints must reach their full optimization as well. Otherwise, the organization *cannot* achieve CMMI level 5. The Data Vault 2.0 Methodology outlines (in some levels of detail) how to tie these components together.

Once the team understands that all work is measured, monitored, and eventually optimized, then Six Sigma mathematics can provide the business with a confidence rating, showing improvement (or not) of the enterprise BI team and their progress as a whole. This is only part of the nature of total cost of ownership (TCO) and reducing TCO while improving return on investment (ROI) for the business.

The Data Vault 2.0 Methodology provides the patterns, artifacts, and repeatable processes for building an enterprise BI solution, effectively and in a measured and applied manner. Six Sigma seeks to assist the optimization of the teams and the implementation methods in order to streamline the agility and improve quality overall. In other words, without Six Sigma, the words "better, faster, cheaper" cannot apply to BI projects.

[§] Six Sigma. (n.d.). In Wikipedia. Retrieved from http://en.wikipedia.org/wiki/Six_Sigma

Total Quality Management

Total quality management (TQM) is the cream of the crop. TQM is necessary in order to keep the moving parts of the enterprise BI solution well-oiled and running smoothly. TQM is the icing on the cake (as it were). As it turns out, TQM plays several roles in the Data Vault 2.0 Methodology. These roles will be briefly introduced and discussed in the following paragraphs. To better understand TQM, a definition is in order:

> *Total quality management (TQM) consists of organization-wide efforts to install and make permanent a climate in which an organization continuously improves its ability to deliver high-quality products and services to customers.*[¶]

The Data Vault 2.0 Methodology incorporates and aligns the goals and functions of TQM with the purpose of producing *better, faster, cheaper* BI solutions. It is actually hard to imagine enterprise-focused projects being run any other way. TQM offers a view consistent with the business users and the deliverables that the enterprise BI project strives to provide. Some of the fundamental primary elements behind TQM include:

- Customer focus
- Total employee involvement (within the reach of the enterprise BI team and business users)
- Process centered
- Integrated system
- Strategic and systematic approach
- Continual improvement
- Fact-based decision making
- Communications**

It is clear by now that TQM plays a vital role in the success of the data warehousing and BI projects. TQM is aligned (as previously described) with the desired outcomes of CMMI, Six Sigma, Scrum agile development, and DAD.

The Data Vault 2.0 Methodology is process-centered, provides for an integrated system, is a strategic and systematic approach, requires total employee involvement, is customer-focused, and relies on transparency and communications. The Data Vault 2.0 model brings fact-based decision making to the table, rather than "truth" or subjectively based decision making. The other part of the fact-based decision making is impacted by the collected KPAs

[¶] Total quality management. (n.d.). In Wikipedia. Retrieved from http://en.wikipedia.org/wiki/Total_quality_management

** Total Quality Management (TQM). (n.d.). In *ASQ Knowledge Center*. Retrieved from http://asq.org/learn-about-quality/total-quality-management/overview/overview.html

and KPIs in the enterprise BI project (don't forget, these are a part of the optimization steps in CMMI level 5).

As it turns out, accountability (both for the system as a whole and the data living in the data warehouse) is a necessary part of TQM as well. How is this possible? TQM is customer focused; the customer (in this case the business user) needs to stand up and take ownership of their data (*not their information* but their *data*).

The only place in the organization that this data exists in raw form, integrated by business key is in the Data Vault 2.0 data warehouse. It is precisely this understanding of facts that draws the business users' attention to Six Sigma metrics, demonstrating quantitatively the gaps between business perception of operation and business reality of data capture over time.

Addressing these gaps by filing change requests to the source systems or renegotiating the service level agreements (SLAs) with the source data provider is part of the TQM process, as well as part of reducing TCO and improving data quality across the enterprise. TQM plays a role in enriching the BI ecosystem, if and only if the business users are forced to be accountable for their own data and decide to engage in gap analysis (the old-fashioned way) by leveraging statistics that show where and what percentage of their current business perception (business requirements) are broken. The Data Vault 2.0 Methodology provides pathways in the project that the teams and business users can follow to achieve these results.

Without the business taking action to *close* the gaps, TQM dissolves to simple data quality initiatives and does not contribute as heavily or as well to the TCO reduction strategy. Improving the quality of the data, and understanding the gaps that exist is vital to the overall success and future of an enterprise BI solution.

INTRODUCTION TO DATA VAULT IMPLEMENTATION

Implementation Overview

The Data Vault system of business intelligence (BI) provides implementation guidelines, rules, and recommendations as standards. As noted in previous sections of this chapter, well-defined standards and patterns are the *key* to success of agile, Capability Maturity Model Integration (CMMI), Six Sigma, and total quality management (TQM) principles. These standards guide the implementation of:

- The data model, finding business keys, designing entities, applying key structures
- The ETL/ELT load processes
- The real-time messaging feeds
- Information mart delivery processes
- Virtualization of the information mart
- Automation best practices
- Business rules – hard and soft
- Write-back capabilities of managed self-service BI

Some of the objectives of managing implementation through working practices include meeting the needs of TQM, embracing master data, and assisting in alignment across business, source systems, and the enterprise data warehouse.

Before going any further, it is necessary to understand that the highest level of optimization can only be reached *if* the process, design, and implementation is pattern based and data driven.

The Importance of Patterns

Patterns make life easier. In the enterprise BI world, patterns enable automation and generation, while reducing errors and error potential. Patterns are the heartbeat of the Data Vault 2.0 BI system. Once the team has accepted the principles that building a data warehouse or BI system is the same as building software, it is possible to extend that thought to pattern driven design. In his book *A Pattern Language* (http://en.wikipedia.org/wiki/A_Pattern_Language), Christopher Alexander says:

> *"A pattern is a recurring solution to a problem within a context."*

Think about it, how often have information technology (IT) teams said they need one pattern for loading history, one pattern for loading current, and yet another pattern for loading data in real time? Other teams have stated that this part of the data model works for these reasons, and this other part of the data model was constructed differently because of exceptions to the design rules. Much of this contributes to what is commonly called "conditional architecture."

Conditional architecture is defined as a pattern that only works for a specific case often based on an *if* condition. When the case changes the boundaries (i.e., volume or velocity or variety), the architecture needs to change. Thus conditional architecture is born.

Conditional architecture is a horrible way to construct or design an enterprise BI solution. The reason is because when volume grows and timelines (velocity changes) shrink, then reengineering takes place to rectify or correct the design. This leads to a solution that continues to cost more and more money and take longer and longer to change. In other words, it leads to a brittle architecture over time. This (especially in a Big Data solution) is a very bad construct.

At some point the business can't or won't be able to pay for the reengineering costs. This is typically when the solution is torn down and rebuilt (greenfield approach). With the patterns of Data Vault 2.0 (both architecture and implementation), re-architecture and reengineering is avoided for 98% of the cases where volume grows, velocity changes, and variety increases.

Having the right pattern or design based on mathematical principles means that the team no longer suffers reengineering because of changing requirements.

Reengineering and Big Data

Reengineering, redesign, and re-architecture happens because Big Data pushes three of the four available axis in the following diagram. The more processing that has to happen in smaller and smaller time frames requires a highly optimized design. The more variety needing to be processed in smaller time frames also requires a highly optimized design. Finally, the more volume needing to be processed in smaller time frames (you guessed it) requires a highly optimized design.

Fortunately for the community, there is a finite set of process designs that have been proven to work at scale; and by leveraging massively parallel processing (MPP), scale-free mathematics, and set logic, these designs work both for small volumes and extremely large volumes without redesign.

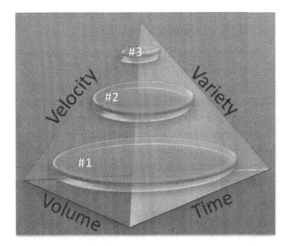

Figure 4.5.1. Architectural Changes and Reengineering

Figure 4.5.1 contains four axis labels: Velocity, Volume, Time, and Variety. In this figure, velocity is the speed of arrival of the data (i.e., latency of arrival); volume is the overall size of the data (on arrival to the warehouse); variety is defined to be the structural, semistructural, multistructural, or nonstructured classification of the data; and time is the allotted time frame in which to accomplish the given task (e.g., loading to the data warehouse). Let's examine a case study for how this impacts reengineering or even conditional architecture.

Scenario 1: 10 rows of highly structured (tab delimited and fixed number of columns) data arrive every 24 hours. The requirement is to load the data to the data warehouse within a six-hour window. How many different architectures or process designs can be put together to accomplish this task? For the sake of argument, let's state that there are 100 possibilities (even typing the data in by hand, or typing it into Excel then loading it to the database). The design that is chosen by this team is to type it in by hand to an SQL prompt as "insert into" statements.

Now the parameters change.

Scenario 2: 1,000,000 rows of highly structured (tab delimited, fixed number of columns) data arrive every 24 hours. The requirement is to load the data warehouse in a four-hour window. Can the team use the same "process design" to accomplish the task? Chances are, the answer is no. *The team must redesign, reengineer, re-architect the process design to accomplish the task in the allotted time frame.*

The redesign is complete. The team now deploys an ETL tool and introduces logic to loading the data set.

Scenario 3: One billion rows of highly structured data arrive every 45 minutes. The requirement is to load the data warehouse in a 40-minute time frame (otherwise the queue of incoming data backs up). Can the team use the same process design they just applied to accomplish this task? Can the team execute without redesign? Again, most likely the answer is no. *The team must once again redesign the process because it doesn't meet the service level agreement (requirements). This type of redesign occurs again and again until the team reaches a CMMI level 5* optimized *state for the pattern.*

The problem is that any *significant change* to any axis on the pyramid causes a *redesign to occur.* The only solution is to mathematically find the right solution, the correct design that will scale regardless of time, volume, velocity, or variety. Unfortunately this leads to unsustainable systems that try to deal (unsuccessfully) with Big Data problems.

The Data Vault 2.0 implementation standards hand these designs to the BI solution team, regardless of the technology underneath. The implementations or patterns applied to the designs for dealing with the data sets scale. They are based on mathematical principles of scale and simplicity, including some of the foundations of set logic, parallelism, and partitioning.

Teams that engage with the Data Vault 2.0 implementation best practices inherit the designs as an artifact for Big Data systems. By leveraging these patterns the team no longer suffers from re-architecture or redesigns just because one or more of the axes or parameters change.

Virtualize Our Data Marts

They should no longer be called "data marts." Because they provide information to the business, they should be called "information marts." There is a split between data, information, knowledge, and wisdom that should be recognized by the BI community.

Virtualization means many things to many people. In this context, they are defined to be view-driven whether or not they are implemented in a relational or nonrelational technology. Views are logical collections of data (mostly structured) on top of physical data storage. Note that it may no longer be a relational table; it might be a key-value pair store, or a nonrelational file sitting in Hadoop.

The more virtualization (or views) that can be applied, the quicker and more responsive the IT team is to change. In other words, less physical storage means less physical management and maintenance costs. It also means faster reaction time for IT to implement, test, and release changes back to the business.

Managed Self-Service BI

Unfortunately the term "self-service BI" is being thrown about in the marketplace. In the 1990s, enterprise information integration (EII) applied to federated query engines. The purpose and use for this type of engine has since morphed into the cloud and virtualization space.

One of the marketing statements by these vendors was that businesses did not need a data warehouse. The industry and the vendors learned that this simply was not a true statement. It wasn't true then, and it certainly isn't true now. Data warehouses (and BI systems) are as important to the enterprise as the operational systems are because the enterprise warehouse captures an *integrated* view of historical information, allowing *gap analysis* to occur across multiple systems.

Look at Figure 4.5.2. If you give children a bunch of finger paint with no training and no instruction, will it make them master artists, or will they simply make a big mess? If children are taught what to do with finger paint and where to paint, then provided some paper and paints, chances are they will paint on the paper instead of themselves.

We can correlate this example with IT. IT wants business to succeed. IT should be an enabler, helping to integrate the proper paints for the right colors and providing the paper along with basic instruction on how to get at the information.

Figure 4.5.2. Illustrating Managed Self-Service BI

What the market realized is that IT is still needed to prepare the data, turn it into information, and make it usable by the business. IT is also needed to secure the data and offer access paths and encrypted information where necessary. Finally, IT is needed to assemble the data and integrate the historical data in an enterprise data warehouse. At the end of the day, *managed* self-service BI is necessary, because IT must manage the information and the systems being used by businesses.

Data Vault 2.0 provides the groundwork for understanding how to properly implement managed self-service BI in enterprise projects. It covers the standards and best practices for achieving optimal goals.

THE OPERATIONAL ENVIRONMENT – A SHORT HISTORY

The computer profession is immature. This is not a pejorative statement about information technology (IT) but simply a fact. When you compare IT versus other professions, it is no contest. The streets of Rome that we use today were laid out by an engineer 2000 years ago. The majority of the hieroglyphics in the pyramids in Egypt were written by ancient accountants and document how much grain was owed the pharaoh. In the mountains of Chile are found skulls that are estimated to be 10,000 years old that indicate that at least an early form of medicine was practiced long ago. So when you compare the profession of IT to the engineering, accounting, and medical professions, it is no contest. The IT profession is immature compared to other professions. That is a historical fact, which is inarguable.

Commercial Uses of the Computer

The very earliest uses of the computer were for the purpose of calculating military matters in World War II. The commercial uses of the computer started around the 1960s. And the commercial use of the computer has being growing and advancing ever since.

The very early days of the computer were (rightfully so) centered on the early technology. In the very earliest days were paper tape, wired boards, and then punched cards as depicted in Figure 5.1.1. The language of the day was "assembler." It was quickly recognized that trying to code and debug assembler was going to be a long and arduous process. Soon there were more sophisticated languages such as COBOL and Fortran.

Soon it was discovered that applications could be built. The first applications used the computer to automate what would otherwise have been tedious human activities. The first applications centered on human resources, payroll, and accounts payables and receivables.

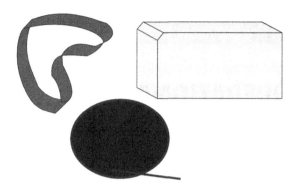

Figure 5.1.1

The First Applications

Figure 5.1.2 depicts the advent of the first applications.

Once organizations discovered that they could write applications, soon applications began to spring up everywhere. In the very earliest days of application development, the coding practices were nonuniform. The code that was produced was difficult to maintain and was often inefficient. In the early days there were no standard coding practices. Everyone did his or her own thing. As a result, the code that was produced was very unstable.

Figure 5.1.3 illustrates the many new applications that were being produced.

Ed Yourdon and the Structured Revolution

Into this fray stepped Ed Yourdon and Tom DeMarco. Yourdon recognized that some discipline was needed in the creation of code and began what was termed the "structured" revolution. Yourdon began with structured programming, then extended his philosophy for discipline into the creation of systems and general design principles. Thus was born structured programming and design. Given the development practices of the day, Yourdon

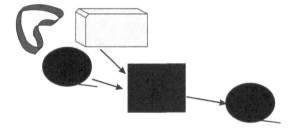

Figure 5.1.2

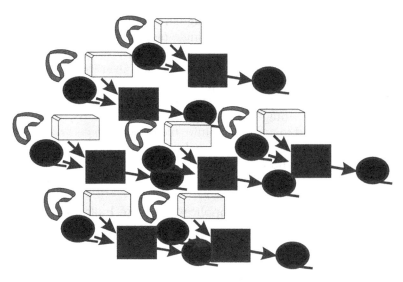

Figure 5.1.3

made significant contributions with the notion that computer systems should be developed with order and discipline.

System Development Life Cycle

One of the significant products of the structured revolution was the notion of the system development life cycle (SDLC), which is shown in Figure 5.1.4. The SDLC is sometimes called the "waterfall" approach to the development of systems.

Disk Technology

At about the same time as structured systems developed came the disk storage device. With disk storage, data could be accessed directly. Prior to the advent of disk storage, data had been stored on magnetic tape files. Even though magnetic tape files could hold

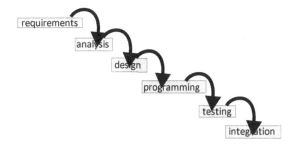

Figure 5.1.4

a lot of data, all the data on the magnetic tapes had to be accessed sequentially. In order to find a single record you had to process the entire file. In addition, magnetic tape files were notoriously unreliable for the long-term storage of data. Over time the oxide stripped off of the magnetic tape files, thus rendering the file unusable. Figure 5.1.5 shows the symbol for a magnetic tape file.

Because disk storage data could be accessed directly, there was no longer a need to access an entire file in order to get to one record. But the first iterations of disk storage were expensive and fragile. Over time, however, the capacity, cost, and stability of the disk files improved. And soon applications were using disk storage, not magnetic tape files.

Figure 5.1.6 shows that applications were built where data could be accessed on disk storage.

Enter the Database Management System

Applications were built with the aid of software called a "database management system" (DBMS). The DBMS allowed the application programmer to focus on the logic of processing. The DBMS focused on the placement and accessing of data stored on the disk.

It wasn't long after the DBMS appeared that it was recognized that since data could be accessed directly, rather than sequentially, that a new type of application could be built. The new application that could be built was the online transaction processing (OLTP) application, which is shown in Figure 5.1.7.

The advent of the online transaction processing application had a profound and long-lasting effect on business. For the first time business was able to incorporate the computer into its very fabric. Prior to online transaction processing, the computer was useful to business, but with online transaction processing, the computer became a normal aspect of the day-to-day processing of business. Suddenly with online transaction processing there were

Figure 5.1.5

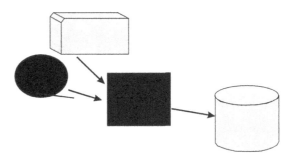

Figure 5.1.6

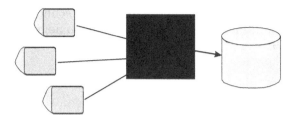

Figure 5.1.7

reservation systems, bank teller systems, ATM systems, and many, many more types of business applications.

Response Time and Availability

With the integration of the computer into business came a new concern. Suddenly the business was concerned with response time and availability. Response time was crucial to the business ability to function properly. When the computer did not yield proper response time, the business directly and immediately suffered. When the computer went down and was unavailable, the business suffered.

Prior to online transaction processing systems, response time and availability were theoretical subjects that were only of passing interest to the business. But in the face of online transaction systems, response time and availability became central concerns of the business.

Because of the elevated importance of response time and availability, there were significant advances in technology. Suddenly the operating system, the DBMS, and other internal components needed to operate with efficiency that was never before needed. Figure 5.1.8 shows the increasing sophistication of the technical environment.

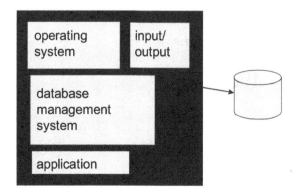

Figure 5.1.8

There have been many advancements in technology. Some of the more prominent advances in early technology are listed in Figure 5.1.9.

1960
Fortran assembler
COBOL punched cards
master files
tape storage
structured analysis, design
SDLC
IBM 360
HIPO chart
data flow diagram
crud chart

1965
functional decomposition

PLI

disk storage

database

1970
database management system
plug compatible computing
extract program
personal computer
spreadsheet

Zachman framework

4GL technology

1975
maintenance backlog nightmare
spider-web systems

data communications monitor

transaction processing

1980
standard work unit

maximum transactions per second

MPP technology

1985
data warehouse

1990
data marts
dimensional model

ERP

1995
dot com fad

ETL

2000

DW 2.0

Figure 5.1.9

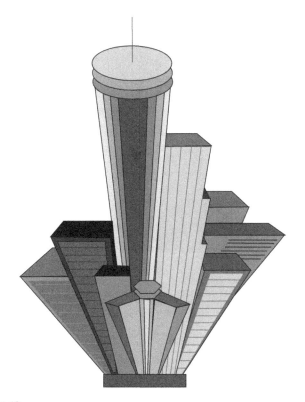

Figure 5.1.10

Corporate Computing Today

The corporate computing environment exists as it is today as a result of many advances. In almost every case, the advances built on top of each other. Figure 5.1.10 depicts the world of corporations and technology today.

THE STANDARD WORK UNIT

At the heart of online transaction processing is good response time. Response time in the online transaction environment is not a nicety, it is a necessity. Organizations depend on their online systems for running day-to-day business. If response time is not good, business suffers. Therefore, in the world of online transaction processing, response time is an absolute necessity.

Elements of Response Time

There are many facets to achieving good response time:
- The organization has to be using the right technology.
- There has to be adequate capacity.
- The workload passing through the system must be understood.
- The data being processed must be understood.

But having all these items in place is not enough. At the heart of success for achieving good response time is something called the "standard work unit." Figure 5.2.1 shows the elements of response time, which is the amount of time from the moment of the initiation of the transaction until the moment in time when the results of the transaction are returned to the end user. Figure 5.2.1 shows that the transaction is initiated, the transaction is sent to the processor, the processor commences execution, the processor goes out and finds data, the data is processed, and the results are sent

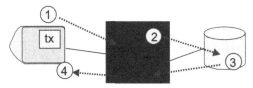

1 - transaction is initiated
2 - transaction goes into execution
3 - data is accessed
4 - response is sent back to user

Figure 5.2.1

to the end user. Typically all of this activity occurs in a second or less. Given all the activity that takes place, it is a wonder that it occurs as fast as it does.

An Hourglass Analogy

To understand how good response time is achieved, it makes sense to study an hour glass. Consider the hour glass shown in Figure 5.2.2.

When you examine the flow of sand through the hourglass, the flow is steady and at an even pace. All things considered, the flow of sand is done efficiently. How does the sand flow through the hour glass in such an efficient manner? Consider the grains of sand as they pass through the center of the hourglass as shown in Figure 5.2.3. One of the reasons (other than gravity) why the hourglass exhibits an even flow of sand is that the grains of sand are small and uniform in size. Consider what would happen if the hourglass were to have pebbles inserted in among the grains of sand as depicted in Figure 5.2.4. The result of placing pebbles in the hourglass is that the flow of sand is interrupted and the flow is erratic and inefficient.

In many ways the transactions that run through an online system are like the grains of sand. As long as the transactions are small and uniform in size, the efficiency of the system is quite good. But when large transactions are mixed in with small transactions in the workload of an online transaction processing system, the flow

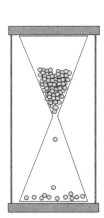

Figure 5.2.2

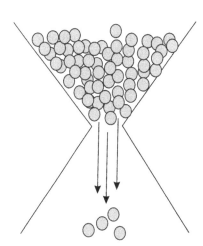

Figure 5.2.3

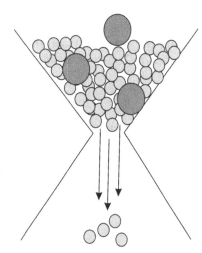

Figure 5.2.4

is very mixed and inefficient. And when the flow is inefficient, the result is poor response time.

The Racetrack Analogy

Another way to express the same thing is seen in Figure 5.2.5.

In Figure 5.2.5 a pathway with different workloads is pictured. You can think of it as a roadway where there are cars running. The cars are all fast and uniform in size. The speeds that are attained are quite high. The roadway could be the old Brickyard in Indianapolis or Daytona. The only cars running on the track are Porsches and Ferraris. Everything is running efficiently.

Now consider another roadway as depicted in Figure 5.2.6. In this roadway there are some small fast cars and some semitrucks. This could be Mexico City at rush hour. Everything is slow.

The difference between the speeds that are attained is remarkable. On one track there are very high rate of speeds. On another track very low rates of speed are attained. The major difference between the tracks is that large, slow vehicles are allowed onto the road. The large vehicles slow everything down.

Your Vehicle Runs as Fast as the Vehicle in Front of It

There is another way of thinking of the speeds that can be attained, which is the vehicle you are in is as slow as the vehicle in front of you. And if the vehicle in front of you is a large, slow vehicle, then that is your optimal speed.

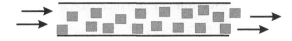

Figure 5.2.5

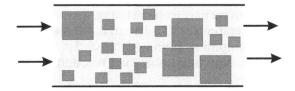

Figure 5.2.6

read 10,000 records
update records

read 3 records
no updates

Figure 5.2.7

The way then to achieve speed and efficiency in the online transaction environment is to allow only small fast-moving transactions into the system.

The size of an online transaction is measured in terms of how much data the transaction accesses and whether the transaction updates. The update a transaction does affects the amount of records that are locked during the update process. In general, an online DBMS "locks" records that might be updated while a transaction is in execution.

Figure 5.2.7 shows what constitutes a "large" online transaction and a "small" online transaction.

The Standard Work Unit

The standard work unit includes transaction time in its definition, that is, in order to achieve good and consistent online transaction time, each online transaction running in the system needs to be small and uniform in size.

The Service Level Agreement

Related to the standard work unit is the notion of a "service level agreement" (SLA). An SLA is an agreement stating what amounts to an acceptable level of performance and service in the online transaction environment. A typical SLA might look like the following:

Monday– Friday between the hours of 7:30 a.m. and 5:30 p.m.

All transactions will execute in no more than 3 seconds.

The will be no outages of greater than 5 minutes.

The SLA covers both average response time and system availability. The SLA covers only working hours. Outside working hours the computer operations staff is free to do whatever is needed to be done to the computer – running large statistical programs, doing maintenance, running database utilities, and so forth.

DATA MODELING FOR THE STRUCTURED ENVIRONMENT

The structured environment contains a lot of complex data with a lot of possibilities for organizing and arranging that data. In the structured environment analysts have the opportunity to shape the data according to their needs. And given the many ways that data can be shaped, the organization needs a roadmap to guide the organization in its efforts to shape the data.

The Purpose of the Road Map

The road map serves several important purposes:
- The road map serves as a direction for the organization to go.
- The road map serves as a guide to different people with different agendas who still must build a collaborative effort.
- The road map allows a large effort to be sustained over time.
- The road map serves as a guide to end users who ultimately must navigate the final product.

There are many reasons then why large, complex organizations need a data model. The data that is modeled is the data that sits at the heart of the business of the company. The data model is shaped around whatever is at the core of the business of the organization.

Granular Data Only

The data model is shaped around *only* the granular detailed data of the organization. Bad things happen when the data modeler allows summarized or aggregated data to enter the data model. When summarized or aggregated data is allowed to enter the data model:
- There is a *huge* amount of data to be modeled.
- The formula for calculating the summarized data changes faster than the modeler can create and change the model.
- Different people have different formula for calculations.

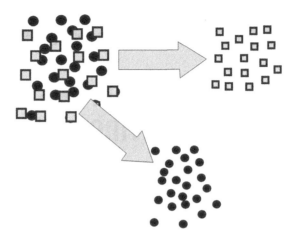

Figure 5.3.1

The first step in building the data model is to remove all derived data – summarized or aggregated– from the data model as shown in Figure 5.3.1.

After the granular data is identified, the next step is to "abstract" the data. The data is abstracted to its highest meaningful level.

As a simple example of abstraction, suppose a corporation has female customers, male customers, foreign customers, corporate customers, and governmental customers. The data model creates the entity known as "customer" and wraps all of the different types of customer together.

Or suppose the company produces sports cars, sedans, SUVs, and trucks. The data model abstracts the data into the entity "vehicle."

The Entity Relationship Diagram

The highest level of abstraction for the data model is called the entity relationship diagram (ERD). The ERD reflects data at its highest level of meaningful abstraction. The entities of the organization are identified, as well as the relationships between those entities. Figure 5.3.2 shows the symbol that identifies the entities and relationships in an ERD.

As an example of the ERD for a manufacturing company, the ERD might look like that seen in Figure 5.3.3.

The ERD is important as a high-level statement of what the data model is all about. But of necessity, there is very little detail found at the ERD level.

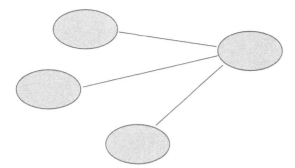

Figure 5.3.2

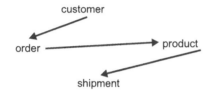

Figure 5.3.3

The DIS

The next level of the data model is the place where much detail is found. This level of the data model is called the "data item set" (DIS).

Each entity identified in the ERD has its own DIS. Using the simple example shown in Figure 5.3.3, there would be one DIS for customer, another DIS for order, another DIS for product, and yet another DIS for shipment.

The DIS contains keys and attributes, and the DIS shows the organization of the data. The symbol for a simple DIS is seen in Figure 5.3.4.

The basic construct of a DIS is a box. In the box are the elements of data that are closely related and that belong together. The different lines between the groupings of data have meaning. A downward pointing line indicates multiple occurrences of data. A line to the right indicates a different type of data.

As a simple example of a DIS consider the DIS shown in Figure 5.3.5. The anchor or primary data is indicated by the box of data that is at the top left of the diagram. The anchor box indicates that the data that relates directly to the key of the box is

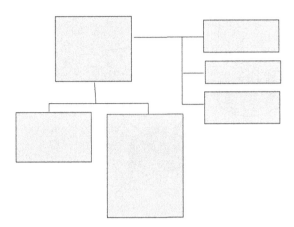

Figure 5.3.4

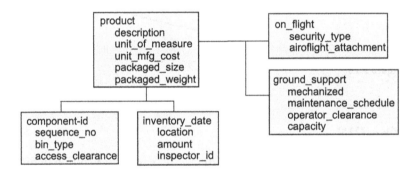

Figure 5.3.5

description, unit of measure, unit manufacturing cost, packaged size, and packaged weight. The elements of data exist once and only once for each product.

Data that can occur multiple times is shown beneath the anchor box of data. One such grouping of data is component id. There can exist multiple components for each product. Another grouping of data that is independent of component id is inventory date and location. The product may have been inventoried in multiple places on different dates.

The lines going to the right of the anchor box indicate different types of data. In this case a product may be used in flight or in ground support.

The DIS indicates the keys, attributes, and relationships for an entity.

```
amannsgtee
  oomdydyd  ppldoie
  ppldodm   plreo
  mnfhfu      nfyur
  mncpdodi  nfdy
  mfjfyr        mvnfh
   mvnvhgf
     mclcp    mcpdfo
     mvcjhfu  pfdl
     fhfyyfh  pfdlofi
  mvjfuf       pflfo
  mvngfuf     mcvudo
```

Figure 5.3.6

Physical Database Design

Once the DIS is created, the physical design of the DIS is created. Each grouping of data in the DIS results in a separate database design. Figure 5.3.6 shows the database design that has resulted from the design of the grouping of data found in the DIS.

The physical database design takes into account the physical structure of the data, the physical characteristics of the data, the specification of keys, the specification of indexes, and so forth. The result of the physical specification of the data is a database design, as shown in Figure 5.3.7.

The elements of the database design include keys, attributes, records, and indexes.

Relating the Different Levels of the Data Model

The different levels of the data model are akin to the different levels of mapping that exist in the world. Figure 5.3.8 shows how the different levels of mapping relate to each other: The ERD is the equivalent to a globe of the world. The DIS is the equivalent to the map of Texas. And the physical database design is the equivalent of the city map of Dallas, Texas. The globe – the ERD – is complete

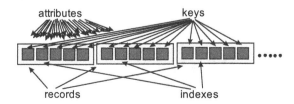

Figure 5.3.7

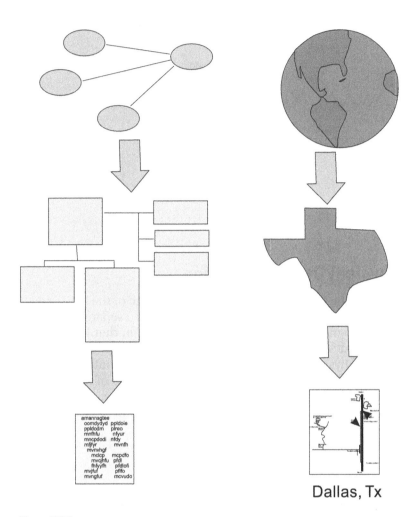

Figure 5.3.8

but not detailed. The map of Texas – the DIS – is incomplete in that you can't find your way to and from Chicago with a map of Texas. But the map of Texas has a great deal more detail than the globe. The city map of Dallas – the physical data model – is even less complete. You cannot find your way from El Paso to Midland with a city map of Dallas. But you have even more details in the city map of Dallas than you do in the state map of Texas.

An Example of the Linkage

The complete linkage of the different forms of data modeling to each other are shown in Figure 5.3.9.

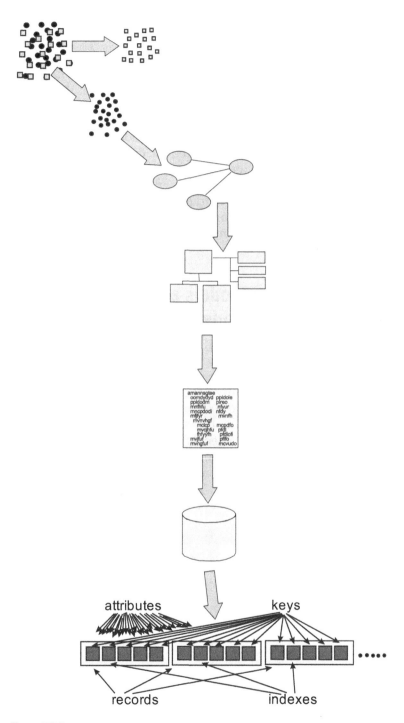

Figure 5.3.9

Generic Data Models

It has been noticed that when a data model is created that it oftentimes applies to companies in the same industry. For example, a bank – ABC – creates a data model. Then one day it is discovered that the data model for bank ABC is very similar to the data model for bank BCD, CDE, and DEF.

Because of the great similarity of data models within the same industry, there are models called "generic data models." The idea behind a generic data model is that it is much less expensive and much faster to acquire a generic data model than it is to build a data model from scratch. It is true that any generic data model is going to need customization. But even with customization, using a generic data model is preferable to having to build the data model by itself.

Operational Data Models and Data Warehouse Data Models

There are different types of data models. There are operational data models and data warehouse data models. An operational data model is one that models the day-to-day operations of the company. The data warehouse data model is one that is based on the informational needs of the organization. The operational data model includes some information that is needed for operational processing only, such as a specific telephone number. The data warehouse data model does not contain data that is specific to operational processing. The data warehouse data model does not contain any summarized data. The data warehouse data model does contain a time stamp for every record in the model.

METADATA

The classical definition of metadata is "data about data." Indeed metadata is the descriptive data that defines important aspects of data to the operating system, the database management system, and the application. When the design sits down and decides what a database is to look like, the designer build metadata definitions of the database.

Typical Metadata

Typically the metadata for a database includes definitions of:
- Table name
- Attributes
- Physical characteristics of those attributes
- Keys
- Indexes and other descriptive information about the data found in the system

Figure 5.4.1 shows the definition of the database that is stored in the form of metadata.

The Repository

Typically the metadata is stored in a repository. There are different kinds of repositories. Some repositories are an extension of the database and are managed by the database management system (DBMS). Other repositories are commercial products that are managed external to the DBMS. Some repositories are passive, in that they are not used interactively in the development process. Other repositories are active, in that they are an integral part of the development process.

Figure 5.4.2 shows that metadata is stored in a repository. And Figure 5.4.3 shows a simple example of what data might look like in a repository.

Figure 5.4.3 shows that a table has been defined. Along with the table, the attributes of the table, the physical characteristic of the table, and keys and indexes have been defined.

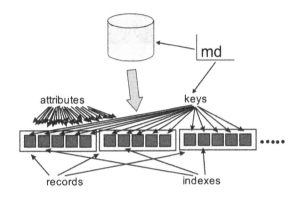

Figure 5.4.1

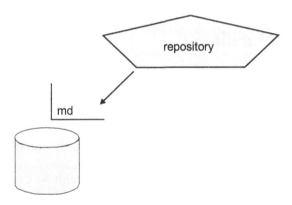

Figure 5.4.2

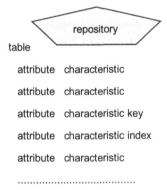

Figure 5.4.3

entity name

relationship name

table

    attribute   characteristic

    attribute   characteristic

    attribute   characteristic key

    attribute   characteristic index

    attribute   characteristic

Figure 5.4.4

Figure 5.4.4 depicts that in addition to a table being defined, the entity belonging to the data model has been defined as well.

Using Metadata

The uses of the metadata are many. There are many communities in the organization who make use of the metadata. Some of the prominent users of metadata include the development community, the data administration community, and the end user community.

The development community uses metadata to determine how new systems must be interfaced with older existing systems. The data administration community uses metadata to determine how the data model needs to be changed. Or if there is a new data model, how the new data model will fit with the existing data model. The end user community uses metadata to help in the creation of queries. The uses of metadata are shown in Figure 5.4.5.

The end user community uses metadata in many ways. The simplest way that metadata is used is in terms of guiding the end user as to what data exists in the system and how that data ought to be used in query processing.

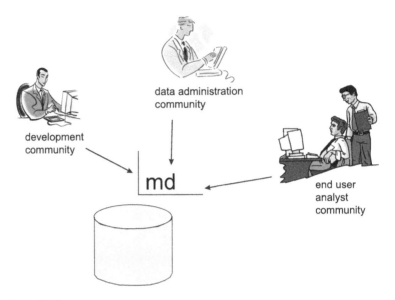

Figure 5.4.5

Analytical Uses of Metadata

But there are other uses as well. Another use of metadata is to determine if a query needs to be done at all. On occasions, the end user will find that the data being sought is already found in another report or database. Preventing the end user from doing unnecessary queries is an important way in which metadata can streamline operations.

Figure 5.4.6 shows the end user looking at metadata as part of the analytical process.

Figure 5.4.6

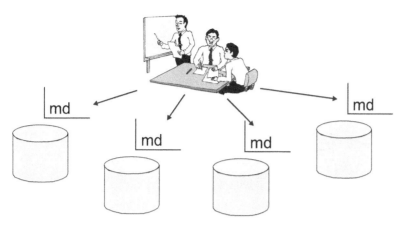

Figure 5.4.7

Looking at Multiple Systems

Another use of metadata is as a basis for determining how to work with multiple systems. Occasionally an organization finds the need to look at information over multiple systems. A good starting point is to look at the metadata in each of the systems that describes the system, as shown in Figure 5.4.7.

The Lineage of Data

Yet another use of metadata in the analytical process is as a basis for understanding the lineage of data. Occasionally the analyst finds some data that looks like it is the right data to use. But to be sure, the analyst needs to know where the data came from. It is normal to find that the data has gone through several transformations and several calculations from the moment the data first entered the corporation.

Looking back and tracing the origins of data is said to be looking at the "lineage" of data. Metadata is the starting point for understanding the lineage of data, as shown in Figure 5.4.8.

Comparing Existing Systems to Proposed Systems

Another important use of metadata comes from the need to compare new proposed systems to existing systems. Sometimes the proposed system is one that will be built internally. In other

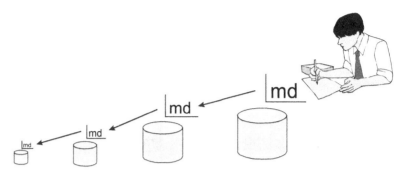

Figure 5.4.8

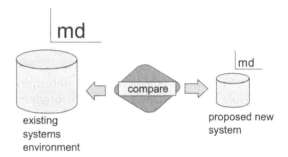

Figure 5.4.9

cases the proposed system is one that may be purchased or otherwise acquired. A good way to start to understand how the systems compare to each other is by looking at their metadata. Figure 5.4.9 shows the comparison of systems by examining the metadata of each system.

DATA GOVERNANCE OF STRUCTURED DATA

For many reasons data in a large corporation winds up being less than perfect. And when data becomes "messed up" corporations find themselves making decisions on data that simply is not correct. When the day arrives where the data is bad enough and the corporation decides to do something about the incorrect data, the organization engages in a practice called "data governance."

A Corporate Activity

Data governance is a corporate wide activity. It often starts in one section of the corporation, but as the data improves, the activity of data governance becomes an activity the organization engages in. Figure 5.5.1 shows that data governance is first and foremost an activity of the organization.

Motivations for Data Governance

There are many reasons why the organization engages in data governance. Sometimes the corporation is just fed up with poor data. But on other occasions there are external forces that motivate the corporation to start a data governance program.

Some of the motivating external factors that push the organization into data governance include compliance with the Sarbanes-Oxley Act, Basel II, and the Health Insurance Portability and Accountability Act (HIPAA) as shown in Figure 5.5.2.

Repairing Data

The essence of data governance is to "fix" broken data. In order to fix the data, you first have to know why it is broken. Indeed, there are many causes of broken data:
- There are multiple and mixed definitions of the same data.
- The data is not integrated at all or has been integrated improperly.

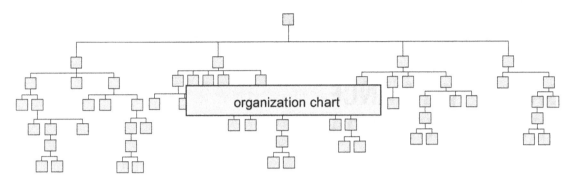

Figure 5.5.1

Sarbanes-Oxley

Basel II

HIPAA

and others

Figure 5.5.2

- The capture of data has not been done correctly.
- There is no properly defined and enforced system of record.
- Calculations and algorithms have been created incorrectly.
- The business requirements have changed while the data has not.

Whatever the cause or causes of incorrect data, the role of data governance is to understand the data and correct whatever problems there are. Figure 5.5.3 shows that the role of data governance is the repair of data.

The work of repair, of course, depends on whatever the problem with might be. And at first, correcting data seems to be a Herculean task, especially for large organizations.

The repair of data only begins with identifying the problem. After the problem is identified, the following steps (at the least) need to be taken:

- The data needs to be redefined.
- The data needs to be re-specified to the system.
- The code that supports the data needs to be modified.

And after all of that, the issue of whether to go back and repair data that has already been written needs to be addressed. The process of repairing data then only begins with the activity of redefining the data.

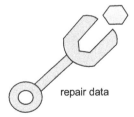

repair data

Figure 5.5.3

Granular, Detailed Data

But the task of repairing data is not as Herculean as it might seem, at least at first glance. The first observation is that data governance applies (or ought to apply) almost exclusively to the granular, detailed data of the organization. If the granular, detailed of the corporation is not correct, it is a sure bet that the derived data will not be correct either. So looking just at the granular, detailed data of the corporation is at least a starting point for "fixing" the data of the corporation.

Figure 5.5.4 shows that separating the granular data from the derived, summarized data is the starting point for the data governance program.

Documentation

Another first step is to document whatever changes are needed. The documentation should be made so that everyone in the corporation has access to the documentation. Figure 5.5.5 shows the need for documentation.

Another important step is the identification and recognition of appropriate subject matter experts (SMEs) and data stewards. The data steward is the person responsible for determining what data is correct and what data is incorrect, and what is to be done about incorrect data. Usually data stewards have other functional responsibilities in the corporation and data stewardship is not a full-time activity.

Data Stewardship

Figure 5.5.6 shows the identification and recognition of data stewards and SMEs.

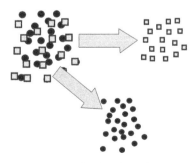

separate granular data from derived data

Figure 5.5.4

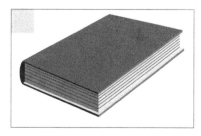

documenting systems

Figure 5.5.5

SMEs and data stewards

Figure 5.5.6

an ongoing effort

Figure 5.5.7

managing the
data governance
project

Figure 5.5.8

It is noted that data governance is an ongoing effort. Usually at the beginning of the data governance effort most of the data is amended. But there still needs to be periodic reviews of data and interaction with data stewards and SMEs, which is depicted in Figure 5.5.7.

Like any other project, data governance needs to be managed. One of the cornerstones of management of the data governance effort is top management buy-in and awareness. Without the support of top management, data governance is doomed to become a backroom, clerical exercise.

Figure 5.5.8 shows that the data governance effort needs to be managed.

6.1

A BRIEF HISTORY OF DATA ARCHITECTURE

Data has been around since the first computer program was written. In many ways data is the gasoline that fuels the engine of the computer. The way that data is used, shaped, and stored has progressed to the point that there is actually now an area of study that can be called "data architecture."

There are many facets to data architecture because, as we shall see, data is complex. The four most interesting aspects of data architecture are:

1. The physical manifestation of data
2. The logical linkage of data
3. The internal format of data
4. The file structure of data

Each of these aspects of data has evolved interdependently over time. Data architecture can best be explained in terms of the evolution of each of these aspects of data architecture. The evolution of data architecture is seen in Figure 6.1.1.

The simplest evolution that has occurred (and has been described in many places) is that of the physical evolution of the media on which data has been stored. Figure 6.1.2 shows this well-documented evolution.

The beginning of the computer industry harks back to paper tape and punched cards. In the very earliest days data was stored by means of paper tape and punched cards. The value of paper tape and punched cards was that it was easy to create storage. But there were many problems with paper tape and cards. Hollerith punched cards were fixed format only (everything was stored in 80 columns). Cards were dropped and soiled. Cards could not be repunched. And cards were expensive.

Figure 6.1.3 shows that punched cards and paper tape were early storage mechanisms for data.

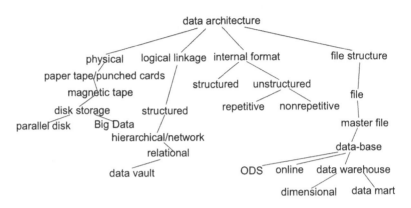

Figure 6.1.1

Only so much data could be stored on cards. Very quickly an alternative to punched cards was needed. Next came magnetic tape. Magnetic tape could store much more data than could ever be stored on punched cards. And magnetic tape was not limited to the single format of a punched card. But there were some major limitations to magnetic tape. In order to find data on a magnetic tape file you had to scan the entire file. And the oxide on magnetic tape files was notoriously unstable.

Figure 6.1.4 shows the symbol for magnetic tape files.

Magnetic tape file represented a major step forward from punched cards, but magnetic tape files had their own serious limitations. After magnetic tape files came disk storage. With disk storage, data could be accessed directly. No longer was it necessary to search the entire file to find a single record.

The early forms of disk storage were expensive and slow. And there was relatively little capacity for the early forms of disk storage. But quickly the costs of manufacturing dropped significantly, the capacity increased, and the speed of access decreased. Disk storage was a superior alternative to magnetic tape files.

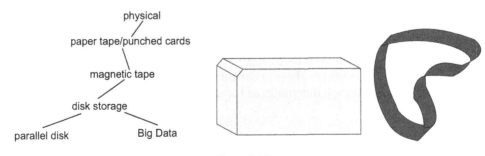

Figure 6.1.2

Figure 6.1.3

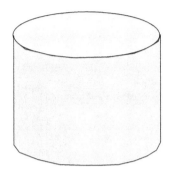

Figure 6.1.4   **Figure 6.1.5**

Figure 6.1.5 shows the symbol for disk storage.

The demand for volumes of data increased dramatically. In short order it was necessary to manage disk storage in a parallel manner. By managing disk storage in a parallel manner, the total amount of data that could be controlled increased significantly. Parallel management of storage did not increase the volume of data that could be managed on a single disk. Instead parallel storage of data decreased the total elapsed time that was required to access and to manage storage.

Figure 6.1.6 shows the symbol for parallel management of storage.

Yet another increase in the volume of data that could be managed on disk arrived in the form of Big Data. Big Data was really just another form of parallelism. But with Big Data even more data could be managed and at an increasingly lower unit cost.

Figure 6.1.7 shows the symbol for Big Data.

Over the years then, the total amount of data that could be managed, at an amazing decrease in the unit storage of data, with an ever-increasing speed of access has evolved. But the physical storage of data was hardly the only evolution that was occurring. Another concurrent evolution that was occurring was the evolution of the way that data was logically organized. It is one thing to physically store data. It is another thing to logically organize data so that it can be easily and rationally accessed.

Figure 6.1.8 shows the evolutionary progression of the logical organization of data.

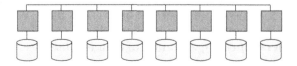

Figure 6.1.6

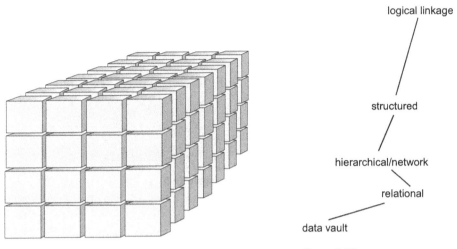

Figure 6.1.7

logical linkage

structured

hierarchical/network

relational

data vault

Figure 6.1.8

In the very earliest days, data was logically organized in almost a random fashion. Every programmer and every designer "did their own thing." To say that the world was in chaos when it came to logical organization of data was an understatement.

Into this world of chaos came Ed Yourdon and Tom DeMarco. Yourdon espoused a concept called the "structured" approach. (Note that the term "structured" as used by Yourdon is quite different than the same term used in describing the internal formatting of data. When Yourdon used the term "structured," he was referring to a logical and organized way of arranging information systems. Yourdon was referring to programming practices, design of systems, and many other aspects of information systems. The term "structured" is also used in describing the internal formatting of data. Even though the terms that are used are the same, they mean something quite different.)

In Yourdon's approach to structured systems, one of the aspects of structure was in reference to how data elements should be logically organized in order to create a disciplined system approach for the building of information systems. Prior to Yourdon there were many schemes for the logical organization of data.

Figure 6.1.9 is a symbol depicting the Yourdon approach to structured programming and development.

A while later came the idea of database management systems (DBMSs) as a means of logically organizing data. With DBMS came the idea of organizing data hierarchically and in a network. An early hierarchical organization of data was used by IBM's IMS. And an early form of network organization of data was Cullinet's IDMS.

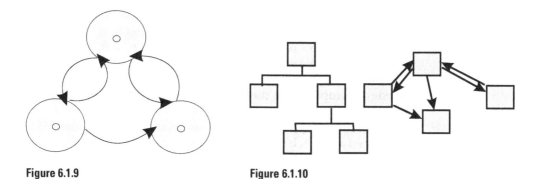

Figure 6.1.9   **Figure 6.1.10**

In the hierarchical organization of data was the notion of a parent/child relationship. A parent could have zero or more children. And a child had to have a parent. Figure 6.1.10 depicts a diagram that has a parent/child relationship and a networked relationship.

DBMS was useful for organizing data both for batch processing and for online transaction processing. Many systems were built running transactions under DBMS.

Soon there came another notion about the way data should be logically organized. That method was through what was termed a "relational database management system."

In the relational database management system, data was "normalized." Normalization meant that there was a primary key for each table and the attributes in the table depended on the key of the table for their existence. The tables were able to be related to each other by means of a key/foreign key relationship. On access of the tables, the tables could be "joined" by means of pairing up the appropriate key and foreign key. Figure 6.1.11 shows a relational table.

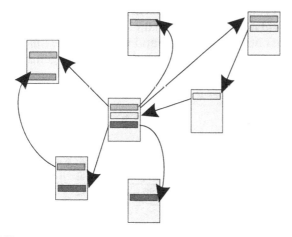

Figure 6.1.11

As interesting and as important as the logical organization of data is, it was not the only aspect of data architecture.

Another aspect of data architecture is that of the internal formatting of data. When you look at the logical organization of data, DBMS only applied to what is called "structured" data. The structured data implies that there is some way that the computer can comprehend the way the data is organized. The structured way of organizing data applies to many aspects of the corporation. The structured approach is used for organizing customer information, product information, sales information, accounting information, and so forth. The structured approach is used for capturing transaction information.

The unstructured approach is for data that is not organized in a manner that is intelligible to the computer. The unstructured approach applies to images, audio information, downloads from satellites, and so forth. But far and away the biggest use of the unstructured approach is for textual data.

Figure 6.1.12 shows the evolution of the internal formatting of data.

The structured approach implies that the data is organized enough to be able to be defined to a DBMS. Typically the DBMS has attributes of data, keys, indexes, and records of data. The "schema" of the data is determined as the data is loaded. Indeed the content of the data and its place in the schema dictate where and how the data is loaded.

Figure 6.1.13 illustrates data loaded in a structured format.

The unstructured internal organization of data contains all sorts of data. There is a wide variety of data here. The unstructured internal organization of data includes email, documents, spreadsheets, analog data, log tape data, and many varieties of data. Figure 6.1.14 shows unstructured internally organized data.

The world of unstructured data is a world where there is a basic division between repetitive and nonrepetitive data. Repetitive unstructured data is data where the data is organized in many records where the structure and content of the records are very

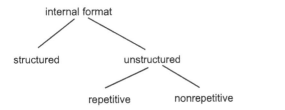

Figure 6.1.12

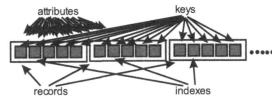

Figure 6.1.13

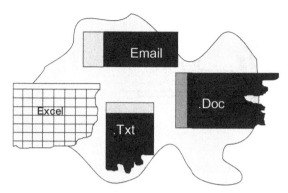

Figure 6.1.14

Figure 6.1.15

similar or even the same. Figure 6.1.15 shows repetitive unstructured data.

The other kind of data found in the unstructured environment is that of nonrepetitive data. With nonrepetitive data there is no correlation between one record of data and any other. If there is a similarity of data between any two records of data in the nonrepetitive environment, it is purely a random event. Figure 6.1.16 depicts the nonrepetitive unstructured environment.

Yet another aspect of data is the file organization of the data. Starting with a very simple file organization, the world has progressed to a very elaborate and sophisticated organization of data. Figure 6.1.17 shows the evolution of file structures of data.

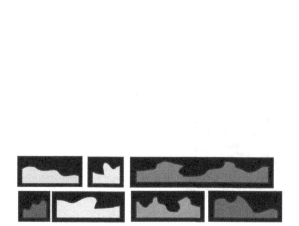

Figure 6.1.16

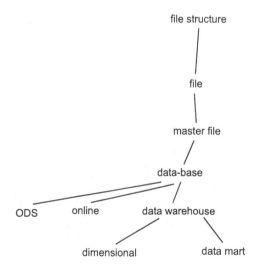

Figure 6.1.17

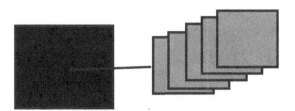

Figure 6.1.18

In the early days there was crude and simple file organization. Soon the vendors of technology recognized that a more formal approach was needed. Thus were born simple files, as shown in Figure 6.1.18. These files were simple collections of data organized in whichever way the designer thought they needed to be organized. In almost every case the files were designed to be optimized around the needs of an application.

But soon it was recognized that the same or very similar information was being collected by more than one application. It was recognized that this overlap of effort was both wasteful and resulted in redundant data being collected and managed. The solution was the creation of a master file. The master file was a place where data could be gathered in a nonredundant manner. Figure 6.1.19 shows a master file.

The master file was a good idea and worked well. The only problem was that a master file existed on a tape file. And tape files were clumsy to use. Soon the idea of a master file evolved into the idea of a database. Thus evolved the database concept, as shown in Figure 6.1.20.

The early notion of a database was as a "place where all data resided for a subject area." In a day and age where lots of data was still lying in files and master files, the idea of a database was appealing. And given that data could be accessed on disk storage in a database, the idea of a database was especially appealing.

Figure 6.1.19   **Figure 6.1.20**

Figure 6.1.21

Soon however the database concept morphed into the online database concept. In the online database concept, not only could data be accessed directly, data could be accessed in a real-time, online mode. In the online, real-time mode, data could be added, deleted, and changed as business needs changed. Figure 6.1.21 depicts the online, real-time environment.

The online database environment opened up computing to parts of the business where never before had any interaction been possible. Soon there were applications everywhere. And in short order the applications spawned what was known as the "spider-web" environment.

With the spider-web environment came the need for integrity of data. Soon the concept of the data warehouse arose. Figure 6.1.22 shows the advent of the data warehouse.

The data warehouse provided the organization with the "single version of the truth." Now there was a basis for reconciliation of data. With the data warehouse – for the first time – came a place where historical data could be stored and used. The data warehouse represented a fundamental step forward for the information processing systems of the organization.

As important as the data warehouse was, there were other elements of architecture that were needed. It was soon recognized that something between a data warehouse and a transactional

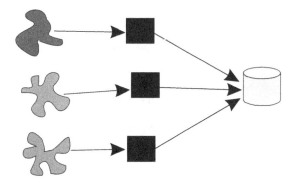

Figure 6.1.22

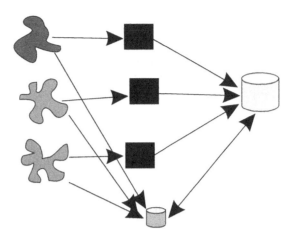

Figure 6.1.23

system was needed. Thus was born the operational data store (ODS). Figure 6.1.23 shows the ODS.

The ODS was a place where online high-performance processing could be done on corporate data. Not every organization had need of an ODS but many did.

At about the time that the data warehouse was born, it was recognized that organizations had need of a place where individual departments could go to and find data for their own individual analytical needs. Into this analytical environment came the data mart, or the dimensional model.

Figure 6.1.24 shows the star join, the foundation of the data mart.

It was then recognized that a more formal treatment of data marts was needed than just having dimensional models. The

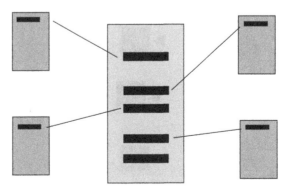

Figure 6.1.24

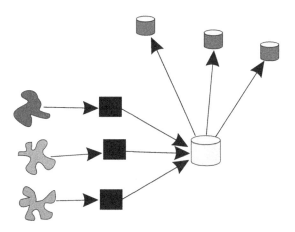

Figure 6.1.25

notion of the dependent data mart was then created. Figure 6.1.25 shows dependent data marts.

The evolution that has been described did not happen independently but concurrently. Indeed the evolution to some levels of development depended on evolutionary developments that occurred in other arenas. For example, the evolution to online databases could not have occurred until the technology that supported online processing had been developed. Or the movement to data warehouses could not have occurred until the cost of storage dropped to an affordable rate.

BIG DATA/EXISTING SYSTEMS INTERFACE

One of the challenges of information systems is determining how they all fit together. In particular, how does Big Data fit with the existing systems environment? There is no question that Big Data brings new opportunities for information and decision making to the organization. And there is no question that Big Data has great promise. But Big Data is not a replacement for the existing systems environment. In fact Big Data accomplishes one task and the existing systems environment accomplishes another task. They are (or should be) complementary to each other.

So exactly how does Big Data need to interface with and interact with the existing systems environment?

The Big Data/Existing Systems Interface

Figure 6.2.1 shows the recommended way in which Big Data and existing systems interface with each other and the overall system flow between Big Data and the existing systems environment. Each of the interfaces will be discussed in detail.

Raw Big Data is divided into two distinct sections (see the "great divide"). There is repetitive raw Big Data and nonrepetitive raw Big Data. Repetitive raw Big Data is handled entirely differently than nonrepetitive raw Big Data.

The Repetitive Raw Big Data/Existing Systems Interface

The interface from repetitive raw Big Data to the existing systems environment in some ways is the simplest interface. In many ways this interface is like a "distillation" process. The mass of data found in raw repetitive Big Data is winnowed down – distilled – into the few records that are of interest.

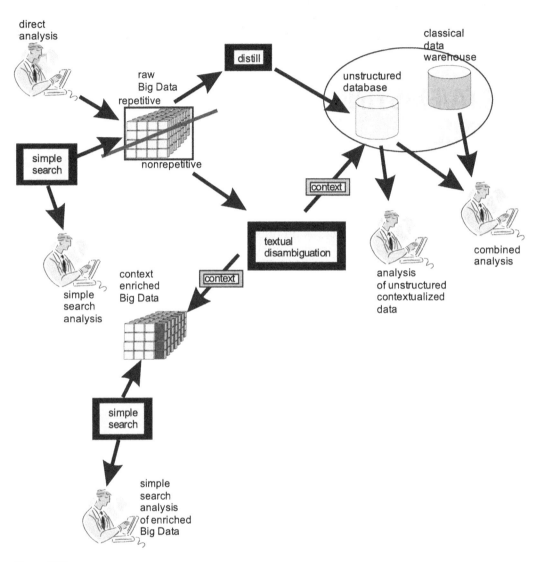

Figure 6.2.1

The repetitive raw Big Data is processed by parsing each record. And when the records that are of interest are located, the records of interest are then edited and passed to the existing systems environment. In such a fashion the data that is of interest is distilled from the mass of records found in the raw repetitive Big Data environment. One assumption made by this interface is that the vast majority of records found in the repetitive component of raw Big Data will not be passed to the existing systems environment. The assumption is that only a few records of interest are to be found.

In order to explain this assumption, consider the following cases of manufacturing, telephone calls, log tape analysis, and metering.

A manufacturer makes a product. The quality of the product is quite high. On the average only 1 out of 10,000 products is defective. However, the defective products are still a bother. All the product manufacturing information is stored in Big Data. But only the information about the defective products is brought to the existing systems environment for further analysis. In this case, based on a percentage basis, very little data is brought to the existing systems environment.

Millions of telephone calls are made on a daily basis. But of those millions of telephone calls, only a handful – maybe three or four – are of interest for call record details. Only the phone calls that are of interest are brought from the Big Data environment to the existing systems environment

For log tape analysis, a log tape of transactions is created. In a day, tens of thousands of log tape entries are created. But only a few hundred entries on the log tape are of interest. Those few hundred log tape entries that are of interest are the only entries that find their way back into the existing systems environment for further analysis.

An organization collects metering data. The vast majority of the metering activity is normal and not of particular interest. But on a few days of the year certain metering data reacts in an unexpected manner. Only those readings that have reacted abnormally are brought to the existing systems environment for further analysis.

And there are many more examples of repetitive raw Big Data being examined for exceptional data.

As a rule when data goes from the Big Data environment to the existing systems environment, it is convenient to place the data in a data warehouse. However, if there is a need, data can be sent elsewhere in the existing systems environment.

Exception-Based Data

Once the data in the raw repetitive Big Data environment is selected (which is usually chosen on an exception basis and is then moved to the existing systems environment) the exception-based data can undergo all sorts of analysis, such as:
• Pattern analysis. Why are the records that have been chosen exceptional? Is there a pattern of activity external to the records that match with the behavior of the records?

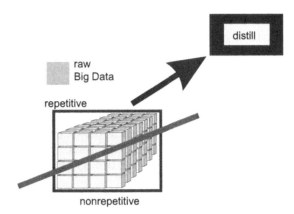

Figure 6.2.2

- Comparative analysis. Is the number of exceptional records increasing? Decreasing? What other events are happening concurrent to the collection of the exceptional records?
- Growth and analysis of exceptional records over time. Over time what is happening to the exceptional records that have been collected from Big Data?

And there are *many* more ways to analyze the data that has been collected.

Figure 6.2.2 shows the interface from Big Data to the existing systems environment.

The Nonrepetitive Raw Big Data/Existing Systems Interface

The interface from the nonrepetitive raw Big Data environment is one that is very different from the repetitive raw Big Data interface. The first major difference is in the percentage of data that is collected. Whereas in the repetitive raw Big Data interface only a small percentage of the data is selected, in the nonrepetitive raw Big Data interface the majority of the data is selected. This is because there is business value in the majority of the data found in the nonrepetitive raw Big Data environment whereas there is little business value in the majority of the repetitive Big Data environment. But there are other major differences as well.

The second major difference in the environments is in terms of context. In the repetitive raw Big Data environment, context is usually obvious and easy to find. In the nonrepetitive raw Big Data environment context is not obvious at all and is not easy to find. It

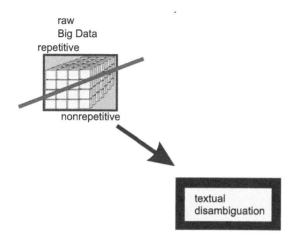

Figure 6.2.3

is noted that context is in fact there in the nonrepetitive Big Data environment; it just is not easy to find and is anything but obvious.

In order to find context, the technology of textual disambiguation is needed. Textual disambiguation reads the nonrepetitive data in Big Data and derives context from the data. (See the chapter on textual disambiguation and taxonomies for a more complete discussion of deriving context from nonrepetitive raw Big Data.)

While *most* of the nonrepetitive raw Big Data is useful, some percentage of data is not useful and is edited out by the process of textual disambiguation. Once the context is derived, the output can then be sent to either of the existing systems environments.

Figure 6.2.3 shows the interface from nonrepetitive raw Big Data to textual disambiguation.

Into the Existing Systems Environment

Once data has come from nonrepetitive raw Big Data and has passed through textual disambiguation, the data can be passed to the existing systems environment.

As the data is passed through textual disambiguation, it is greatly simplified. Context is inferred and each unit of text that passes the filtering process is turned into a flat file record. The flat file record is reminiscent of a standard relational record. There is a key and dependent data, as is found in a relational format.

The output can be sent to a load utility so that the output data can be placed in whatever DBMS is desired. Typical output DBMSs include Oracle, Teradata, UDB/DB2, and SQL Server.

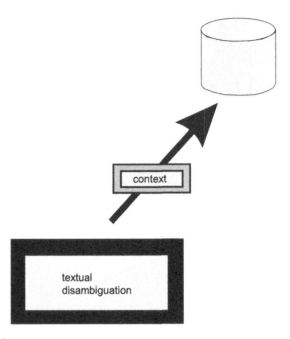

Figure 6.2.4

Figure 6.2.4 shows the movement of data into the existing systems environment in the form of a standard DBMS.

The "Context-Enriched" Big Data Environment

The other route that data can take after it passes through textual disambiguation is that the output of data can be placed back into Big Data. There may be several reasons for wanting to send output back into Big Data. Some of the reasons include:

- The volume of data. There may be a lot of output from textual disambiguation. The sheer volume of data may dictate that the output data be placed back into the Big Data environment.
- The nature of the data. In some cases the output data may have a natural fit with the other data placed in the Big Data environment. Future analytical processing may be greatly enhanced by placing output data back into Big Data.

In any case, after data passes through textual disambiguation and is placed back into Big Data, it enters Big Data in a very different state. When data has passed through textual disambiguation and is placed back into the Big Data environment, it is placed into the environment with the context of the data clearly identified and prominently a data part of the data in Big Data.

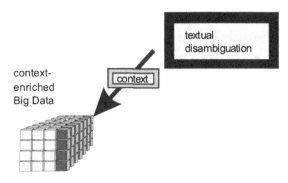

Figure 6.2.5

By placing the output of textual disambiguation back into Big Data, there now is a section of Big Data that can be called the "context-enriched" section of Big Data. From a structural standpoint, the context-enriched component of Big Data looks to be very similar to repetitive raw Big Data. The only difference is that the context-enriched component of Big Data has context open and obvious and attached to the base data in this component of Big Data.

Figure 6.2.5 shows that output data from textual disambiguation can be placed back into Big Data. Another perspective of the Big Data environment is shown in Figure 6.2.6.

Figure 6.2.6 shows that there is the division of Big Data into the repetitive and nonrepetitive sections. However, in the repetitive section, it is seen that when context-enriched Big Data is added to the Big Data environment, context-enriched data simply becomes another type of repetitive data. Stated differently, there are two types of repetitive data in Big Data – simple repetitive data and context-enriched repetitive data.

This division becomes important when doing analytical processing. Repetitive data is analyzed in a completely different fashion than context-enriched repetitive data.

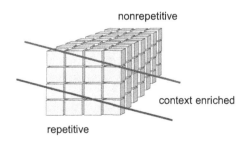

Figure 6.2.6

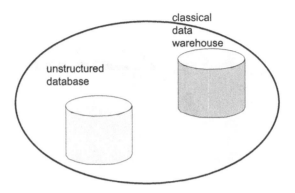

Figure 6.2.7

Analyzing Structured Data/Unstructured Data Together

The final interface of interest in the Big Data environment is that data that has come from Big Data either through the distillation process or textual disambiguation. The data that arrives here can be placed into a standard DBMS.

Figure 6.2.7 shows the database that has been created from unstructured data being placed in the same environment as the classical data warehouse. Of course the data in the classical data warehouse has been created from structured data entirely.

Figure 6.2.7 shows that data whose origin is quite different can be placed in the same analytical environment. The DBMS may be Oracle or Teradata. The operating system may be Windows or Linux. In any case doing analytical processing against the two databases is as easy as doing a relational join. In such a manner it is easy and natural to do analytical processing against data from the two different environments. This means that structured data and unstructured data can be used together analytically. By combining these two types of data together, entirely new vistas of analytical processing open up.

THE DATA WAREHOUSE/ OPERATIONAL ENVIRONMENT INTERFACE

As interesting as the Big Data/existing systems interface is, it is not the only interface the data architect needs to know about. The other major interface in the corporate systems environment that is of interest is the interface between the operational environment and the data warehouse.

The Operational/Data Warehouse Interface

Figure 6.3.1 shows the interface between the operational environment and the data warehouse environment.

The operational environment is the place where day-to-day corporate decisions are made at the detailed level. The data warehouse environment is the place where the data that serves as the basis for corporate decision making is stored.

The Classical ETL Interface

The interface between the two environments is called the "ETL" layer. ETL stands for extract/transform/load. It is in the ETL interface that application data is transformed to corporate data. The transformation is one of the most important transformations of data the corporation has.

Figure 6.3.2 shows the classical ETL interface.

The transformation of data in this interface is from application data to corporate data. The operational data is defined by each application. As a consequence there are inconsistent definitions of data, inconsistent formulas, inconsistent structures of data, and so forth. But when the data passes through the ETL layer, the inconsistencies are resolved.

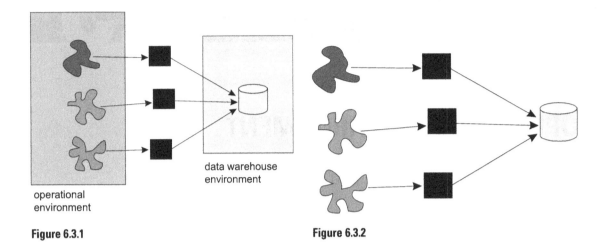

Figure 6.3.1   **Figure 6.3.2**

The Operational Data Store/ETL Interface

There are, however, several variations to the classical ETL interface between the operational environment and the data warehouse environment. One of those variations is the inclusion of the operational data store (ODS) into the interface. Figure 6.3.3 shows that the ODS can participate in the interface.

Data that flows to the ODS can flow directly into the ODS from the operational environment or data that passes to the ODS can pass through the ETL transformation layer. Whether or not the

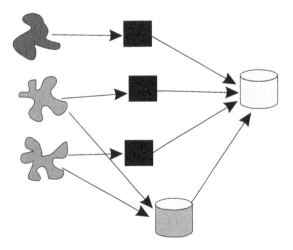

Figure 6.3.3

data passes through the ETL layer depends entirely on the class of the ODS. In the case of a class I ODS, data passes directly from the operational system to the ODS. In the case of a class II or class III ODS, data passes through the ETL interface.

Not every corporation has or needs an ODS. Usually it is those corporations where there is a high degree of online transaction processing where the ODS is found.

The Staging Area

Another variation of the classical ETL interface between the operational environment and the data warehouse environment is the case where there is a staging area. Figure 6.3.4 shows a staging area.

There are some very specific cases where a staging area is called for. One of those cases is where data from two or more files must be merged and there is a timing issue. The data from file ABC is ready for merger at 9:00 a.m. and the data from file BCD is not ready for a merger until 5:00 p.m. In this instance, the data from file ABC must be "staged" until the merge is ready to occur.

A second case for the staging area is where there is a large volume of data and the data must be separated into different workloads in order to accommodate the parallelization of the ETL process. In this case a staging area is needed to separate the volume of data.

A third case for the staging area is where the data coming from the operational environment must pass through a "preprocessing" step. In the preprocessing step, data passes through an edit and correction process.

One of the issues with the staging area is whether or not analytical processing can be done against data found in the staging area. As a rule, data in the staging area is not used for analytical

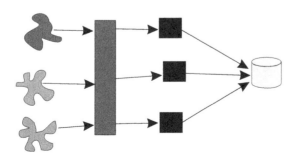

Figure 6.3.4

processing. This is because the data found in the staging area has not yet been passed through the transformation process. Therefore it does not make sense to do any analytical processing against data found in the staging area.

Note that a staging area is optional and most organizations do not need one.

Changed Data Capture

Yet another variation on the classical interface between operational systems and data warehouse systems is the "changed data capture" (CDC) option. For high-performance online transaction environments it is difficult or inefficient to scan the entire database every time data needs to be refreshed into the data warehouse environment. In these environments it makes sense to determine what data needs to be updated into the data warehouse by examining the log tape or journal tape. The log tape is created for the purposes of online backup and recovery in the eventuality of a failure during online transaction processing. But the log tape contains all the data that needs to be updated into the data warehouse. The log tape is read offline and is used to gather the data that needs to be updated into the data warehouse.

Figure 6.3.5 depicts the CDC option.

Inline Transformation

Another alternative to the classical operational-to–data warehouse interface is that of the inline transformation. In the inline transformation, the data that needs to flow to the data

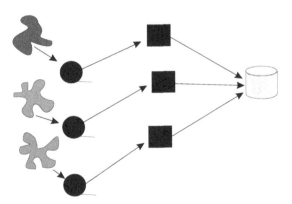

Figure 6.3.5

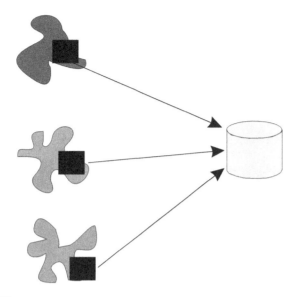

Figure 6.3.6

warehouse is captured and processed as part of online transaction processing.

Online transformation is not used very often because the coding needs to be part of the original coding specifications and because of the resource consumption that is required during high-performance online transaction processing. In truth, most code for online transaction processing is created before any one realizes that the results of online transaction processing need to be reflected in the data warehouse environment. However, on occasion this option is seen.

Figure 6.3.6 shows the inline transformation option.

ELT Processing

A final variation on the classical ETL interface is one that can be called the ELT interface. The ELT interface is one where the data is loaded directly from the operational environment to the data warehouse. Once in the data warehouse, the data is then transformed.

The problem with the ELT option is that there is the temptation to simply not execute the "T" step (i.e., the transformation step). In this case the data warehouse turns into a "garbage dump." And once the data warehouse is loaded with garbage, it becomes worthless as a foundation for decision making.

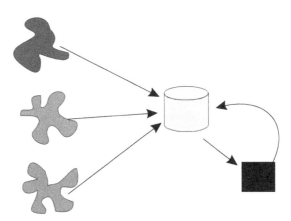

Figure 6.3.7

If an organization has the will power to not neglect to do the "T" step, then there is nothing wrong with the ELT approach. But few organizations have the willpower and discipline to use the ELT approach properly.

Figure 6.3.7 illustrates the ELT approach to interfacing operational systems and data warehouses.

DATA ARCHITECTURE – A HIGH-LEVEL PERSPECTIVE

One of the aspects of architecture is to provide a high-level perspective as shown in the diagram in Figure 6.4.1.

A High-Level Perspective

Figure 6.4.1 shows representative components. For example, on the left-hand side where there are cathode ray tubes (CRTs) emanating from an application, the diagram is representative of online transaction processing systems. In reality there are *many* applications and *many* databases represented by the application, database, and CRTs.

The diagram also shows that there are two major types of Big Data – repetitive data and nonrepetitive data. And of the repetitive data there is simple repetitive data and context-enriched repetitive data. The typical sources of the different types of Big Data are shown as well.

The diagram shows that repetitive data is distilled into data that can be placed into the analytical data warehouse environment. In addition, nonrepetitive data can be disambiguated and placed either in the data warehouse or back into Big Data as context-enriched repetitive Big Data.

Redundancy

There are many issues raised by the diagram in Figure 6.4.1. One of the issues is that of redundant data. One look at the diagram and it appears that there is redundant data everywhere. In fact rather than redundant data there is data that has been transformed. And if a value of data remains the same after transformation, then you may want to consider the data to be redundant. Then again, you may not.

Consider redundancy in the real world. Take the time of day. You can find the time of day on the Internet, on the telephone, on the radio, on television, and many other places for that matter.

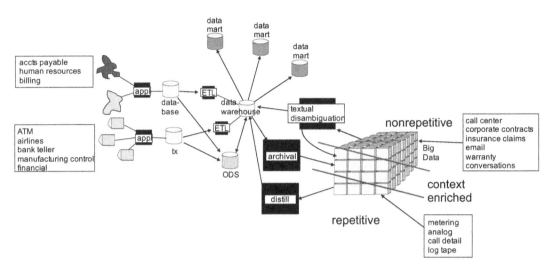

Figure 6.4.1

Does the fact that time of day appears redundantly in many places become a bother? The only time it becomes a bother is if there is no way to determine what the accurate time is. If there were no definitive source of time, then having time appear redundantly would be a problem. But as long as there is some definitive source somewhere and as long as most redundant sources adhere to that definitive source, then there is no problem. In fact, having redundant sources of time is actually quite helpful, as long as there is no problem with the integrity of that time.

Therefore having redundant data across the enterprise as shown in Figure 6.4.1 is not an issue as long as the integrity of the data is not an issue.

The System of Record

The integrity of the data in data architecture is established by what can be called the "system of record." The system of record is the one place where the value of data is definitively and singularly established. Note that the system of record applies only to detailed granular data. The system of record does not apply to summarized or derived data.

In order to understand the system of record, think of a bank and your bank account balance. For every account in every bank, there is a system of record for account balance. There is one and only one place where the account balance is established and managed from. Your bank account balance may appear in many places

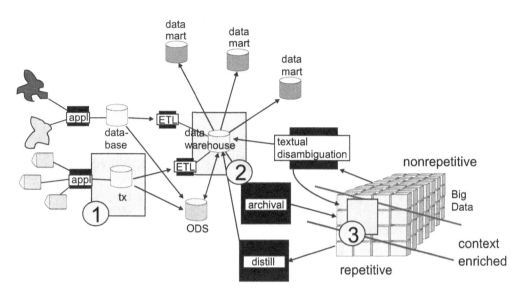

Figure 6.4.2

throughout the bank. But there is only one place where the system of record is kept.

The system of record moves throughout the data architecture that has been described and is depicted in Figure 6.4.2.

Figure 6.4.2 shows that as data is captured, especially in the on-line environment, which the data has as its first system of record. Location 1 shows that the system of record for current valued data is found in the online environment. You can think of calling the bank and asking for your account balance that exists right now, and the bank looks into its online transaction processing environment to find your account balance right now.

Then one day you have an issue with a bank transaction that occurred two years ago. Your lawyer requires you to go back and prove that you made a payment two years ago. You can't go to your online transaction processing environment. Instead you go to your record in the data warehouse. As data ages, the system of record for older data moves to the data warehouse. That is location 2 in the diagram.

Time passes and you get audited by the Internal Revenue Service (IRS). You have to go back 10 years in time to prove what financial activity you have had. Now you go to the archival store in Big Data. That is location 3 in the diagram.

So as time passes the system of record for data changes in data architecture.

Another way to look at the data found in data architecture is in terms of what types of questions are answered in different parts of

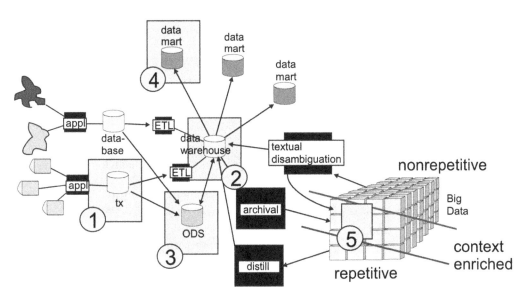

Figure 6.4.3

the architecture. Figure 6.4.3 shows that different types of questions are answered in different parts of the architecture.

Figure 6.4.3 shows that in location 1, detailed up-to-the second questions are answered. Here is where you ask for up-to-the second accurate account balance information.

Location 2 indicates that in the data warehouse you look at your historical activity that has been passed through your bank account.

Location 3 is the ODS. In the ODS you find up-to-the second accurate integrated information. In the ODS you look across information such as *all* your account information – your loans, your savings accounts, your checking account, your IRA, and so forth.

In location 4 are the data marts. In the data marts is where bank management combines your account information with thousands of other accounts and looks at the information from the perspective of a department. One department looks at the data in the data marts from an accounting perspective. Another department looks at the data from the perspective of marketing, and so forth.

There is yet another perspective of data afforded by the data found in location 5. Big Data is found in location 5. There is deep history there as well as a variety of other data. The kinds of analysis that can be done in location 5 are miscellaneous and diverse.

Of course the differences in data and the types of analysis that can be done are different for different industries. The example that has been used is of a bank for the purposes of making the example clear. But for other industries, there are other types of usage information.

Different Communities

Different communities use the information found in data architecture. In general, the clerical community uses information found in location 1 and 2. Everyone uses the data found in location 3. The data warehouse serves as a crossroad for information throughout the organization. Different functional departments use the information found in location 4. And location 5 serves as an omnibus for the entire organization.

REPETITIVE ANALYTICS – SOME BASICS

There are some basic concepts and practices regarding analytics that are pretty much universal. These practices and concepts apply to repetitive analytics and are essential for the data scientist.

Different Kinds of Analysis

There are two distinct types of analysis – open-ended continuous analysis and project-based analysis. Open-ended continuous analysis is analysis that it typically found in the structured corporate world but is occasionally found in the repetitive data world. In open-ended continuous analysis, the analysis starts with the gathering of data. Once the data is gathered, the next step is to refine the data and analyze the data. After the data is analyzed, one decision or a set of decisions are made and the results of those decisions affect the world. Then more raw data is gathered and the process starts over again.

The process of gathering data, refining it, analyzing it, and then making decisions based on the analysis on an ongoing basis is actually very common. An example of such a continuous feedback loop might be a bank's decision to raise or lower the loan rate. The bank gathers information about loans applications and loans payments. Then the bank digests that information and decides to raise or lower loan rates. The bank raises the rate then tests to see what the results have been. Such is an example of an open-ended continuous analytical loop.

The other type of analytical system is a project-based analysis. In a project-based analysis the intent is to do the analysis just once. For example the government may do an analysis on how many illegals have been integrated successfully into society. The intent is to make such a study exactly once. There may be safety studies conducted by an automobile manufacturer. Or there may be chemical analysis of a product. Or there may be a study about the content of ethanol in gasoline. There can be any sort of one-time studies.

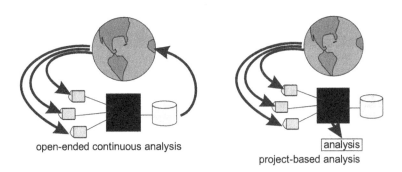

open-ended continuous analysis

analysis
project-based analysis

Figure 7.1.1

Figure 7.1.1 shows that there are two types of analytical studies.
Whether a study happens one time or is ongoing greatly affects the infrastructure surrounding the study. In a continuous study there needs to be an ongoing infrastructure that is created. In a onetime study there is a very different infrastructure that is created.

Looking for Patterns

However the analytical study is done, the study typically looks for patterns. Stated differently, the organization identifies patterns that lead to conclusions. The patterns are tipoffs that important previously unknown events are occurring. By knowing these patterns the organization can then have insights that allow the organization to manage itself more efficiently, more safely, or more economically, or whatever the end goal of the study is.

The patterns can come in different forms. Sometime the patterns are in the form of measurements of occurrences. In other cases a variable is measured continuously. Figure 7.1.2 shows two common forms in which patterns are measured.

Where there are discrete occurrences, the occurrences are pasted onto a "scatter chart." The scatter chart is merely a collection of the points placed onto a chart. There are many issues that

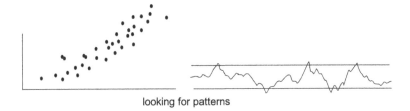

looking for patterns

Figure 7.1.2

relate to the creation of a scatter chart. One of the more important issues is that of determining if a pattern is relevant. On occasion there may be points that have been collected that should not have been collected. On other occasions there may be points on the chart that have been created that form more than one pattern. A professional statistician is needed to be able to determine the accuracy and the integrity of the points found on a scatter diagram.

Another form of finding patterns is to look at a continuously measured variable. In this case there typically are levels of thresholds that are of interest. As long as the continuous variable is within the limits of the threshold, there is no problem. But the moment the variable exceeds one or more level of the threshold, then the analyst takes interest. Usually the analysis centers on what else occurred when the variable exceeded the threshold value.

Once the points of events have been captured and fit to a graph, the next issue is that of identifying false-positives. A false-positive is an event that has occurred but for reasons unrelated to the study. If enough variables are studied, there will be occurrences of false-positives merely by the fact that enough variables have been correlated to each other.

There once was a famous false-positive correlation that occurred that was widely known and discussed. That false-positive correlation was one that stated that if the AFC won the Super Bowl, then the stock market would go down for the next year. But if the NFC won the Super Bowl, then the stock market would rise. Based on this false-positive, one could make money in the stock market knowing what who the winner of the Super Bowl was. Figure 7.1.3 shows this infamous false-positive correlation.

In reality there is no real correlation between the winner of the Super Bowl and the performance of the stock market. Winning a football game is no indicator of economic performance. The fact that for many years there actually was a correlation proves that

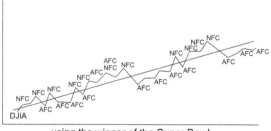

using the winner of the Super Bowl
as a stock market predictor

Figure 7.1.3

if enough trends are compared, somebody will find a correlation somewhere even if the correlation occurs by simple coincidence.

There may be many reasons why false-positive readings occur. Consider an analysis of Internet sales. One looks at the results of a sale and starts to draw conclusions. In many cases the conclusion is correct and valid. But one Internet sale occurred because someone's cat walked across the keyboard at just the wrong time. There is no legitimate conclusion that can be drawn from an occurrence such as that.

False-positive readings can occur for a huge number of unknown and random reasons as depicted by Figure 7.1.4.

Heuristic Processing

Analytical processing is fundamentally different than other types of process. In general, analytic processing is known as "heuristic" processing. In heuristic processing the requirements for analysis are discovered by the results of the current iteration of processing. In order to understand the dynamics of heuristic processing, consider classical system development life cycle (SDLC) processing. Figure 7.1.5 shows a classical SDLC development effort.

In classical SDLC processing the first step is to gather requirements. In classical SDLC, the intent is to gather *all* requirements before the next step of development occurs. This approach is sometimes called the "waterfall" approach because of the need to gather all requirements before engaging in the next step of development.

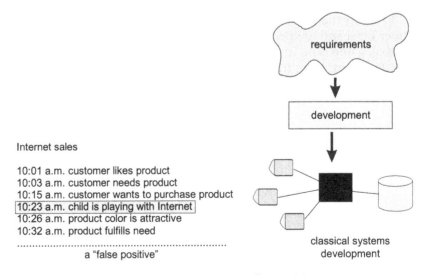

Internet sales

10:01 a.m. customer likes product
10:03 a.m. customer needs product
10:15 a.m. customer wants to purchase product
10:23 a.m. child is playing with Internet
10:26 a.m. product color is attractive
10:32 a.m. product fulfills need

a "false positive"

Figure 7.1.4

classical systems
development

Figure 7.1.5

But heuristic processing is fundamentally different than the classical SDLC. In heuristic processing you start with some requirements. You build a system to analyze those requirements. Then, after you have results, you sit back and rethink your requirements after you have had time to reflect on the results that have been achieved. You then restate the requirements and redevelop and reanalyze again. Each time you go through the redevelopment exercise is called an "iteration." You continue the process of building different iterations of processing until such time as you achieve the results that satisfy the organization that is sponsoring the exercise.

Figure 7.1.6 depicts the heuristic approach to analysis.

One of the characteristics of the heuristic process is that at the beginning, it is impossible to know how many iterations of redevelopment will be done. It just simply is impossible to know how long the heuristic analytical process will take. Another characteristic of the heuristic process is that the requirements may change very little or the requirements may completely change of the life of the heuristic process. Again, it is impossible to know what the requirements will look like at the end of the heuristic process.

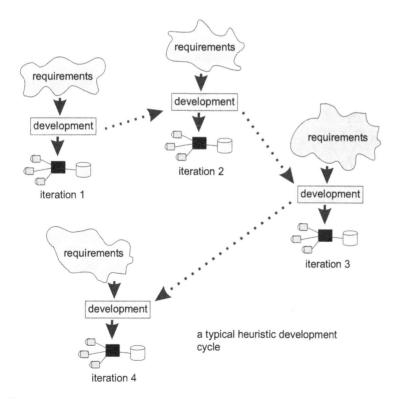

a typical heuristic development cycle

Figure 7.1.6

Because of the iterative nature of the iterative process, the development process is much less formal and a lot more relaxed than the development process found in the classical SDLC environment. The essence of the heuristic process is on speed of development and the quick production of results.

Another characteristic of the heuristic process is for the need for data to be "frozen" from time to time. In the heuristic process, the algorithms that process data are constantly changing. If the data that is being operated on is also being changed at the same time, the analyst can never tell whether the new results are a result of the change in algorithms or a change in the data. Therefore, as long as the algorithms going against the data are changing, it is useful to freeze the data that is being operated on.

The notion that data needs to be frozen is antithetical to other forms of processing. In other forms of processing, there is a need to operate on the most current data possible. In other forms of processing, data is being updated and changed as soon as possible. Such is not the case at all in heuristic processing.

Figure 7.1.7 shows the need to freeze data as long as the algorithms processing the data are changing.

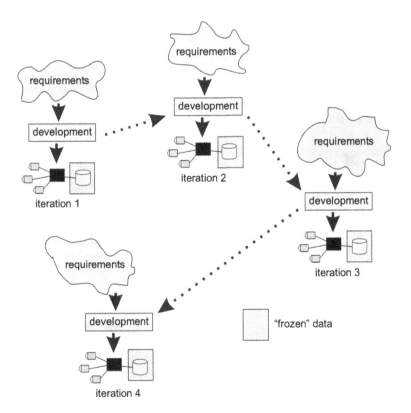

Figure 7.1.7

The Sandbox

Heuristic processing is done in what is called the "sandbox." The sandbox is an environment where the analyst has the opportunity to go and "play" with data. The analyst can look at data one way one day and another way another day. The analyst is not restricted in what kind of processing or in terms of how much processing can be done.

The reason why there is a need for a sandbox is that in standard corporate processing there is a need for tight control of processing. One reason for the need for tight control of processing in the standard environment is because of resource limitations. In the standard corporate operating environment, there is a need to control the resources that are used for processing by all analysts. That is because there is a need for high performance in the standard operating environment. But in the sandbox environment, there is no such restriction on the analyst. In the sandbox environment, there is no need for high performance. Therefore, analysts are free to do whatever analytical investigation that they wish to do.

But there is another reason for the sandbox environment. That reason is that in the standard operating environment there is a need for tight control of data access and calculation. That is because in the standard operating environment, there are security concerns and data governance concerns. But in the sandbox there are no such concerns.

The converse of processing in the sandbox is that because there are no controls in the sandbox environment, the results of processing in the sandbox environment should not be used in a formal manner. The results of processing in the sandbox can lead to great new and important insight. But after the insight has been captured, the insight is translated into a more formal system and is incorporated into the standard operating environment. The sandbox environment then is a great boon to the analytics community.

Figure 7.1.8 shows the sandbox environment.

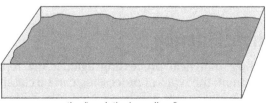

the "analytical sandbox"

Figure 7.1.8

a "normal" profile
- female
- 35 years of age
- college educated
- married
- 2.7 children
- drives a Honda
- mortgage of $256,000
- plays tennis
- likes Italian food

....

Figure 7.1.9

The "Normal" Profile

One of the most important things that an analyst can develop is something that can be called the "normal" profile. The normal profile is the composite of the audience that is being analyzed. In the case of people, the normal profile may contain such things as gender, age, education, location, number of children, and marriage status. Figure 7.1.9 shows a "normal" profile.

The normal profile for a corporation may include such attributes as size of corporation, locations, type of product or service created, and revenue of the corporation. There are different definitions of what is normal for different environments.

There are many reasons why a normal profile is useful. One reason is that the profile is just plain interesting. The normal profile tells management at a glance what is going on inside a system. But there is another very important reason why a normal profile is useful. When looking at a large body of data, it is oftentimes useful to look at a single record and measure just how far from the norm the record is. And you can't determine how far from the norm a record is unless you first understand the norm.

In many cases the further from the norm a record is the more interesting it becomes. But you can't spot a record that is far from the norm unless you first understand what the norm is.

Distillation, Filtering

When doing analytical processing against the repetitive Big Data environment, the types of processing can be classified in one of two ways. There is what can be termed "distillation" processing and there is what can be termed "filtering" processing. Both of these processes can be done depending on the needs of the analyst.

In distillation processing, the results of the processing are a single set of results, such as the creation of a profile. In retail operations, the desire might be to create a normal profile. In banking, the result of distillation might be to create the new lending rate. In manufacturing, the result might be to determine the best materials for manufacture.

In any case the results of the distillation process is a single occurrence of a set of values.

In filtering, the results are quite different. In filtering, the result of processing is the selection of and the refinement of multiple records. In filtering, the objective is to find all records that satisfy some criteria. Once those records have been found, the records can then edited, manipulated, or otherwise altered to suit the needs of the analyst. Then the records are output for further processing or analysis.

In a retail environment, the results of filtering might be the selection of all high-value customers. In manufacturing, the results of filtering might be the selection of all end products that failed quality tests. In healthcare, the results of filtering might be all patients afflicted with a certain condition, and so forth.

The processing that occurs in distillation and in filtering is quite different. The emphasis in distillation is on analytical and algorithmic processing and the emphasis in filtering is on selection of records and the editing of those records.

Figure 7.1.10 illustrates the types of processing that can be done against repetitive data.

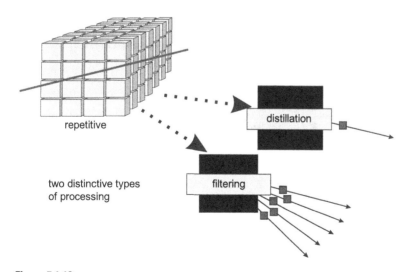

Figure 7.1.10

Subsetting Data

One of the results of filtering is the creation of subsets of data. As repetitive data is read and filtered, the result is the creation of data into different subsets. There are lots of practical reasons of subsetting data. Some of those reasons are:

- The reduction in volume of data that has to be analyzed. It is much easier to analyze and manipulate a small subset of data than it is to analyze that same data mixed in with many other nonrelevant occurrences of data.
- Purity of processing. By subsetting data, the analyst can filter out unwanted data, so that the analysis can focus on the data that is of interest. Creating a subset of data means that the analytical algorithmic processing that occurs can be very focused on the objective of the analysis.
- Security. Once data is selected into a subset, it can be protected with even higher levels of security than when the data existed in an unfiltered state.

Subsetting data for analysis is a technique that is used commonly and has been used as long as there was data and a computer.

One of the uses of subsetting of data is to set the stage for sampling.

In data sampling, processing goes against a sample of data rather than against the full set of data. In doing so, the resources used for creating the analysis are considerably less and the time that it takes to create the analysis is significantly reduced. And in heuristic processing, the turnaround time to do an analysis can be very important.

Sampling is especially important when doing heuristic analysis against Big Data because of the sheer volume of data that has to be processed.

Figure 7.1.11 shows the creation of an analytical sample.

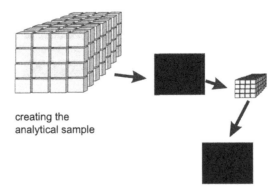

creating the
analytical sample

Figure 7.1.11

There are some downsides to sampling. One downside is that the analytical results obtained when processing the sample may be different than the processing results achieved when processing against the entire database. For example, the sampling may produce the results that the average age of a customer is 35.78 years. When the full database is processed, it may be found that the average age of the customer is really 36.21 years old. In some cases this small differential between results is inconsequential. In other cases the difference in results is truly significant. Whether there is significance or not depends on how much difference there is and the importance of accuracy.

If there is not much of a problem with slight inaccuracies of data, then sampling works well. If in fact there is a desire to get the results as accurate as possible, then the algorithmic development can be done against sampling data. When the analyst is satisfied that the sampling results are being done properly, then the final run can be made against the entire database, thereby satisfying the needs to do analysis quickly and the need to achieve accurate results.

One issue that arises with sampling is the bias of the sample. When data is selected for inclusion in the sampling database, there is *always* a bias of the data. What the bias is and how badly the bias colors the final analytical results is a function of the selection process. In some cases there is a bias but the bias of the data really doesn't matter. In other cases there is a real effect made on the final results because of the bias of the data selected for the sampling database.

The analyst must constantly be aware of the existence of and the influence of the bias of the sampling data.

Figure 7.1.12 shows that there is an expensive marginal value of accuracy when processing sampling data.

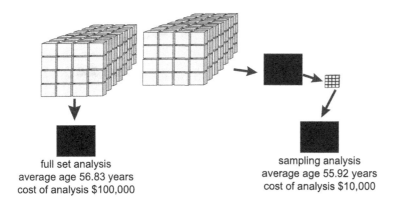

full set analysis
average age 56.83 years
cost of analysis $100,000

sampling analysis
average age 55.92 years
cost of analysis $10,000

Figure 7.1.12

Filtering Data

There are many reasons why filtering data – especially Big Data – is a common practice. The actual of filtering data can be done on almost an attribute or any attribute value found in the database. Figure 7.1.13 shows that filtering data can be done many ways.

While data can be filtered, at the same time the data can be edited and manipulated. It is common practice for the output of the filtering process to create records that have some means of ordering the records. Usually the ordering is done by the inclusion of uniquely valued attributes. For example, the output relating to a person may have the data relating to the person's social security number as part of the output. Or the filtered output for manufacturing goods may have attributes of the part number along with lot number and date of manufacture. Or if the filtered data were from real estate, there may be property address that is an attribute that is included as a key.

Figure 7.1.14 shows that the data that is produced as part of the filtering process usually contains uniquely valued attributes.

One result of filtering is the production of subsets of data. In fact when data is filtered, the result is the creation of a subset of data. However, the analyst creating the filtering mechanism may want to use the creation of a subset of data as an opportunity to prepare for future analysis. Stated differently, when a subset is created, it may be useful to put a little planning into the process to create the subset so that it will be useful to future analytical processing. Figure 7.1.15 shows that subsets of data are created when data is filtered.

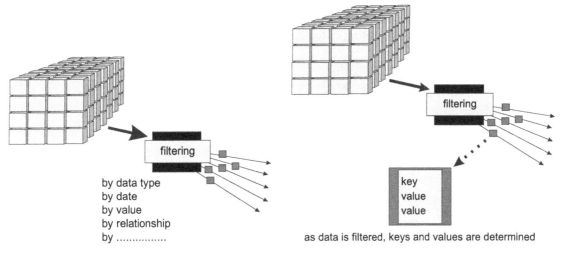

by data type
by date
by value
by relationship
by ....

Figure 7.1.13

as data is filtered, keys and values are determined

Figure 7.1.14

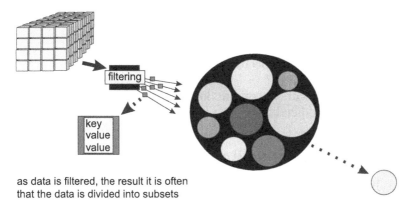

as data is filtered, the result it is often
that the data is divided into subsets

Figure 7.1.15

Repetitive Data and Context

In general, repetitive data yields its context easily and readily. In general because repetitive data has so many occurrences of
data and because repetitive data is all similarly structured, finding
context is easy to do.

When data is in the world of Big Data, the data is unstructured
in the sense that the data is not being managed by a standard database management system. Because the data is unstructured, in
order to be used, the repetitive data has to pass through the parsing process (as does all unstructured data). But because the data is
structurally repetitive, once the analyst has parsed the first record,
all subsequent records will be parsed in exactly the same manner. Because of this, parsing repetitive data in Big Data still must
be done. But doing parsing for repetitive data is an almost trivial
thing to do.

Figure 7.1.16 shows that context for repetitive data is usually
easy to find and determine.

When looking at repetitive data, most data is fairly unexceptional as shown in Figure 7.1.17. About the only interesting data
that occurs is in terms of values that occur inside repetitive data.
As an example of interesting values occurring, consider retail
sales. Most retail sales for a retailer are from $1.00 to $100.00. But

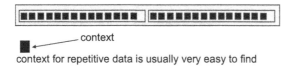

context for repetitive data is usually very easy to find

Figure 7.1.16

occasionally an order is for greater than $100.00. These exceptions are of great interest to the retailer.

The retailer is interested in such issues as:

- How often do they occur?
- How large are they?
- What else occurs in conjunction with them?
- Are they predictable?

Linking Repetitive Records

Repetitive records by themselves have value. But occasionally repetitive records that have been linked together tell an even larger picture. When records are linked together where there is a logical reason for the linkage, a more complex story can be derived from the data.

Repetitive records can be linked together in many ways. But the most common way to link them together is through common occurrence of data values. For example, there may be a common customer number that links the records. Or there may be a common part number. Or there may be a common retail location number, and so forth.

There are in fact many different ways to link together repetitive records, depending on the business problem being studied.

Figure 7.1.18 shows it sometimes make sense to link repetitive records together based on a business relationship of the records.

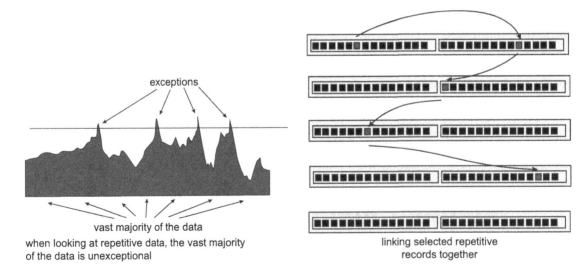

exceptions

vast majority of the data

when looking at repetitive data, the vast majority of the data is unexceptional

linking selected repetitive records together

Figure 7.1.17   **Figure 7.1.18**

Log Tape Records

It is common in examining Big Data to encounter log tapes. Many organizations create log tapes only to wake up one day and discover that there is a wealth of information on those tapes that has never been used.

As a rule, log tapes contain information that is stored in a cryptic manner. Most log tapes are written for purposes other than analytical processing. Most log tapes are written for purposes of backup and recovery or for the purpose of creating a historical events. As a consequence, log tapes require a utility to read and decipher the log tape. The utility reads the log tape, infers the meaning of the data found on the log tape, then reformats the data into an intelligible form. Once the data is read and reformatted, the analyst can then start to use the data found on the log tape.

Most log tape processing requires the elimination of irrelevant data. Much data appears on the log tape that is of no use to the analyst.

Figure 7.1.19 shows a schematic of what a typical log tape might look like and shows that many different kinds of records are found on the log tape. Typically these records are written onto the log tape in a chronological manner. As a business event occurs, a record is written to reflect the occurrence of the event.

At first glance this data might look like nonrepetitive data. Indeed from a physical occurrence of data standpoint that is a valid perspective. But there is another way to look at the data found on a log tape. That perspective is that the log tape is merely a chronological accumulation of a bunch of repetitive records. A "logical" perspective of a log tape is seen on the right in Figure 7.1.20.

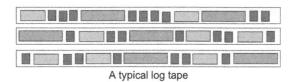

A typical log tape

Figure 7.1.19

the physical log tape   the logical log tape

Figure 7.1.20

Figure 7.1.20 shows that logically a log tape is merely a sequential collection of different types of records. The perspective shown in Figure 7.1.20 shows that the data logically appears to be repetitive records of data.

Analyzing Points of Data

One of the ways in which data is analyzed is through the graphing of collection of points of reference data. This technique is called the creation of a scatter diagram and is seen in Figure 7.1.21.

While gathering and plotting these points can lead to simple observations, there is a mathematical means to expressing the scatter diagram. A line can be drawn through the points. The line represents a mathematically calculated formula using what is called the "least squares method." In the least squares approach, the line represents the mathematical function where the square of the distance from each point to the line is the least value.

On occasion there is a point of reference that does not seem to fit with all the other points. If this is the case, the point of reference can be discarded. Such a point of reference is referred to as an "outlier."

In the case of an outlier, the theory is that some other factors were relevant to the calculation of the point of reference. Removing the outlier will not hurt the implications created by the calculation of the least squares regression analysis. Of course if there are too many outliers, then the analyst must indulge in deeper analysis of why the outliers occurred. But as long as there are only a few outliers and there are reasons why the outliers should be removed, then removal of outliers is a perfectly legitimate thing to do

Figure 7.1.22 depicts a scatter diagram with linear regression analysis and a scatter diagram with outliers.

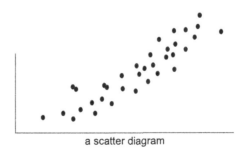

a scatter diagram

Figure 7.1.21

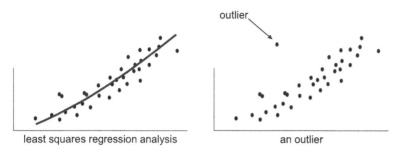

least squares regression analysis   an outlier

Figure 7.1.22

Data Over Time

It is normal to look at data over time. Looking at data over time is a good way to get insight that would otherwise not be possible.

One of the standard ways to look at data over time is through a Pareto chart. Figure 7.1.23 depicts data found in a Pareto chart.

While looking at data over time is a standard and a good practice, there is an insidious aspect to looking at data over time. If the data being examined over time is being examined for a short period of time, then there is no problem. But if the data being examined is being examined over a lengthy enough period of time, then the parameters over which the examination is made change can affect the data.

This effect of looking at data over limited moments of time is illustrated by a simple example. Suppose there is an examination of the gross national product (GNP) of the United States over decades. One way to measure GNP is by looking at GNP measured against dollars. So you plot the national GNP every 10 years or so. The problem is that over time, the dollar means different things in terms of value. The worth of the dollar in 2015 is not the same thing at all as the dollar in 1900. If you do not adjust your parameters

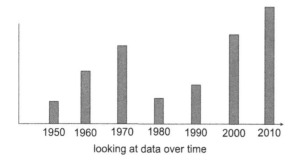

looking at data over time

Figure 7.1.23

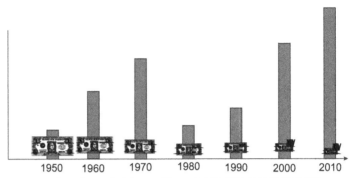

over time the metadata used to measure data *always* changes

Figure 7.1.24

of measurement for inflation, your measurement of GNP means nothing.

Figure 7.1.24 shows that over time the meaning of the basic measurement of the dollar is not the same over decades.

The fact is that the dollar and inflation are well-understood phenomena. What is not so well understood is that there are other factors over time that cannot be as easily tracked as inflation.

As an example, suppose one were tracking the revenue of IBM over decades. The revenue of IBM over decades is easy enough to find and track because IBM is a publicly traded company. But what is not so easy to track are all the acquisitions of other companies that IBM has made over the years. Looking at IBM in 1960 and then looking at IBM in 2000 is a little misleading, because the company that IBM was in 1960 is a very different company than the company that IBM is in 2000.

There is constant change in the parameters of measurement of *any* variable over time. The analyst of repetitive data does well to keep in mind that given enough time, the very patterns of measurement of data over time gradually change.

ANALYZING REPETITIVE DATA

Much of the data found in Big Data is repetitive. Analyzing repetitive data in the Big Data environment is quite different than analyzing data in the nonrepetitive environment. As a point of departure, we need to look at what the repetitive Big Data environment looks like. Figure 7.2.1 shows that data in the repetitive Big Data environment looks like lots of units of data laid end to end.

Repetitive data can be thought of as being organized into blocks, records, and attributes. Figure 7.2.2 shows this organization.

A block of data is a large allocation of space. The system knows how to find a block of data. The block of data is loaded with units of data. These units of data can be thought of as records. Within the record of data are attributes of data.

As an example of the organization of data consider the record of telephone calls. In the block of data are found the information about many phone calls. In the record for each phone call is found some basic information, such as:
- Date and time of the phone call
- Who was making the phone call
- To whom the call was made
- How long the telephone call was made

There may be other incidental information such as was the phone call operator assisted or was the phone call an international phone call. But at the end of the day, the same attribution of information is found over and over again, for every phone call.

When the system goes to look for data, the system knows how to find a block of data. But once the system finds a block of data, it is up to the analyst to make sense of the data found in the block. The analyst does this by "parsing" the data. The analyst reads the data in the block. Then the analyst determines where a record is. On finding a record, the analyst then determines what attribute is where.

The process of parsing would be onerous if there were not a high degree of similarity of the records tucked into the block. Figure 7.2.3 shows that upon encountering a block of data in Big Data there is a need to parse the block.

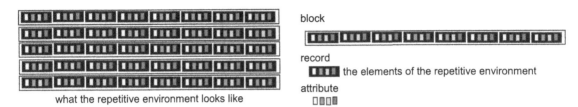

what the repetitive environment looks like

Figure 7.2.1

block

record

▮▮▮▮ the elements of the repetitive environment

attribute

▯▮▮▮

Figure 7.2.2

parse ← how the analyst knows what data is in the repetitive environment

Figure 7.2.3

Log Data

One of the most common forms of Big Data is log data. Indeed much important corporate information is tucked into the form of logs.

When one looks at log data, log data does not appear to look much like other repetitive data. Consider the comparison seen in Figure 7.2.4 in which repetitive data does not look like log data at all. It appears that in log data many different kinds of records appear. And indeed they do. But this apparent contradiction can be resolved by understanding that *logically* the log tape is nothing more than an amalgamation of repetitive records. This phenomenon is shown by Figure 7.2.5.

Even though a log tape record is composed of multiple records and must be parsed, the good news is that there typically are a finite number of record types that have to be parsed. (Unlike other

repetitive data   log data

Figure 7.2.4

physical log data   logical log data

Figure 7.2.5

nonrepetitive records where there are anything but a finite number of record types that need to be parsed.) Figure 7.2.6 shows that there are a finite number of records that need to be examined when parsing a log tape.

The analysis of repetitive data starts with access to the means by which Big Data is stored. In many instances Big Data is stored in Hadoop. However, there are other technologies (such as Huge Data) that can manage and store large amounts of data.

In an earlier day and age where there were only structured database management systems (DBMSs), the DBMS itself did much of the basic data management. But in the world of Big Data, much of the management of the data is up to the user.

Figure 7.2.7 shows some of the different ways in which basic data management needs to be done in Big Data. For example, with Hadoop you can access and analyze data through an interface; you can access and parse data; you can directly access the data and do

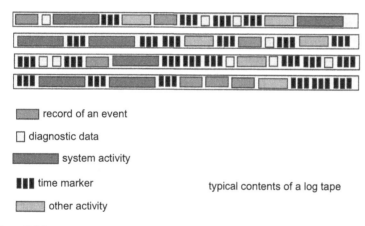

Figure 7.2.6

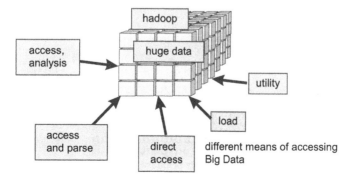

Figure 7.2.7

basic functions yourself; there are load utilities, and there are other data management utilities. Most of the focus on the technology that directly accesses data in Big Data is concerned with two things:

1. The reading and interpretation of the data
2. The management of large amounts of data

The management of large amounts of data is a consuming issue because there are indeed large amounts of data that need to be handled. There is a science to the handling of large amounts of data unto itself. Notwithstanding the need to manage large amounts of data, there is still a need for creating an architecture of data.

Active/Passive Indexing of Data

One of the most useful design techniques the architect can use is that of creating different kinds of indexes of data. In any case, an index is useful in helping find data. It is always faster to locate data through an index than it is to search the data directly. So indexes have their place in analytical processing.

The way that most indexes are built is through starting with a user requirement to access data then building an index to satisfy that requirement. When an index is built in this manner, it can be called an "active index" because there is an expectation that the index will be actively used.

But there is another type of index that can be built and that index is a passive index. In a passive index there is no user requirement to start with. Instead the index is built "just in case" somebody in the future wants to access the data according to how the data is organized. Because there is no active requirement for the building of the index, it is called a "passive" index.

Figure 7.2.8 shows both active and passive indexes that can be built.

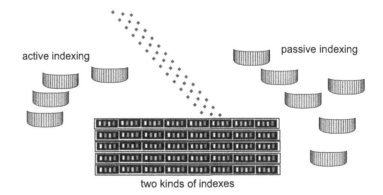

two kinds of indexes

Figure 7.2.8

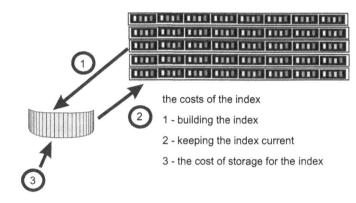

the costs of the index

1 - building the index

2 - keeping the index current

3 - the cost of storage for the index

Figure 7.2.9

With any index there is a cost. There is the cost of initially building the index. Then there is the cost of keeping the index current. Then there is the cost of storage for the index. In the world of Big Data, indexes are typically built by technology called "crawlers." The crawler technology is constantly searching the Big Data creating new index records. As long as the data remains stable and unchanged, the data has to only be indexed once. But if data is added or if data is deleted, then there needs to be constant updates to the index in order to keep the index current. And in any case, there is the cost of storage for the index itself.

Figure 7.2.9 shows the costs of building and maintaining an index.

Summary/Detailed Data

Another issue that arises is whether detailed and summary data should be kept in Big Data and if both summary and detailed data are kept in Big Data, should there be a connection between the detailed and summary data.

First, there is no reason why summary and detailed data should not be stored in Big Data. Big Data is perfectly capable of holding both kinds of data. But if Big Data can hold both detailed and summary data, should there be a logical connection between the detailed data and the summary data. In other words should the detailed data add up to the summary data?

The answer is that even though detailed and summary data can both be stored in Big Data, there is no necessary connection between the data once stored in Big Data. The reason for this is that when the data is calculated and the summary data is created, it is necessary to have an algorithm. The algorithm most likely is *not* stored in Big Data. So, as long as an algorithm is not stored in Big Data, there is no necessary logical connection between detailed data and summary data. For this reason, detailed data may or may not add up to the related summary data that can be stored in Big Data.

Figure 7.2.10 shows this relationship of data inside Big Data.

But if detailed data and summary data should both be kept in Big Data and if detailed data should not necessarily add up to the summary data found there, at the very least there should be documentation of the algorithm that was used to create the summary data. Figure 7.2.11 shows that documentation of algorithms and selection of detailed data should be documented alongside the summary data stored in Big Data.

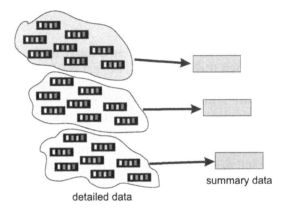

summary data

detailed data

Figure 7.2.10

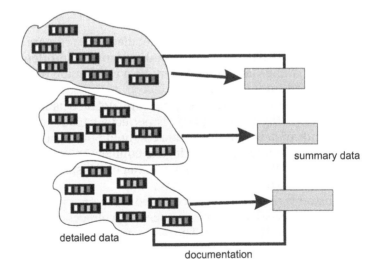

summary data

detailed data

documentation

Figure 7.2.11

Metadata in Big Data

While data is the essence of what is stored in Big Data, it is important not to neglect another type of data. That data is metadata. There are *many* forms of metadata, and each of them is important. Two of the more important forms of metadata are native metadata and derived metadata. Native metadata is metadata that addresses the immediate descriptive needs of the data. Typical native metadata includes such information as:

- Field name
- Field length
- Field type
- Field identifying characteristics

Native metadata is used to identify and describe data that is stored in Big Data. Derived metadata takes many forms. Some of the forms of derived metadata include:

- Description of how data was selected
- Description of when data was selected
- Description of the source of data
- Description of how data was calculated

Figure 7.2.12 depicts the different types of metadata.

With metadata stored in Big Data, there arises the issue of where metadata should be stored. Traditionally, metadata has been stored in a separate repository. The repository is stored physically separately from the data itself. But in the world of Big Data, there are some very good reasons for managing metadata differently. In Big Data, it often makes sense to store the descriptive metadata physically in the same location and same data set as the data being described.

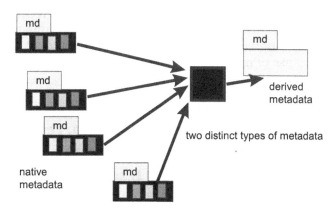

Figure 7.2.12

There are several very good reasons for the physical storage of metadata in the same physical location as the data itself. Some of those reasons are:

- Storage is cheap. There is no reason why the cost of storage needed to store the metadata should ever be an issue.
- The world of Big Data is undisciplined. Having the metadata stored directly with the data being described means that the metadata will never be lost or misplaced.
- Metadata changes over time. When the metadata is stored directly with the data being described there is *always* a direct relationship between the metadata and the data being described. In other words, the metadata *never* goes out of touch with the data being described
- Simplicity of processing. When the analyst starts to process data in Big Data, there is never a search for the metadata. It is always easy to locate because it is always with the data being described.

Figure 7.2.13 shows that embedding metadata along with the data stored in Big Data is a good idea.

Note that storing metadata directly with the data stored in Big Data does not preclude the possibility of having a repository of metadata for Big Data. There is nothing to say that metadata cannot be stored in the data with Big Data AND reside in a repository as well.

Linking Data

One of the fundamental issues of data is that of how data is linked to each other. This issue is an issue in Big Data just as it has been an issue in other forms of information processing.

In classical information systems, linkage of data was accomplished by matching data values. As an example, one record contained social security numbers and another record contained social security numbers as well. The two units of data could then be linked because of the existence of the same value residing in the

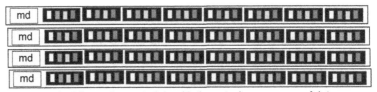

embedding native metadata with the actual occurrences of data

Figure 7.2.13

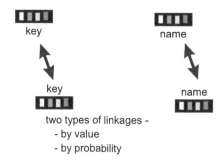

key

name

key

name

two types of linkages -
- by value
- by probability

Figure 7.2.14

record. The analyst could be 99.99999% assured that there was a basis for linkage. (Curiously, since the government reissues social security numbers at the death of an individual, the analyst cannot be 100% assured that the linkage is valid.)

But with the unstructured data (i.e., textual data) that comes with Big Data, it is necessary to accommodate another type of relationship involving the linkage of data. In this case it is necessary to accommodate what can be called a "probable linkage of data." A probable linkage of data is linkage that is based on probability rather than an actual value. Probabilistic linkages arise wherever there is text.

As an example of a probabilistic linkage consider the linkages of data based on name. Suppose there are two names in different records, Bill Inmon and William Inmon. Should these values be linked? There is a high probability that these names should be linked. But it is only a probability, not a certainty. Suppose there are two records where the name William Inmon is found. Should these records be linked? One record refers to a serial killer in Arizona and another record refers to a data warehouse writer in Colorado. (This is a true example – look it up on the Internet to verify.) When text is involved, linkage is accomplished on the basis of probability of a match, not the certainty of a match.

Figure 7.2.14 depicts the different kinds of linkages that are found in Big Data.

REPETITIVE ANALYSIS

Internal, External Data

Because the cost of storage is so inexpensive with Big Data, it is possible to consider storing data that comes from other than internal sources.

In an earlier day the cost of storage was such that the only data that corporations considered to store was internally generated data. But with the cost of storage diminished by the advent of Big Data, it is now possible to consider storing external data as well as internal data.

One of the issues with storing external data is that of finding and using identifiers. But textual disambiguation can be used on external data just as it can against internal data, so it is entirely possible to establish discrete identifiers for external data.

Figure 7.3.1 shows that storing external data in Big Data is a real possibility.

Universal Identifiers

As data is stored in Big Data and as textual disambiguation is used to bring the data into a standard database format, the subject of universal identifiers or universal measurement arises. Because data comes such diverse sources, because there is little or no discipline or uniformity of data across disparate sources, and because there is a need to relate data to common measurements there is a need for uniform measurement characteristics across the universe from which data comes.

Some universal measurements are fairly obvious; other universal measurements are not.

Three standard or universal measurements of data might include:
- Time – Greenwich Mean Time
- Date – Julian data
- Money – U.S. dollar

Undoubtedly there are other universal measurements. And each of these measurements has its own quirks.

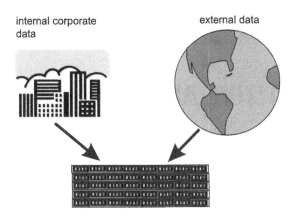

internal corporate data

external data

Figure 7.3.1

Greenwich Mean Time (GMT) is the time that occurs at the meridian that runs through Greenwich, England. The good news about GMT is that there is universal understanding as to what that time is. The bad news is that it is not in agreement with 23 other time zones in the world. But at least there is an agreed-on understanding of time in at least one other place in the world.

Julian date is the sequential count of dates starting from day 0, which occurred at January 1, 4713 BC. The value of Julian date is that it is universal and that it reduces the number of days to an ordinal number. In a standard calendar, calculating how many days there are between May 16, 2014 and January 3, 2015, is a complex thing to do. But with Julian date, such a calculation is very simple to do.

The U.S. dollar is as good a measurement of currency as any other measure. But even with the U.S. dollar there are challenges. For example the conversion rate between the dollar and other currencies is constantly changing. If you calculate a value on February 15, converting the dollar against another currency, chances are excellent that you will get a different value if you make the same currency conversion on August 7. But all other factors being equal, the U.S. dollar serves as a good economic measurement of wealth.

Figure 7.3.2 shows some of the universal measurements.

time - GMT

date - Julian

money - dollar

some standard measurements of data

Figure 7.3.2

security is an issue

Figure 7.3.3

Security

Another significant and serious concern of data (anywhere, not just in Big Data) is that of security. There are literally hundreds of reasons why data needs to be secure, including:
– Healthcare data needs to be secure because of privacy reasons.
– Personal financial data needs to be secure because of theft and personal loss.
– Corporate financial data needs to be secure because of insider trading laws.
– Corporate activity needs to be secure because of the need to keep trade secrets actually secret

There are a multitude of reasons why certain data needs to be treated with the utmost of care when it comes to security, which is depicted in Figure 7.3.3.

There are many facets to security. Only a few of them will be mentioned here. The simplest (and one of the most effective) forms of security is that of encryption. Encryption is the process of taking data and substituting encrypted values for actual values. For example, you might take the text "Bill Inmon" and substitute "Cjmm Jmopm" in its place. In this case we have merely substituted the next letter in the alphabet for the actual value. It would have taken a good cryptographer about a nanosecond to decrypt the data. But a good encryption analyst could figure out many more ways to encrypt the data that would stump even the most sophisticated of analysts.

In any case, the process of encrypting data is commonly used. Typically, fields of data are encrypted inside a database. In healthcare, for example, only the identifying information is encrypted. The remaining data is left untouched. This allows the data to be used in research without endangering the privacy of the data. Figure 7.3.4 shows encryption being done on a field of data.

There are many issues that relate to encryption. Some of the issues are:
– How secure is the encrypting algorithm?
– Who can decrypt the data?

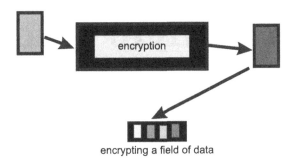

encrypting a field of data

Figure 7.3.4

- Should fields that need to be indexed be encrypted?
- How should decryption keys be protected?

One of the more interesting issues is consistency of encryption. Suppose you encrypt the name "Bill Inmon." Suppose that a later place you need to once again encrypt the name "Bill Inmon." You need to ensure that the name "Bill Inmon" is encrypted the same everywhere there is a need for encryption. You need to ensure consistency of encryption everywhere encryption is needed. This is necessary because if you need to link records based on an encrypted value, you cannot do so if there is no consistency of encryption. Figure 7.3.5 shows the need for consistency of encryption.

Another interesting aspect of security is looking at who is trying to look at encrypted data. The access and analysis of encrypted may be purely innocent. Then again it may not be innocent at all. By examining log tapes and seeing who is trying to access what data, the analyst can determine if someone is trying to access data they shouldn't be looking at. Figure 7.3.6 shows that examining log tapes is a good practice in determining if there are breaches of security.

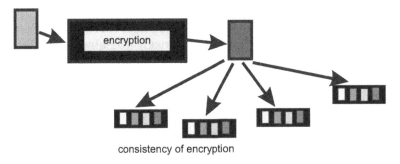

consistency of encryption

Figure 7.3.5

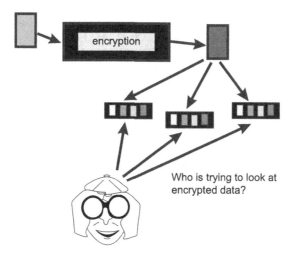

Figure 7.3.6

Filtering, Distillation

There are two basic kinds of processing that occur in the analysis of repetitive data – distillation and filtering.

In distillation of data, repetitive records are selected and read. Then the data is analyzed, looking for average values, total values, exceptional values, and the like. After the analysis has concluded, a single result is achieved and becomes the out-of-distillation process.

As a rule, distillation is done on a project basis or on an irregular unscheduled basis. Figure 7.3.7 shows the process of distillation of repetitive data.

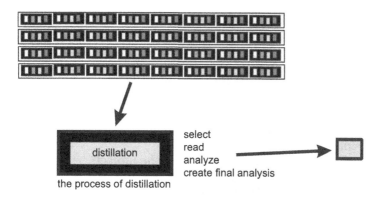

Figure 7.3.7

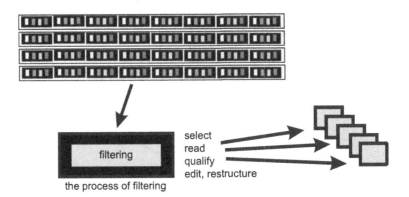

the process of filtering

Figure 7.3.8

The other type of processing done against repetitive data is that of filtering repetitive and reformatting the repetitive data. Filtering of data is similar to distillation in that data is selected and analyzed. But the output of filtering of data is different. In filtering there are many records that are the output of processing. And filtering is done on a regular, scheduled basis. Figure 7.3.8 depicts the filtering of repetitive records of data.

Archiving Results

Much of the analytical processing that is done against repetitive data is of the project variety, and there is a problem with analytical processing done on a project basis. The problem is that once the project is finished, the results are either discarded or "mothballed." There is no problem until such time as it comes to do another project. When starting a new project, it is convenient to see what analysis has preceded this analysis. There may be overlap. There may be complementary processing. If nothing else, a description of how the previous analyses have been developed can be useful.

Therefore, at the end of a project it is useful to create an archive of the project. Typical information that might go into the archive might include:

- What data went into the project?
- How was data selected?
- What algorithms were used?
- How many iterations were there in the project?
- What results were attained?
- Where are the results stored?

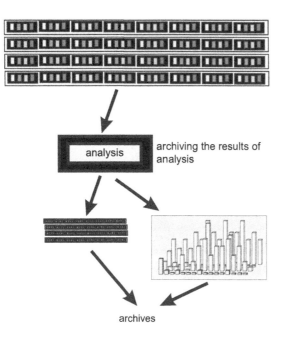

archiving the results of analysis

archives

Figure 7.3.9

– Who conducted the project?
– How long did it take to conduct the project?
– Who sponsored the project?

Figure 7.3.9 shows that an archive of projects is a worthwhile thing to do. At the very least, the results created by the project should be gathered and stored, as shown in Figure 7.3.10

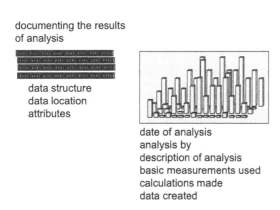

documenting the results of analysis

data structure
data location
attributes

date of analysis
analysis by
description of analysis
basic measurements used
calculations made
data created

Figure 7.3.10

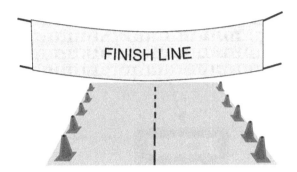

Figure 7.3.11

Metrics

At the outset of the repetitive analysis it is worthwhile to establish the metrics that will establish whether a project has met its objectives. The optimal time to outline such metrics is at the very outset of the project.

There is a problem with delineating the metrics at the beginning. That problem is that in a heuristically run project, many of the metrics cannot be definitively established. Nevertheless,

outlining the metrics at the very least gives the project a sense of focus.

The metrics can be described in very broad terms. There is no need to have the metrics defined to a very low level of definition. Figure 7.3.11 shows that metrics define when a project has been successful or less than successful.

NONREPETITIVE DATA

There are two types of data that reside in the Big Data environment – repetitive data and nonrepetitive data. Repetitive data is relatively easy to handle because of the repetitive nature of the structure of the data. But nonrepetitive data is anything but easy to handle because every unit of data in the nonrepetitive environment must be individually interpreted before it can be used for analytical processing.

Figure 8.1.1 shows a representation of nonrepetitive data as it resides in a raw state in the Big Data environment.

The nonrepetitive data found in Big Data is called "nonrepetitive" because each unit of data is unique. Figure 8.1.2 shows that each unit of data in the nonrepetitive environment is different from the preceding unit of data.

There are many examples of nonrepetitive data in the Big Data environment. Some of the examples include:

• Email data
• Call center data
• Corporate contracts
• Warranty claims
• Insurance claims

It is possible for two units of repetitive data to actually be the same. Figure 8.1.3 shows this possibility. As an example of two units of nonrepetitive data being the same, suppose there are two emails that contain one word – the word "yes." In this case the emails are identical. But the fact that they are identical is merely an act of randomness.

In general, when text finds its way into the Big Data environment, the units of data stored in Big Data are nonrepetitive. One

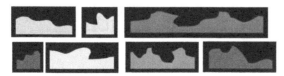

nonrepetitive data

Figure 8.1.1

267

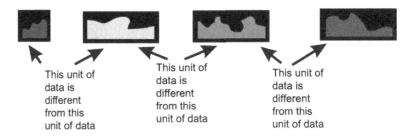

Figure 8.1.2

approach to processing nonrepetitive data is to use a search technology. While search technology accomplishes the task of scanning the data, search technology leaves a lot to be desired. The two primary shortcomings of search technology are that searching data does not leave a database that can be subsequently used for analytical purposes, and search technology does not look at or provide context for the text being analyzed. There are other limitations of search technology as well.

In order to do extensive analytical processing against nonrepetitive data, it is necessary to read the nonrepetitive data and to turn the nonrepetitive data into a standard database format. Sometimes this process is said to take unstructured data and turn it into structured data. That indeed is a good description of what occurs.

The process of reading nonrepetitive data and turning it into a database is called "textual disambiguation" or "textual ETL." Of necessity textual disambiguation is a complex process because the language it processes is complex. There is no getting around the fact that processing text is a complex process.

The result of processing nonrepetitive data in Big Data with textual disambiguation is the creation of a standard database. Once data is put into the form of a standard database, it can then be analyzed using standard analytical technology. The mechanics of textual disambiguation are shown in Figure 8.1.4.

The general flow of processing in textual ETL is as follows. The first step is to find and read the data. Normally this step is straightforward. But occasionally the data has to be "untangled" in order

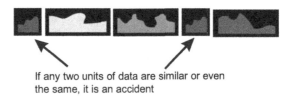

Figure 8.1.3

for further processing to continue. In some cases the data resides in a unit-by-unit basis. This is the "normal" (or easy) case. But in other cases the units of data are combined into a single document and the units of data must be isolated in the document in order to be processed.

The second step is to examine the unit of data and determine what data needs to be processed. In some cases all the data needs to be processed. In other cases only certain data needs to be processed. In general this step is straightforward.

The third step is to "parse" the nonrepetitive data. The word "parse" is a little misleading because it is in this step that the system applies great amounts of logic. The word "parsing" implies a straightforward process, and the logic that occurs here is anything but straightforward. The remainder of this chapter discusses this logic.

After the nonrepetitive data has been parsed, the attributes of data, the keys of data, and the records of data are identified. Once the keys, attributes, and records are identified, it is a straightforward process to turn the data into a standard database record.

That then is what takes place in textual disambiguation. The heart of textual disambiguation is the logic of processing that occurs when nonrepetitive data is analyzed and turned into keys, attributes, and records.

The activities of logic that occur here can be roughly classified into several categories. Figure 8.1.5 shows those categories.

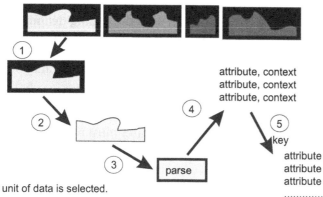

attribute, context
attribute, context
attribute, context

key
attribute
attribute
attribute
....

parse

1 - The unit of data is selected.
2 - The data within the unit of data that is of interest
  is selected.
3 - The data of interested is "parsed" (or passe d through
  "textual disambiguation").
4 - The basic attributes and context are identified.
5 - A basic data base record is created.

Figure 8.1.4

textual ETL

textual disambiguation
  - contextualization
  - standardization
  - basic editing

Figure 8.1.5

The basic activities of logic applied by textual disambiguation include the activities of:

- Contextualization, where the context of data is identified and captured
- Standardization, where certain types of text are standardized
- Basic editing, where basic editing of text occurs

Indeed there are other functions of textual disambiguation, but these three classifications of activities encompass most of the important processing that occurs.

The remainder of this chapter will be an explanation of logic that is found in textual disambiguation.

Inline Contextualization

One form of contextualization is a form that is called "inline contextualization" (or sometimes called "named value" processing). Inline contextualization only applies when there is a repetition and predictability of text. It is noted that in many cases there is no predictability of text, so inline contextualization cannot be used in these cases.

Inline contextualization is the process of inferring the context of a word or phrase by looking at the text immediately preceding and immediately following the word or phrase. As a simple example of inline contextualization consider the raw text "2. This is a PAID UP LEASE."

The context name would be Contract Type. The beginning delimiter would be "2. This is a" and the ending delimiter would be "." The system would produce an entry into the analytical database that would look like:

Doc name, byte, context – contract type, value – PAID UP LEASE.

Figure 8.1.6 shows the activity the system does in processing raw text to determine inline contextualization.

Note that the beginning delimiter must be unique. If you were to specify "is a" as a beginning delimiter, then every occurrence

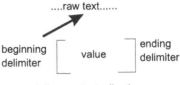

inline contextualization

Figure 8.1.6

where the term "is a" is found would be qualified. And there may be many places where the term "is a" is found that do not specify inline contextualization.

Also note that the ending delimiter must be specified exactly. In this case if the term does not end in a ".", then the system will not consider the entry to be a hit.

Because the ending delimiter must be specified accurately, the analyst also specifies a maximum character count. The maximum character count tells the system how far to search to determine whether the ending delimiter has been found.

On occasion the analyst wants the inline contextualization search to end on a special character. In this case the analyst specifies the special character that is needed.

Taxonomy/Ontology Processing

Another powerful way to specify context is through the usage of taxonomies and ontologies. There are many important things that taxonomies do for contextualization. The first is applicability. Whereas inline contextualization requires repetitive and predictable occurrences of text to be applicable, taxonomies do not have such a requirement. Taxonomies are applicable just about everywhere. A second valuable feature of taxonomies is that they can be applied externally. This means that in choosing the taxonomy to be applied, the analyst can greatly influence the interpretation of the raw text.

For example, suppose the analyst were going to apply a taxonomy to the phrase "President Ford drove a Ford." If the interpretation that analyst wished to infer were about cars, then the analyst would choose one or more taxonomy that would allow "Ford" to be interpreted as an automobile. But if the analyst were to choose a taxonomy relating to the history of the presidents of the United States, then the term "Ford" would be interpreted to be a former president of the United States.

The analyst then has great power in applying the correct taxonomy to the raw text that is to be processed. The mechanics of how a taxonomy processes against raw text is seen in Figure 8.1.7.

As a simple example of the application of a taxonomy to raw text, consider the following example.

Raw text: "…she drove her Honda into the garage…" The simple taxonomy used looks like this:

Car
   Porsche
   Honda
   Toyota

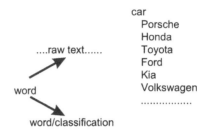

Figure 8.1.7

Ford
Kia
Volkswagen
Etc.

When the taxonomy is passed against the raw text, the results look like this:

Doc name, byte, context – car, value – Honda

In order to accommodate other processing, on some occasions it is useful to create a second entry such as this:

Doc name, byte, context – car, value car

The reason why it is sometimes useful to produce a second entry into the analytical database is that on occasion you want to process all the values and you want the context to be processed as a value. That is why that on occasion the system produces two entries into the analytical database.

Note that textual ETL operates on taxonomies/ontologies as if the taxonomies were a simple word pair. In fact taxonomies and ontologies are much more complex that simple word pairs. But even the most sophisticated taxonomy can be decomposed into a series of simple word pairs.

In general the usage of taxonomies as a form of contextualization is the most powerful tool the analyst has in determining the context of raw text.

Custom Variables

Another very useful form of contextualization is that of the identification of the creation of what can be termed "custom variables." Almost every organization has custom variables. A custom variable is a word or phrase that is recognizable entirely from the format of the word or phrase. As a simple example, a manufacturer may have its part numbers in the form of "AK-876-uy." Looking at a part number generically, the generic form of the part number

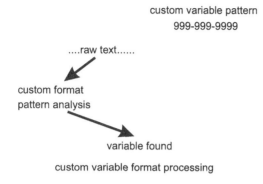

custom variable pattern
999-999-9999

....raw text......

custom format
pattern analysis

variable found

custom variable format processing

Figure 8.1.8

would be "CC-999-cc." In this case "C" indicates a capital character, "-" indicates the literal "-", "9" indicates any numeric digit, and
"c" indicates a lowercase character.

By looking at the format of a word or phrase, the analyst can tell
immediately the context of the variable.

Figure 8.1.8 shows how raw text is processed using custom
variables.

As an example of the use of custom variables, consider the following raw text:

"…I want to order two more cases of TR-0987-BY to be deliv-
ered on…"

On processing the raw text, the following entry would be created inside the analytic database:

Doc name, byte, context – part number, value – TR-0987-BY

Note that there are a few common custom variables in common use. One (in the United States) is 999-999-9999, which is the
common pattern for telephone number. Or there is 999-99-9999
which is the generic pattern for social security number.

The analyst can create whatever pattern he or she wishes for
processing against the raw text. The only "gotcha" that sometimes
occurs is the case where, on occasion, more than one type of variable will have the same format as another variable. In this case
there will be confusion in trying to use custom variables.

Homographic Resolution

A powerful form of contextualization is known as "homographic resolution." In order to understand homographic resolution,
consider the following (very real) example. Some doctors are trying
to interpret doctors' notes. The term "ha" gives the doctors a problem. When a cardiologist writes "ha" the cardiologist is referring to

"heart attack." When an endocrinologist writes "ha," the endocrinologist is referring to "hepatitis A." When a general practitioner writes "ha," the general practitioner is referring to "headache."

In order to create a proper analytic database, the term "ha" must be interpreted properly. If the term "ha" is not interpreted properly, then people that have had heart attacks, hepatitis A, and headaches will all be mixed together, and that surely will produce a faulty analysis.

There are several elements to homographic resolution. The first element is the homograph itself. In this case the homograph is "ha." The second element is the homograph class. The homograph class in this case includes cardiologist, endocrinologist, and general practitioner. The homographic resolution is that for cardiologists "ha" means "heart attack," for endocrinologists "ha" means "hepatitis A," and that for general practitioners, "ha" means "headache."

The fourth element of homographic resolution is that each of the homographic classes must have typical words assigned to the class. For example, a cardiologist may be associated with words such as "aorta," "stent," "bypass," and "valve."

There are then four elements to homographic resolution:
1. Homograph
2. Homograph class
3. Homograph resolution
4. Words associated with the homograph class

Figure 8.1.9 shows how homographic processing is done against raw text.

Suppose the raw text looks as follows: "…120/68, 168 lb, ha, 72 bpm, f, 38,…"

On processing the raw text, the entry into the database might look like:

Document name, byte, context -headache, value – ha

Care must be taken with the specification of homographs. The underlying work done by the system to resolve the homograph is considerable. So system overhead is a concern. In addition, the

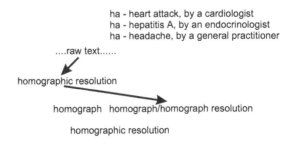

Figure 8.1.9

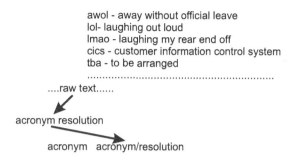

awol - away without official leave
lol- laughing out loud
lmao - laughing my rear end off
cics - customer information control system
tba - to be arranged
....
....raw text......

acronym resolution

acronym   acronym/resolution

Figure 8.1.10

analyst can specify a default homographic class should none of the homographic classes be qualified. In this case, the system will default to the homograph class specified by the analyst

Acronym Resolution

A related form of resolution is that of acronym resolution. Acronyms are found everywhere in raw text. Acronyms are a standard part of communication. Furthermore, acronyms tend to be clustered around some subject area. There are IBM acronyms, military acronyms, instant messaging acronyms, chemical acronyms, Microsoft acronyms, and so forth. In order to clearly understand a communication, it is advisable to resolve acronyms.

Textual ETL is equipped to resolve acronyms. When textual ETL reads raw text and spots an acronym, textual ETL replaces the acronym with the literal value. Figure 8.1.10 shows the dynamics of how textual ETL reads raw text and resolves an acronym when it is found.

As an example of how acronym resolution works, suppose there were the following text:

"Sgt Mullaney was awol as of 10:30 pm on Dec 25…"

The following entry would be placed in the analytical database:

Document name, byte, context – away without official leave, value awol

Textual ETL has organized the terms of resolution by category class. Of course the terms of resolution can be customized upon loading into the system.

Negation Analysis

On occasion, text will state that something did not happen, as opposed to saying that something happened. If standard contextualization is used, there will be a reference to something that did

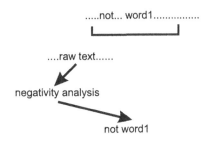

Figure 8.1.11

not happen. In order to make sure that when a negation is stated in text, the negation needs to be recognized by textual ETL.

For example, if a report says, "…John Jones did not have a heart attack…," there does not need to be a reference to John Jones having a heart attack. Instead there needs to be a reference to the fact that John did *not* have a heart attack.

There are actually many different ways that negation analysis can be done by textual ETL. The simplest way is to create a taxonomy of negative terms, "none, not, hardly, no, …" and keep track of the negations that have occurred. Then, if a negative term has occurred in conjunction with another term in the same sentence, the inference is made that something did not happen.

Figure 8.1.11 shows how raw text can be treated to create one form of negation analysis.

As an example of negation analysis, consider the raw text "… John Jones did not have a heart attack…"

The data that would be generated would look like the following:

Document name, byte, context – negation, value – no

Document name, byte, context – condition, value – heart attack

Care must be taken with negation analysis because not all forms of negation are easily handled. The good news is that most forms of negation in language are straightforward and are easily handled. The bad news is that some forms of negation require elaborate techniques for textual ETL management.

Numeric Tagging

Another useful form of contextualization is that of numeric tagging. It is normal for a document to have multiple numeric values on the document. It is also normal for one numeric value to mean one thing and another numeric value to mean something else.

For example a document may have the following items:

Payment amount

Late fee charge

....raw text......

date/numeric tagging

tag:date/tag:numeric

Figure 8.1.12

Interest amount

Payoff amount

It is most helpful to the analyst who will be analyzing the document to "tag" the different numeric values. In doing so, the analyst can simply refer to the numeric value by its meaning. This makes the analysis of documents that contain multiple numeric values quite convenient. (Stated differently, if the tagging is not done at the time of textual ETL processing, the analyst accessing and using the document will have to do the analysis at the time the document is being analyzed, which is a time-consuming and tedious process. It is much simpler to tag a numeric value at the moment of textual ETL processing.)

Figure 8.1.12 shows how raw text is read and how tags are created for numeric values.

As an example of how textual ETL might read a document and tag a numeric value, consider the following raw text:

"…Invoice amount – "$813.97,…""

The data placed onto the analytic database would look like the following:

Document name, byte, context – invoice amount, value – 813.97

Date Tagging

Date tagging operates on the same basis as numeric tagging. The only difference is that date tagging operates on dates rather than numeric values

Date Standardization

Date standardization comes in useful when there are multiple documents that have to be managed or when a single document requires analysis based on date. The problem with a date is that it can be formatted so many ways. Some common ways that a date can be formatted include: –

May 13, 2104

23rd of June, 2015

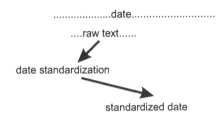

Figure 8.1.13

2001/05/28
14/14/09
While a human being can read these forms of data and understand what is meant, a computer cannot.

Data standardization by textual ETL reads a data, recognizes it as a date, recognizes what date value is being represented in text, and converts the date value into a standard value. The standard value is then stored in the analytical database. Figure 8.1.13 shows how textual ETL reads raw text and converts date values into standardized values.

As an example of the processing done by textual ETL against raw text, consider the following raw text:

"…she married on July 15, 2015, at a small church in Southern Colorado…"

The database reference generated for the analytical database would look like the following:

Document name, byte, context – date value, value – 20150715.

List Processing

Occasionally text contains a list. And occasionally the list needs to be processed as a list, rather than as a sequential string of text.

Textual ETL can recognize and process a list if asked to do so. Figure 8.1.14 shows how raw text is read and processed into a recognizable list in textual ETL.

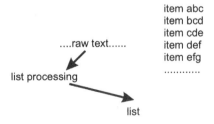

Figure 8.1.14

Consider the following raw text:
"recipe ingredients –
1 – rice
2 – salt
3 – paprika
4 – onions
…"
Textual could read the list and process it as follows:
Document name, byte, context – list recipe element 1, value – rice
Document name, byte, context – list recipe element 2, value – salt
Document name, byte, context – list recipe element 3, value – paprika

Associative Word Processing

Occasionally there are documents that are repetitive in structure but not in terms of words or content. In cases like these it may be necessary to use a feature of textual ETL called "associative word processing."

In associative word processing, an elaborate definitional structure of data is created, then the words inside the structure are defined according to a common meaning of words. Figure 8.1.15 depicts associative word processing.

As an example of associative word processing, consider the following raw text:

"Contract ABC, requirements section, required conferences – every two weeks,…"

The output to the analytical database might look like the following:

Document name, byte, scheduled meeting, value – required conference

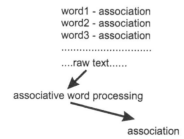

Figure 8.1.15

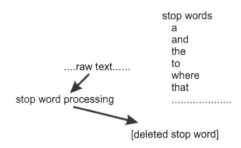

Figure 8.1.16

Stop Word Processing

Perhaps the most straightforward processing done in textual ETL is that of stop word processing. Stop words are words that are necessary for proper grammar but are not useful or necessary for the understanding of the meaning of what is being said. Typical English stop words are "a," "and," "the," "is," "that," "what," "for," "to," "by," and so forth. Typical stop words in Spanish include "el," "la," "es," "de," "que," and "y." All Latin-based languages have stop words.

In doing textual ETL processing stop words are removed and the analyst has the opportunity to customize the stop word list, which is shipped with the product. Removing unnecessary stop words has the effect of reducing the overhead of processing raw text with textual ETL.

Figure 8.1.16 shows raw text that is being processed for stop words by textual ETL.

In order to envision how stop word processing works, consider the following raw text:

"…he walked up the steps, looking to make sure he carried the bag properly…"

After stops words are removed, the resulting raw text would look like the following:

"…walked steps looking carried bag…"

Word Stemming

Another sometimes useful editing feature of textual ETL is that of stemming. Latin-based and Greek-based words have word stems. There are usually many forms of the same word. Consider the stem "mov." The different forms of the word stem "mov" include move, mover, moves, moving, and moved. Note that the stem itself may or may not be an actual word.

Oftentimes it is useful to make associations of text that uses the same word stems. It is easy to reduce a word down to its word stem in textual ETL, as shown in Figure 8.1.17.

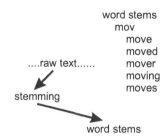

Figure 8.1.17

In order to see how textual processes word stems, consider the following raw text:

"…she walked her dog to the park…"

The resulting database entry would look like the following:

Document name, byte, stem – walk, value – walked

Document Metadata

On occasion it is useful to create an index of the documents that are being managed by the organization. The index can be created where there is only the index or the index can be created in conjunction with all the other features available in textual ETL. There are business justifications for both types of design.

Typical contents for a document index include such data as:

- Date document created
- Date document last accessed
- Date document last updated
- Document created by
- Document length
- Document title or name

Figure 8.1.18 shows that document metadata can be created by textual ETL.

Suppose an organization has a contract document. Running textual ETL against the contract document can produce the following entry into the analytical database:

Figure 8.1.18

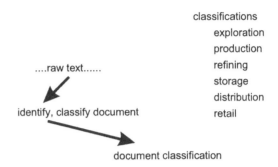

Figure 8.1.19

Document name, byte, document title – Jones Contract, July 30, 1995, 32651 bytes, by Ted Van Duyn,…

Document Classification

In addition to document metadata being able to be gathered, it is also possible to classify documents into an index. As an example of classifying documents, suppose the company is an oil company. One way of classifying documents in an oil company is according to how the documents belong to a part of the organization. Some documents are about exploration, some are about oil production, some are about refining, and so forth. Textual ETL can read the document and determine which classification the document belongs in.

Figure 8.1.19 shows the reading of raw text and the classification of documents.

As an example of document classification, suppose the corporation has a document on deep-water drilling. The database entry that would be produced looks like the following:

Document, byte, document type – exploration, document name - …………………

Proximity Analysis

Occasionally the analyst needs to look at words or taxonomies that are in proximity to each other. For example when a person sees the words "New York Yankees," the thought is about a baseball team. But when the words "New York" and "Yankees" are separated by two or three pages of text, the thought is something entirely different.

Therefore it is useful to be able to do what is referred to as "proximity analysis" in textual ETL. Proximity analysis operates on actual words or taxonomies (or any combination of these elements. The analyst specifies the words or taxonomies that are

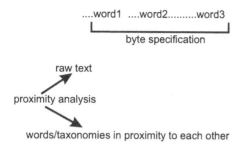

Figure 8.1.20

to be analyzed, gives a proximity value for how close the words need to be in the text, and gives the proximity variable a name. Figure 8.1.20 shows proximity analysis operating against raw text.

As an example of proximity analysis against raw text, suppose there were raw text that looked like the following:

"…away in a manger no crib for a child…"

Suppose the analyst had specified that the words manger, child, and crib were the words that composed the proximity variable, which is baby Jesus.

The results of the processing would look like the following:

Document name, byte, context – manger, crib, child, value – baby Jesus

Care must be taken with proximity analysis as a great amount of system resources can be expended if there are many proximity variables to be sought.

Functional Sequencing within Textual ETL

There are many different functions that occur within textual ETL. Given the document and the processing that needs to occur, the sequence the functions are done in has a great effect on the validity of the results. In fact the sequence of the functions may determine whether the results that are achieved are accurate or not.

Therefore, one of the more important features of textual ETL is the ability to sequence the order in which functions are executed.

Figure 8.1.21 shows that the different functions can be sequences at the discretion of the analyst.

Internal Referential Integrity

In order to keep track of the many different variables and the many different relationships, textual ETL has an elaborate internal structure. In order for any given iteration of textual ETL to exe-

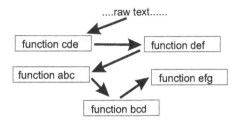

sequencing the functions of textual disambiguation

Figure 8.1.21

cute properly, the internal relationships *must* be defined properly. Stated differently, if the internal relationships inside textual ETL are not properly defined, textual ETL will not execute properly and the results obtained will not be valid and accurate.

As an example of internal relationships inside textual ETL, there is a need to define a document. Once a document is defined, the different indexes that can be created for the document can be defined. Once the different indexes are defined, the delimiters that define the index must be defined. This entire infrastructure must be in place before textual ETL can operate accurately.

In order to ensure that ALL internal relationships are accurately defined, textual ETL has to have verification processing executed before textual ETL can be run.

Figure 8.1.22 shows the need for verification processing.

If any one or more internal relationship is found to be out of place or not defined, the verification process sends a message identifying the relationship that is out of order and declares that the verification process has not been properly passed.

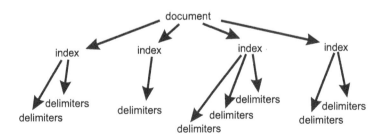

There is an internal structuring of data definitions that requires that the referential integrity of the relationship be checked before processing

Figure 8.1.22

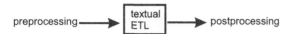

There are both preprocessing and post processing of
text that possibilities with textual ETL

Figure 8.1.23

Preprocessing, Postprocessing

There is a lot of complexity to the processing inside textual
ETL. In most cases a document can be processed entirely within
the confines of textual ETL. However, on occasions, it is possible
to either preprocess a document or postprocess the document (or
do both) if necessary as shown in Figure 8.1.23.

Textual ETL is designed to do as much processing as possible
within the scope of the program. The reason why neither preprocessing nor postprocessing is a normal part of the work flow is
because of overhead. When you do either preprocessing or postprocessing, the overhead of processing is elevated.

There are several activities that occur in preprocessing, if in
fact it is necessary to run preprocessing. Some of those activities
include the following:
- Filtering unwanted and unneeded data
- Fuzzy logic repair of data
- Classification of data
- Raw editing of data

Figure 8.1.24 shows the processing that occurs inside the preprocessor.

Occasionally there is a document that simply cannot be processed by textual ETL without being first processed by a preprocessor. In cases like this a preprocessor comes in handy.

After ETL processing it is possible to postprocess a document. The
functions accomplished in postprocessing are seen in Figure 8.1.25.
On occasion an index entry needs to be edited before it is clean. Or
data needs to be merged before it is in the form the end user expects.
These are all typical activities that can occur in postprocessing.

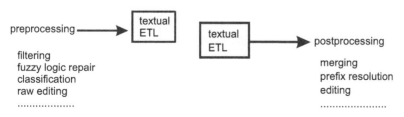

Figure 8.1.24   **Figure 8.1.25**

MAPPING

Mapping is the process of defining the specifications of how a document is to be processed to textual ETL. There is a separate mapping for each type of document to be processed. One of the nice features of textual ETL is that the analyst can build on the specification of previous mappings when it comes time to build a new mapping. On many occasions, one mapping will be very similar to another mapping. It is not necessary for the analyst to create a new mapping if a previous mapping has been created that is similar.

At first glance, creating mappings is a bewildering process. It is like the airline pilot at the control of the airplane. There are many control panels and many switches and buttons. To the uninitiated, flying an airplane seems to be an almost monumental task.

However, once an organized approach is taken, learning to do mapping is a straightforward process. Figure 8.2.1 shows the questions analysts need to ask as they do the mapping process. Most of the questions are straightforward, but a few deserve an explanation.

The first observation is that there is a difference between repetitive and nonrepetitive records of text and structural text repetition. It is true that the words "repetition and nonrepetition" appear in this book. But they do not mean the same thing at all.

Repetitive records of data refers to records of data that repeatedly appear and are very similar in structure and even in context. Nonrepetitive records are records that appear where there is little or no repetition of records from one record to the next.

But repetitive text is something entirely different. Repetitive text refers to text appearing the same way or in a very similar way across more than one document. A simple example of repetitive text are boiler plated contracts. In boiler plated contracts, a lawyer has taken a basic contract and added a few words to it. The same contract appears over and over again in a repetitive manner. Another example of repetitive text is blood pressure. In blood pressure readings, blood pressure is written as "bp – 124/68." The first number is the diastolic reading and the second reading is the systolic reading. When one encounters "bp 176/98," one know exactly what is meant by the text. The text is repetitive.

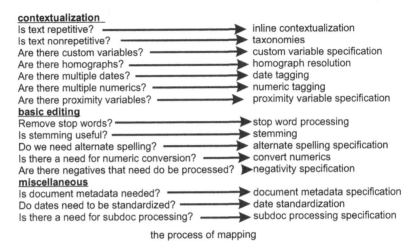

the process of mapping

Figure 8.2.1

Of course you can use as many techniques and specifications are as applicable. You can use taxonomies, inline contextualization, and custom formatting, all at once. Or you can use only taxonomy processing. Or only inline contextualization. The data and what you want to do with the data dictate how you will choose to do what is needed.

One of the issues is choosing names for variables. For example, when you create a custom format you choose a name for the variable. Suppose you wanted to pick up telephone number. You could use a specification of "999-999-9999." You need to name the variable that is created in a meaningful manner. The variable name becomes the context.

For example, for a telephone number, the name "variable001" would be a terrible name. No one would know what you meant when they encountered "variable001." Instead, a name such as "telephone_number001" is much more appropriate. When a person reads "telephone_number001," it is immediately obvious what is meant.

The definition of a mapping is meant to be done in an iterative manner. It is *highly* unlikely that you will create a mapping and that the mapping you create becomes the final mapping. It is *much more* likely that you will create a mapping, run the mapping against the document, then go back and make adjustments to the mapping. Documents are complex and language is complex. There are plenty of nuances in language that people take for granted. Therefore it is unrealistic to think that you will create the perfect mapping the first time you create one. It just doesn't happen with even the most experienced people.

Textual ETL often has multiple ways to handle the same interpretation. In many cases the mapper will be able to accomplish the same results in more than one way. There is no right way or wrong way to do something in textual ETL. You can choose whatever way makes the most sense to you.

Textual ETL is sensitive to resource consumption. In general, textual ETL operates in an efficient manner. The only things to be avoided are the following:

- Looking for more than four or five proximity variables. It is possible to swamp textual ETL by looking for many proximity variables,
- Looking for many homographs. It is possible to swamp textual ETL by looking for more than four or five homograph resolutions
- Taxonomy processing. Loading more than 1000 words in a taxonomy can slow the system down.
- Date standardization. Date standardization causes the system to use many resources. Do not use date standardization unless you really need to use it.

ANALYTICS FROM NONREPETITIVE DATA

There is a wealth of information hidden in nonrepetitive data that is unable to be analyzed by traditional means. Only after the nonrepetitive data has been unlocked by textual disambiguation can analysis be done. There are many examples of rich environments where there is a wealth of information in nonrepetitive data, such as:

- Email
- Call center
- Corporate contracts
- Warranty claims
- Insurance claims
- Medical records

But talking about the value of analysis of nonrepetitive data and actually showing the value are two different things. The world is not convinced until it sees concrete examples.

Call Center Information

Most corporations have call centers. A call center is a corporate function where the corporation staffs phone operators to have conversations with customers. With a call center, the consumer has a voice of the corporation with whom a conversation can be made. In many ways the call center becomes the direct interface the consumer has to the corporation. The conversations that occur in the call center are many and diverse:

- Some people want to complain.
- Some people want to buy something.
- Some people want product information.
- Some people just want to talk.

There is then a wealth of information that transpires in the conversations that corporations with their customer or prospect base.

So what does management of the corporation know about what takes place in their call center? The answer is that management knows very little about what transpires in the call center.

At best management knows how many calls occur daily and how long those calls are. But other than that, management knows very little about what is being discussed in their call center.

And why does management know so little about what takes place in the call center? The answer is that management needs to look at conversations and conversation is nonrepetitive data. And prior to textual disambiguation, the computer could not handle nonrepetitive data for the purposes of analytical processing. However, with textual disambiguation, organizations can now start to understand the content of what is being discussed in call center conversations.

Figure 8.3.1 shows the first step in doing analytics against telephone conversations.

The first step in analyzing conversations is to capture the conversations. Recording conversations is an easy thing to do. You just get a tape recorder and record (and make sure you are not breaking a law in doing so).

After the conversation is recorded, the next step is to use voice recognition technology to convert the conversation to an electronic form. Voice transcription technology is not perfect. There are accents that need to be accounted for. There is slurred speech. There are people that talk very softly. There are angry people who shout. So voice transcription is not a perfect science. But if enough

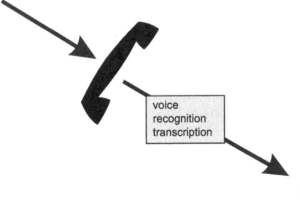

voice recognition transcription

DEANNACALLEDINWITHISSUESWITHHERNEWCABLEBOX
SHOWINGNODATACONNECTIVITY,THEOTHERBOXESSEEMTO
WORKFINE.
WEDAUG2100:16:52EDT2013ISSUE:ONEOFCUSTOMER'SSTBHAS
FOUR8'SONDISPLAYACTION:RESEATCOAXANDPOWERCABLES;
RENEWINITSTBFINALRESUL
WEDAUG2100:17:04EDT2013TONYCISAYINGTHATTHESTBTHAT
WEREPLACESTILLTHESAMETHNG--DROPSHIP
CYNTHIAHORNADAY-VOD271.STBSPOLL,BHRONLINE.GROUPS
TAB.TTFS,CONFIRMEDOUTAGE.ADVCX.
CUSTOMERHASNOONDEMAND.AFFECTEDBYOUTAGE.
WEDAUG2100:19:59EDT2013CSTCALLEDINWITHSTBHAVING
MULTIPLEISSUESSUCHASUNABLETOMAKERECORDINGS,
FREEZING,NOPAUSEORREWINDFUNCTIONFO
CUSTISUPSETTOGETMIS-LEADEDBYLASTFIELDTECHTHATSHE
CANRECORDFROMTHEDVRTODVD.

Figure 8.3.1

DEANNACALLEDINWITHISSUESWITHHERNEWCABLEBOX
SHOWINGNODATACONNECTIVITY,THEOTHERBOXESSEEMTO
WORKFINE.
WEDAUG2100:16:52EDT2013ISSUE:ONEOFCUSTOM   STBHAS
FOUR8'SONDISPLAYACTION:RESEATCOAXANDPOWERCABLES,
RENEWINITSTBFINALRESUL
WEDAUG2100:17:04EDT2013TONYCISAYINGTHATTHESTBTHAT
WEREPLACESTILLTHESAMETHNG--DROPSHIP
CYNTHIAHO   VOD271.STBSPOLL,BHRONLINE.GROUPS
TAB.TTFS,CONFIRMEDOUTAGE.ADVCX.
CUSTOMERHASNOONDEMAND.AFFECTEDBYOUTAG
WEDAUG2100:19:59EDT2013CSTCALLEDINWITHSTBHAVING
MULTIPLEISSUESSUCHASUNABLETOMAKERECORDINGS
FREEZING,NOPAUSEORREWINDFUNCTIONFO
CUSTISUPSETTOGETMIS-LEADEDBYLASTFIELDTECHTHATSHE
CANRECORDFROMTHEDVRTODVD.

a wealth of information

Figure 8.3.2

people speak where their words can be understood, then voice
transcription works adequately.

Once the voice recordings have been recorded and transcribed,
a wealth of information opens up to the analyst. Figure 8.3.2 depicts the world that has opened up.

The first step in unlocking the information found in the call
center conversations is mapping the transcriptions. Mapping is
the process of defining to textual disambiguation how to interpret
the conversations. Typical mapping activities include:
- Editing of stop words
- Identification of homographs
- Identification of taxonomies
- Acronym resolution

While mapping must be done, the mapping that is created
on day 1 can be used until day n. In other words, mapping is a
onetime-only activity. The mapping done the first day can be used
thereafter. The analyst only has to do mapping once.

Figure 8.3.3 shows that mapping is done from the transcriptions.

Once mapping is done, textual disambiguation is ready to process the transcriptions. The input to textual disambiguation is the
raw text, the mapping, and taxonomies. The output from textual
disambiguation is an analytical database. The analytical database
is in the form of any standard database that is used for analytical
processing. By the time the analyst gets his or her hands on the
database, it appears to be just like any other database the analyst
has ever processed. The only difference is that the source of data
for this database is nonrepetitive text.

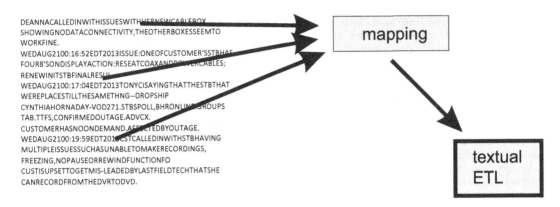

DEANNACALLEDINWITHISSUESWITHHERNEWCABLEBOX
SHOWINGNODATACONNECTIVITY,THEOTHERBOXESSEEMTO
WORKFINE.
WEDAUG2100:16:52EDT2013ISSUE:ONEOFCUSTOMER'SSTBHAS
FOUR8'SONDISPLAYACTION:RESEATCOAXANDPOWERCABLES;
RENEWINITSTBFINALRESUL
WEDAUG2100:17:04EDT2013TONYCISAYINGTHATTHESTBTHAT
WEREPLACESTILLTHESAMETHNG--DROPSHIP
CYNTHIAHORNADAY-VOD271.STBSPOLL,BHRONLINEGROUPS
TAB.TTFS,CONFIRMEDOUTAGE.ADVCX.
CUSTOMERHASNOONDEMAND.AFFECTEDBYOUTAGE.
WEDAUG2100:19:59EDT2013CSTCALLEDINWITHSTBHAVING
MULTIPLEISSUESSUCHASUNABLETOMAKERECORDINGS,
FREEZING,NOPAUSEORREWINDFUNCTIONFO
CUSTISUPSETTOGETMIS-LEADEDBYLASTFIELDTECHTHATSHE
CANRECORDFROMTHEDVRTODVD.

Figure 8.3.3

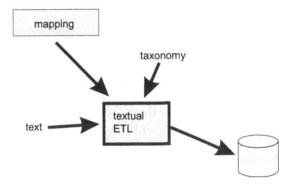

Figure 8.3.4

Figure 8.3.4 shows the processing that occurs inside textual disambiguation.

The output of textual disambiguation is a standard database, often thought of as being in the form of relational data. In many ways the database that has been produced has text that has been "normalized." There are business relationships that are buried in the database. These business relationships are a result of the mapping and the text that has been interpreted by the mapping.

Figure 8.3.5 shows the database that has been produced.

After the database has been created by textual disambiguation, the next step is the selection of an analytical tool (or tools).

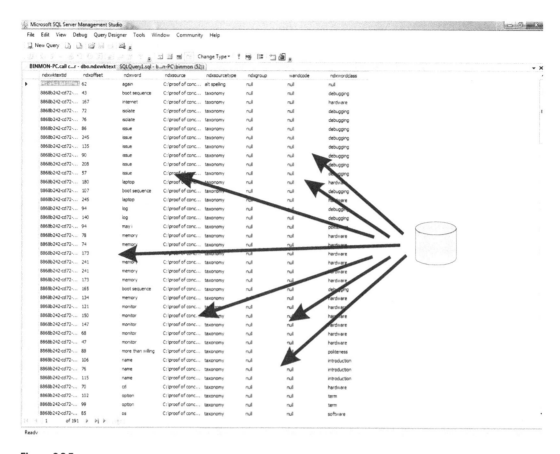

Figure 8.3.5

Depending on the analysis to be done it may be necessary to choose more than one analytical tool for analysis. The analytical tool that is chosen only has to be able to process relational data. That is the only requirement for the analytical tool.

Figure 8.3.6 shows that an analytical tool needs to be selected.

After the analytical tool has been selected, then analysis can commence. The analyst takes the data derived from the database that was derived from the transcriptions and does the analysis.

Each analytical tool has its favored method of presenting data. Figure 8.3.7 shows a dashboard created by using Tableau for analyzing the call center information.

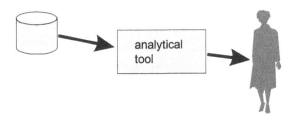

Figure 8.3.6

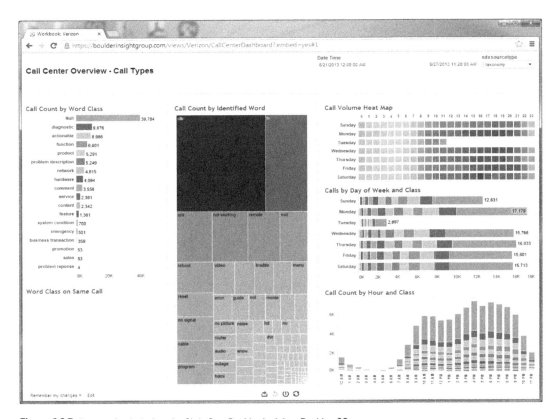

Figure 8.3.7   Source: Analysis done by Chris Cox, Boulder Insights, Boulder, CO.

The dashboard reflects the content of the activity that has transpired within the call center. With the dashboard the analyst can see among other things:

- When activities were processed
- What kind of activities were processed

- The actual content of calls
- The demographics of what was discussed

The dashboard gives a wealth of information that is organized and is graphical. In a glance, management can see what is transpiring in the call center.

As an example of the information contained in the dashboard, consider Figure 8.3.8, which shows a ranked survey. The diagram in Figure 8.3.8 is a synopsis of the type of call that has passed through the call center. Each call is categorized as to what the major purpose of the call was. Then the calls are ranked as to how many of which type occurred during the reporting period. If there were no other information on the dashboard, this information is extremely useful by itself.

Another type of information found on the dashboard is the information relating to what time of day the calls came in at. Figure 8.3.9 shows this information. Not only is the hour of day identified, the classification by type of call is identified as well. It is worth noting

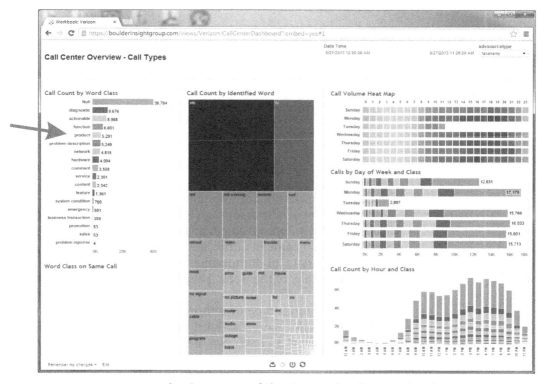

a ranked survey of the type of calls received

Figure 8.3.8

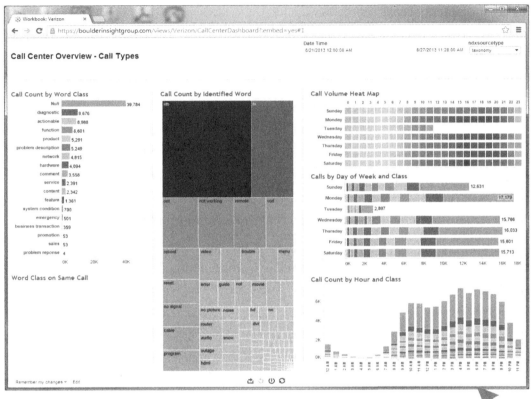

an hour-by-hour analysis of the calls received

Figure 8.3.9

that using the dashboard approach, drill-down processing is a possibility. For each hour for each category of call, the analyst can invoke drill-down processing to investigate more thoroughly each class of call that came in during any given hour.

A related type of information that is available is type of phone call by day of the week. This type of information is seen in Figure 8.3.10.

And yet another type of information that is available on the dashboard is information about the day of the month when calls occurred. Figure 8.3.11 shows a "heat map" depicting the pattern of calls throughout the month.

But perhaps the most useful information on the dashboard is the information shown by Figure 8.3.12, which shows in the form of a histogram the actual subjects that were discussed during call center activity. The most discussed subject has the black box that is largest. The next most discussed subject is the next largest box. By

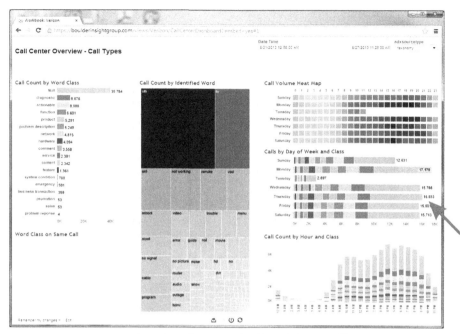

a day-by-day analysis of the traffic

Figure 8.3.10

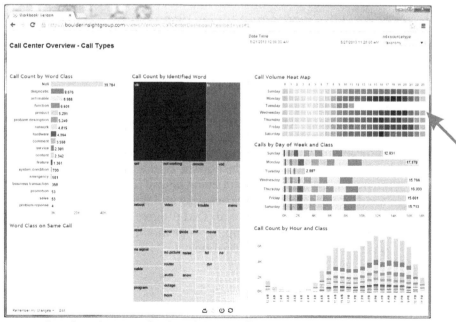

a day-by-day analysis of the traffic throughout the month

Figure 8.3.11

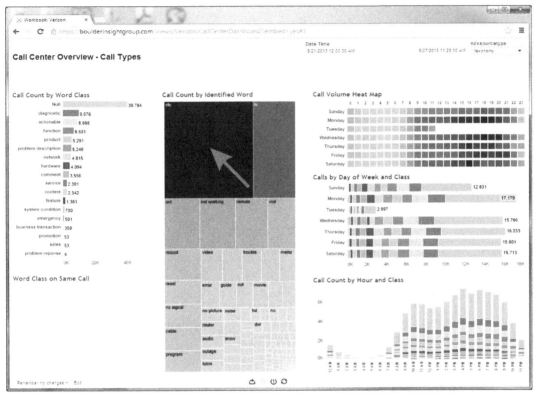

a histogram showing the words and topics discussed
in call center conversations

Figure 8.3.12

looking at the histogram, management has a very good idea what
subjects are on the minds of their customers. Looking at the dashboard tells management in a glance what management needs to
know about what is going on in the call center.

As impressive as the dashboard is, the dashboard would not
be possible without the data being placed in a standard database.
There is a progression of processing and data that makes possible
the creation of the dashboard. That progression looks like this:

Repetitive data → Mapping → Textual ETL → Standard database → Analytical tool → Dashboard

Medical Records

Call center records are important and are at the center of business value. But call center records are hardly the only form of
nonrepetitive records that are valuable. Another form of valuable

nonrepetitive data is medical records. Medical records are written usually as a patient goes through a procedure or some event of medical care. The records, once written, are valuable to many people and organizations, including the physician, patient, hospital or provider, and research organizations.

The challenge with medical records is that they contain narrative information. Narrative information is necessary and useful to the physician. But narrative information is not useful to the computer. In order to be used in analytical processing, the narrative information must be put into the form of a database in a standard database format. This is a classic case of nonrepetitive data being placed in the form of a database. What is needed is textual ETL.

In order to see how textual ETL is used, consider a medical record. (Note that the medical record being shown in Figure 8.3.13 is a real record, however, it is from a country other than the United States and is not subject to the regulations of the Health Insurance Portability and Accountability Act [HIPAA].)

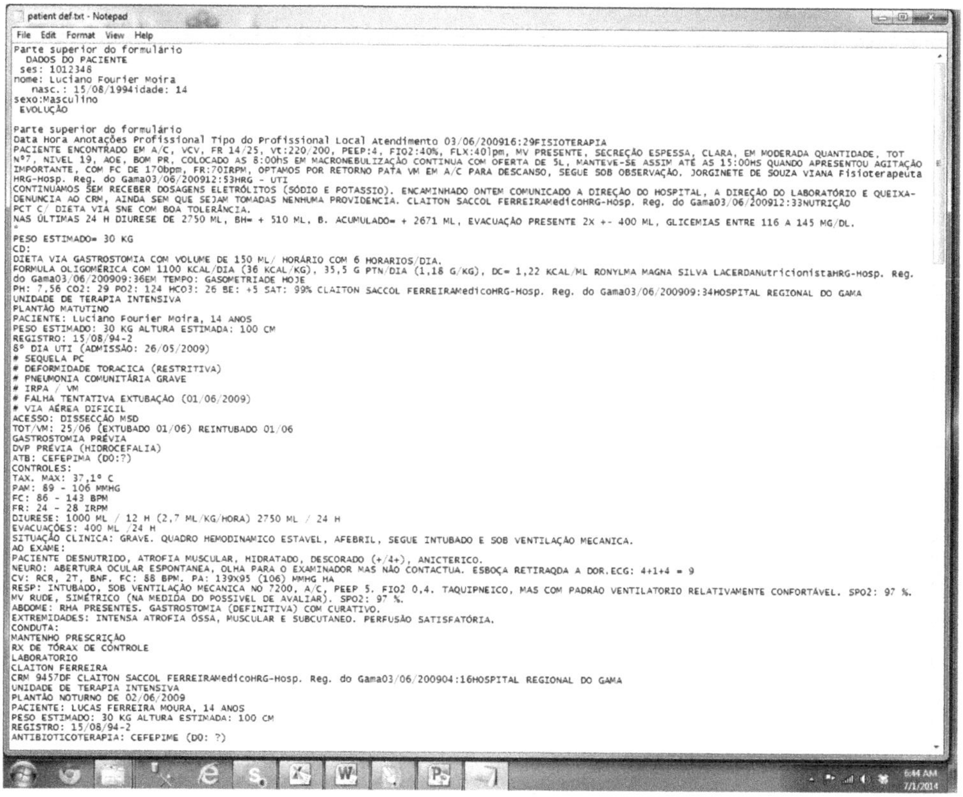

```
patient def.txt - Notepad
File Edit Format View Help
Parte superior do formulário
  DADOS DO PACIENTE
 ses: 1012348
nome: Luciano Fourier Moira
   nasc.: 15/08/1994idade: 14
sexo:Masculino
 EVOLUÇÃO

Parte superior do formulário
Data Hora Anotações Profissional Tipo do Profissional Local Atendimento 03/06/200916:29FISIOTERAPIA
PACIENTE ENCONTRADO EM A/C, VCV, FR 14/25, Vt:220/200, PEEP:4, FIO2:40%, FLX:40lpm, MV PRESENTE, SECREÇÃO ESPESSA, CLARA, EM MODERADA QUANTIDADE, TOT
N°7, NIVEL 19, AOE, BOM PR, COLOCADO AS 8:00hS EM MACRONEBULIZAÇÃO CONTINUA COM OFERTA DE 5L, MANTEVE-SE ASSIM ATÉ AS 15:00HS QUANDO APRESENTOU AGITAÇÃO
IMPORTANTE, COM FC DE 170bpm, FR:70IRPM, OPTAMOS POR RETORNO PATA VM EM A/C PARA DESCANSO, SEGUE SOB OBSERVAÇÃO. JORGINETE DE SOUZA VIANA Fisioterapeuta
HRG-Hosp. Reg. do Gama03/06/200912:53HRG - UTI
CONTINUAMOS SEM RECEBER DOSAGENS ELETRÓLITOS (SÓDIO E POTASSIO). ENCAMINHADO ONTEM COMUNICADO A DIREÇÃO DO HOSPITAL, A DIREÇÃO DO LABORATÓRIO E QUEIXA-
DENUNCIA AO CRM, AINDA SEM QUE SEJAM TOMADAS NENHUMA PROVIDENCIA. CLAITON SACCOL FERREIRAMedicoHRG-Hosp. Reg. do Gama03/06/200912:33NUTRIÇÃO
PCT C/ DIETA VIA SNE COM BOA TOLERÂNCIA.
NAS ÚLTIMAS 24 H DIURESE DE 2750 ML, BH= + 510 ML, B. ACUMULADO= + 2671 ML, EVACUAÇÃO PRESENTE 2X +- 400 ML, GLICEMIAS ENTRE 116 A 145 MG/DL.

PESO ESTIMADO= 30 KG
CD:
DIETA VIA GASTROSTOMIA COM VOLUME DE 150 ML/ HORÁRIO COM 6 HORARIOS/DIA.
FORMULA OLIGOMÉRICA COM 1100 KCAL/DIA (36 KCAL/KG), 35,5 G PTN/DIA (1,18 G/KG), DC= 1,22 KCAL/ML RONYLMA MAGNA SILVA LACERDANutricionistaHRG-Hosp. Reg.
do Gama03/06/200909:36EM TEMPO: GASOMETRIADE HOJE
PH: 7,56 CO2: 29 PO2: 124 HCO3: 26 BE: +5 SAT: 99% CLAITON SACCOL FERREIRAMedicoHRG-Hosp. Reg. do Gama03/06/200909:34HOSPITAL REGIONAL DO GAMA
UNIDADE DE TERAPIA INTENSIVA
PLANTÃO MATUTINO
PACIENTE: Luciano Fourier Moira, 14 ANOS
PESO ESTIMADO: 30 KG ALTURA ESTIMADA: 100 CM
REGISTRO: 15/08/94-2
8° DIA UTI (ADMISSÃO: 26/05/2009)
# SEQUELA PC
# DEFORMIDADE TORACICA (RESTRITIVA)
# PNEUMONIA COMUNITÁRIA GRAVE
# IRPA / VM
# FALHA TENTATIVA EXTUBAÇÃO (01/06/2009)
# VIA AÉREA DIFICIL
ACESSO: DISSECÇÃO MSD
TOT/VM: 25/06 (EXTUBADO 01/06) REINTUBADO 01/06
GASTROSTOMIA PRÉVIA
DVP PRÉVIA (HIDROCEFALIA)
ATB: CEFEPIMA (D0:?)
CONTROLES:
TAX. MAX: 37,1° C
PAM: 89 - 106 MMHG
FC: 86 - 143 BPM
FR: 24 - 28 IRPM
DIURESE: 1000 ML / 12 H (2,7 ML/KG/HORA) 2750 ML / 24 H
EVACUAÇÕES: 400 ML /24 H
SITUAÇÃO CLINICA: GRAVE. QUADRO HEMODINAMICO ESTAVEL, AFEBRIL, SEGUE INTUBADO E SOB VENTILAÇÃO MECANICA.
AO EXAME:
PACIENTE DESNUTRIDO, ATROFIA MUSCULAR, HIDRATADO, DESCORADO (+/4+), ANICTERICO.
NEURO: ABERTURA OCULAR ESPONTANEA, OLHA PARA O EXAMINADOR MAS NÃO CONTACTUA. ESBOÇA RETIRAQDA A DOR.ECG: 4+1+4 = 9
CV: RCR, 2T, BNF. FC: 88 BPM. PA: 139X95 (106) MMHG HA
RESP: INTUBADO, SOB VENTILAÇÃO MECANICA NO 7200, A/C, PEEP 5. FIO2 0,4. TAQUIPNEICO, MAS COM PADRÃO VENTILATORIO RELATIVAMENTE CONFORTÁVEL. SPO2: 97 %.
MV RUDE, SIMÉTRICO (NA MEDIDA DO POSSIVEL DE AVALIAR). SPO2: 97 %.
ABDOME: RHA PRESENTES. GASTROSTOMIA (DEFINITIVA) COM CURATIVO.
EXTREMIDADES: INTENSA ATROFIA ÓSSA, MUSCULAR E SUBCUTANEO. PERFUSÃO SATISFATÓRIA.
CONDUTA:
MANTENHO PRESCRIÇÃO
RX DE TÓRAX DE CONTROLE
LABORATORIO
CLAITON FERREIRA
CRM 9457DF CLAITON SACCOL FERREIRAMedicoHRG-Hosp. Reg. do Gama03/06/200904:16HOSPITAL REGIONAL DO GAMA
UNIDADE DE TERAPIA INTENSIVA
PLANTÃO NOTURNO DE 02/06/2009
PACIENTE: LUCAS FERREIRA MOURA, 14 ANOS
PESO ESTIMADO: 30 KG ALTURA ESTIMADA: 100 CM
REGISTRO: 15/08/94-2
ANTIBIOTICOTERAPIA: CEFEPIME (D0: ?)
6:44 AM
7/1/2014
```

a medical record

Figure 8.3.13

When looking at medical records, the records start to take a recognizable pattern. The first part of the medical record is the identification part. In this part of the record, one or more identifying criteria are found. In the second part of the medical record, there is narrative information. In the narrative section, a doctor or nurse has written down some characterization of a medical event such as a diagnosis, procedure, or observation. In the third section of the medical record are laboratory test results that are relevant to the reason why the patient is in medical care.

Figure 8.3.14 shows a typical medical record. In a medical record there is a narrative every time a medical event occurs. Figure 8.3.15 shows that there is more than one narrative section relating to a patients visit in the hospital.

The techniques used in processing the medical record include all the ways that textual ETL can process text. Figure 8.3.16 shows

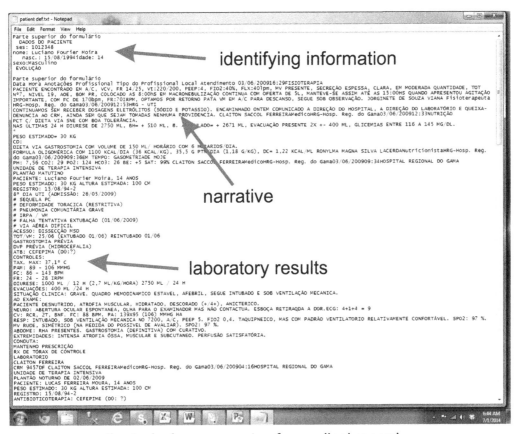

the typical components of a medical record

Figure 8.3.14

a narrative is made of each medical event

Figure 8.3.15

some of the techniques used to identify data

Figure 8.3.16

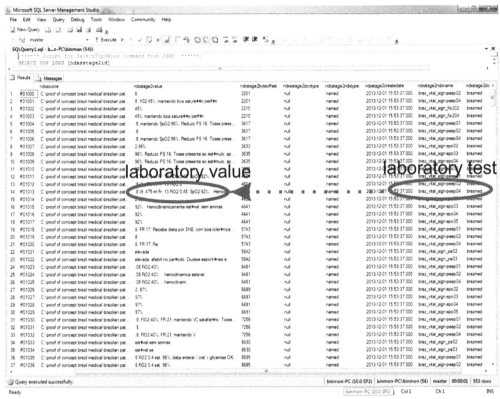

a sample data base output from medical record ETL processing

Figure 8.3.17

some of the ways that medical records are processed. The result of textual ETL processing the medical record is a normalized database. Figure 8.3.17 shows the normalized textual based database that has resulted from textual ETL processing a medical record.

Once the text has been placed in a standard relational database, it is useful for analytic processing. Now millions of medical records can be analyzed.

9.1

OPERATIONAL ANALYTICS

Analytics can be used throughout the computing environment. Indeed one of the values of computerizing a system is to be able to do analytics.

One of the most important environments in corporate computing is that of the operational environment. The operational environment is one that is the place where detailed, up-to-the-second decisions are made. The operational environment is used primarily by the clerical community. The operational environment is where the business of the corporation is transacted.

Figure 9.1.1 shows that there are two primary processing and decision-making environments in most corporations. There is the operational environment and there is the management decision environment.

There are several criteria that enhance the success of the operational environment. Some of those criteria include the ability to:

Create, update, and delete individual transactions

Access data

Have integrity of transaction processing

Handle large volumes of data

Handle data systematically

Execute quickly

Of all of these factors, the ability to access and process data quickly is the most important in operational systems.

Figure 9.1.2 shows that performance, which is the ability to execute transactions quickly, is the most important criteria in the operational environment. There are many reasons why speed of execution is so important in the operational environment. The reason is that the computer has been integrated into the day-to-day business of the running of the corporation. When there is a problem with performance, the day-to-day business of the corporation grinds to a halt.

To understand the importance of speed of transaction execution, consider the following circumstances:

- In a bank, a teller must wait 60 seconds for a transaction to process. The bank teller and the customer being served are both irritated.

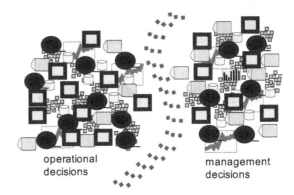

operational
decisions

management
decisions

Figure 9.1.1

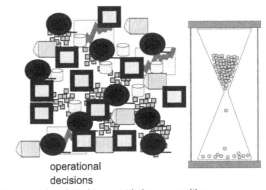

operational
decisions

The operational environment is hypersensitive
to the amount of time that it takes to run a process

Figure 9.1.2

- In an airline reservation, the airline clerk must wait 60 seconds to conduct business across the network. Long queues build up waiting for the system to finish processing.
- In an ATM environment, customers drive away angry when the ATM machine takes 60 seconds to complete a transaction.
- On the Internet, when using a site, viewers go away when the site takes a long time to complete a transaction.

And there are many, many other circumstances where transaction response time affects the business of the corporation. Figure 9.1.3 shows that transaction response time is essential to the satisfactory running of the business.

With transaction processing, the computer began
to be essential to the running of day-to-day business

Figure 9.1.3

Transaction Response Time

Transaction response time is the most important element of the operational environment. What then are the elements of response time? Figure 9.1.4 shows the elements of transaction response time.

At step 1, a transaction is initiated. A customer wants to see how much money is in his or her account. A shelf stocker wants to place an item on the shelf of a store. A clerk wants to mark the successful manufacture of an order. An airline wants to upgrade a customer. These are all forms of initiating a transaction.

At step 2, the transaction arrives at the computer. The program goes into execution. Variables are initialized. Calculations are made. Algorithms are executed. Then, somewhere along the line of doing its processing, the computer program discovers that it needs to go to a database and find some data in order to execute.

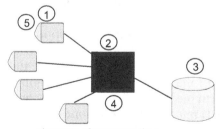

elements of response time
1 - transaction is initiated
2 - processor commences execution
3 - data is accessed
4 - data is returned and processed
5 - results are sent to user

Figure 9.1.4

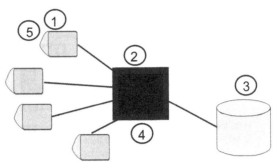

response time measured from (1) to (5)

Figure 9.1.5

At step 3, a request is made to the database management system (DBMS) to find data. The DBMS honors the request and goes off to search for some data. Upon finding the data, the DBMS packages the data and sends it back to the computer.

The program commences processing again. The program discovers that it needs more data so the program issues another request for data to the DBMS. Data is returned to the program.

Finally upon conclusion of the program, step 4, the program inside the computer is ready to return results to the user making the request.

The results are returned to the user at step 5.

Response time inside the computer is measured from the length of time it takes for steps 2, 3, and 4 to execute. On the average, response time is typically between one and two seconds. Given all the computer had to go through, it is amazing that response time is as fast as it is. Figure 9.1.5 shows how response time is measured.

Far and away the biggest element of response time (i.e., steps 2, 3, and 4) is the amount of time needed to search and retrieve data. The processing inside the computer – steps 2 and 4 – occur very quickly. It is step 3 that chews up the most amount of time.

There is a term for step 3. That term is an "input/output" (I/O) operation. An I/O refers to the work done by the system in making either an input or an output to the system. Figure 9.1.6 depicts an I/O operation.

There are two kinds of speeds found in a computer – electronic speeds and mechanical speeds. Electronic speeds are measured typically in nano seconds. Mechanical speeds are measured in terms of milliseconds. The difference in speeds is akin to flying on a jet airplane and riding a bicycle. There is that much difference between the two types of speeds.

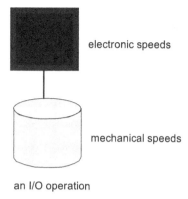

electronic speeds

mechanical speeds

an I/O operation

Figure 9.1.6

The internal operations of a computer operate in electronic speeds. The I/O operations operate at mechanical speeds. In order to get a program to operate quickly, the analyst needs to minimize the number of I/Os that are being done. Minimizing the number of I/Os being done has the effect of speeding a program in its execution. But minimizing I/Os also has the effect of reducing the speed of every other transaction that is awaiting execution.

In a computer, a single program executes at a time. The other programs that need to execute wait while the one program that is in execution finishes. The time the other programs have to wait is called "queue" time. Figure 9.1.7 illustrates queue time.

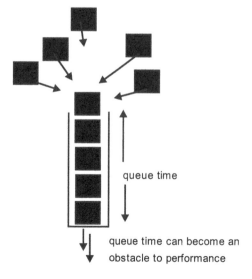

queue time

queue time can become an obstacle to performance

Figure 9.1.7

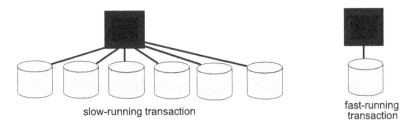

slow-running transaction

fast-running
transaction

Figure 9.1.8

There are two primary ways that queue time can build inside a computer – either a single program takes a long time to execute or the rate at which transactions arrive at the queue exceeds the average execution time. In any case. in many computers it is queue time that causes slowdowns in processing.

Another way of looking at the phenomenon of performance is in terms of the number of I/Os being done by a transaction. Figure 9.1.8 shows two different kinds of transactions. The transaction of the left is not going to be a fast running transaction. It has too many I/Os that it has to do. The transaction on the right has a much better chance of being a fast running transaction. It has only one or two I/Os that it must do. Therefore looking at the number of I/Os that a transaction must do is a good way to look at the performance characteristics of a transaction.

There is a way to reduce the amount of I/Os that a transaction has to do. Consider the transaction shown in Figure 9.1.9, which shows that lots of different kinds of data are needed in order to execute the transaction. If the transaction goes and looks on disk storage for all the different places where the data resides, the transaction will not be a fast running transaction.

What the database designer could do is to combine all or some of the data into a single database design. There is nothing that says

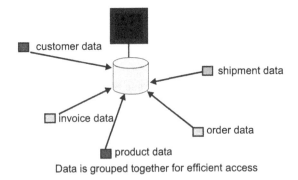

customer data

shipment data

invoice data

order data

product data

Data is grouped together for efficient access

Figure 9.1.9

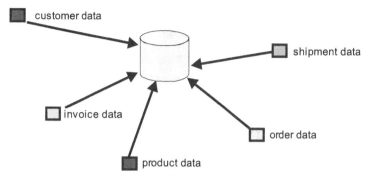

This type of data design is called denormalization

Figure 9.1.10

Every now and then it is
necessary to access a lot
of records in a single
transaction

Figure 9.1.11

that data of different types must be placed in different databases.
In order to enhance performance, the analyst could combine all
the data (or even some of the data) into a single database. This type
of design is referred to as a "denormalized" design. Figure 9.1.10
shows that data can be denormalized.

Once the data is denormalized, the number of I/Os needed to
execute the transaction is reduced. The transaction now becomes
a fast running transaction.

Every now and then it happens that a transaction needs to
look at a lot of data, regardless of how the data is organized. Such
programs are typical of report programs that look at the day's activities, or the month's activities. Figure 9.1.11 shows one of these
long-running programs.

What happens if one of these long-running programs is mixed
with a lot of short-running programs, as shown in Figure 9.1.12?
The answer is performance for the entire system comes to a halt.
The minute the long-running program goes into execution, the
queue builds behind the long-running program. And that defeats
the purpose of the operational environment.

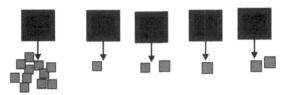

Having one transaction that accesses a lot of data mixed in with transactions that access little data is disruptive to everyone's performance

Figure 9.1.12

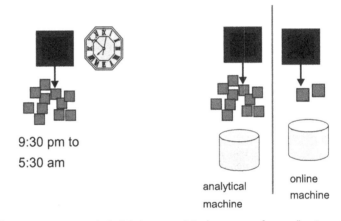

9:30 pm to
5:30 am

analytical
machine

online
machine

There are many ways to isolate large analytical processes from online transactions

Figure 9.1.13

So what can the analyst do if it is necessary to run a long-running program (which is a fact of life)? Figure 9.1.13 shows some solutions to allowing the system to run long-running programs and to have online transaction response time.

One solution to resolving the conflict between long-running programs and the need for consistent response time is to partition off the time slots for running on the computer. All fast running transactions run during the daytime when business needs for there to be good response time, and long-running programs are able to be executed in the wee hours of the morning, when no one else is using the machine.

An alternative is to execute long-running programs on a different machine on a different DBMS than the database and machine that the transactions are operating on. This alternative works whenever there is no need for the long-running program to access the actual data that is being transacted against.

10.1

OPERATIONAL ANALYTICS

The operational environment is one where the day-to-day activities of the corporation take place. Sales are made. Bank deposits are made. Insurance policies are sold. Grocery shelves are stocked. In short, the world operates in a modern efficient manner when the operational world runs properly. The data that is generated by operational processing is of enormous value to the world. Figure 10.1.1 depicts the operational environment.

Operational analytics consist of the decisions that are made as a result of the execution of transactions in the operational environment. Those points of data that are at the heart of operational analytics are generated by operational systems. Operational systems are those systems that run transactions and manage data inside a database management system.

There are many characteristics of operational systems. The essence of operational applications is depicted in Figure 10.1.2. Operational systems have the mission of being speedy in execution, operating against data at a detailed level, and bound together in applications.

Because of the need for speedy execution of transaction, data is often denormalized. Denormalization is the design technique that the designer needs to use in order enhance performance. But because data is denormalized it is "pulled apart." One unit of data is found in one database and the same unit of data is found in another database. The fragmentation of data into separate databases is a natural result of the need for denormalization of data in a high-performance environment. Denormalization of data in the high-performance transaction-processing environment is a normal, natural phenomenon.

But there is a side effect of denormalization of data. Because data is denormalized in the operational environment, data is not integrated. The same unit of data often exists in several places. (Or in the worst case, the same unit of data exists in many, many, many places.) The net effect of the same data existing in many places is that the data loses its integrity. One user accesses the data in one place and gets one value. Another user accesses the same data in another place and gets a very different value. Both users think they have the correct value of data. And both users have very different values. This lack of integrity of data is seen in Figure 10.1.3.

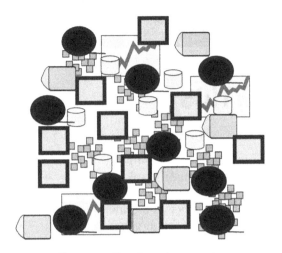

the operational environment

Figure 10.1.1

the essence of operational applications

1 - speed of processing

2 - operation at the detailed level

3 - applications

Figure 10.1.2

One can see the frustration across the organization. How in the world can decisions be made when no one knows that the correct value of data is? But the lack of integrity is not the only problem with operational applications. Another problem with operational applications is that there is only a minimal amount of historical data to be found in operational applications.

There is a good reason for there being minimal history in operational applications. The reason for the minimal amount of historical data is that the need for high performance trumps all other operational objectives. System tuners long ago discovered that the more data there is in a system, the slower the system runs. Therefore, in order to have optimal performance, system tuners jettisoned historical data. Because operational systems have a need for high performance, of necessity, there is little historical data found in the operational environment. Figure 10.1.4 shows that there is minimal historical data found in the operational environment.

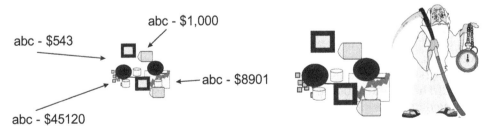

lack of integrity of data

no historical data

Figure 10.1.3   **Figure 10.1.4**

But there is a problem with jettisoning historical data. That problem is that historical data is useful for many purposes. Historical data is useful for:

Spotting and measuring trends

Understanding the long-term habits of customers

Looking at developing patterns

Because of the lack of integrity of data and because of the need to have a place to house historical data, there arose a need for a different kind of architectural structure than the operational application. Because of the need to do analytic processing (as opposed to transactional processing), there appeared in the world a structure called the "data warehouse." Figure 10.1.5 shows the emergence of the data warehouse.

The definition of a data warehouse has been around since the beginning of data warehousing. A data warehouse is a subject-oriented, integrated, nonvolatile, time-variant collection of data in support of management's decisions. A data warehouse contains detailed, integrated data that is historical.

Another way of thinking about a data warehouse is that a data warehouse is a "single version of the truth." The data warehouse is the detailed, integrated bedrock data that can be used for decision-making purposes throughout the organization.

The data model that best serves as a basis for the data warehouse is the relational model. The relational model is normalized data and is good for representing data at its most granular level. Figure 10.1.6 shows the relational model that serves as a design foundation for the data warehouse.

data warehouse

  - subject oriented

  - integrated

  - time variant

  - nonvolatile

collection of data in support

of management's decisions

the single version of the truth

Figure 10.1.5

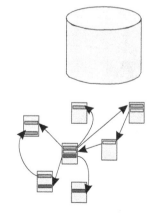

The relational model supports integrated, detailed, historical data

Figure 10.1.6

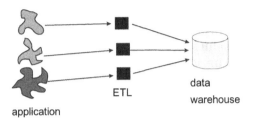

loading data into the data warehouse

Figure 10.1.7

Data is loaded into the data warehouse from the operational applications. Data in the operational applications resides in the applications in a denormalized state. Data is loaded into the data warehouse through technology known as "ETL" ("extract/transform/load") as depicted in Figure 10.1.7.

In fact data is not "loaded" into the data warehouse at all. The reality is that data is transformed as it passes from the operational environment into the data warehouse environment. In the operational environment, data is designed into a denormalized state. In the data warehouse, data is designed into the normalized state. The purpose of ETL processing is to transform application data into corporate data. To the uninitiated this transformation doesn't seem to be a difficult process. But in fact it is. In order to understand the transformation accomplished by textual ETL, refer to the transformation depicted in Figure 10.1.8

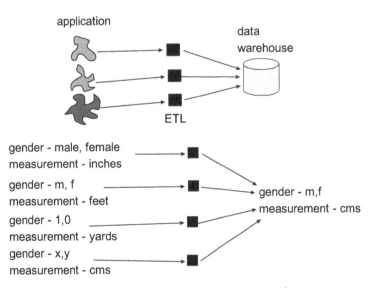

Figure 10.1.8   transforming application data into corporate data

In Figure 10.1.8 application data holds different renditions of data for gender and measurement. In one application, gender is indicated by the values – male and female. In another application, gender is indicated by 1 and 0. In one application, measurement is made in inches. In another application, measurement is made in centimeters.

In the data warehouse there is one indicator for gender – m and f. In the data warehouse there is one unit of measurement – centimeters. The transformation from application data to corporate data is made during the ETL process. The diagram in Figure 10.1.8 is a good illustration of what is meant by the difference between application data and corporate data.

A fundamental concept to the integrity of data and the establishment of corporate data is the "system of record." The system of record is the definitive data of the corporation. In the operational environment the system of record is the data that feeds values to the data warehouse. Figure 10.1.9 illustrates the system of record in the operational environment.

It is worthwhile noting that the system of record moves from one environment to the next. The system of record for operational data resides in the operational environment. But as data passes into the data warehouse, the system of record also passes into the data warehouse. The difference is the timeliness of the data. Data in the operational environment is accurate as of the moment of access. Stated differently, data in the operational environment is up-to-the-second accurate data. But when the system of record data moves to the data warehouse, the system of record data becomes accurate as to the moment in history that is reflected in the data warehouse. The system of record is historically accurate in the data warehouse.

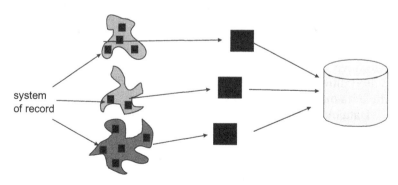

system
of record

The actual data elements that provide data for
the data warehouse are called the system of record

Figure 10.1.9

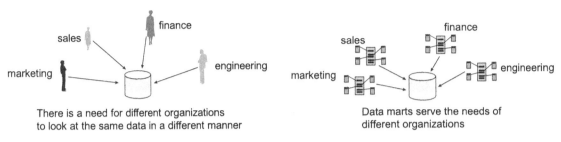

There is a need for different organizations
to look at the same data in a different manner

Figure 10.1.10

Data marts serve the needs of
different organizations

Figure 10.1.11

One of the most important functions of the data warehouse is
the ability to serve as a foundation for different organizations to
look at the same data differently and still have the same foundation of data. Figure 10.1.10 shows this capability.

The reason the data warehouse can serve as a foundation of data
for different organizations is that the data in the data warehouse is
granular and integrated. You can think of the data in the data warehouse as grains of sand. Sand can be shaped into many different
final goods – silicon chips, wine glasses, automobile headlights,
body parts, and so forth. And by the same token, marketing can look
at data in the data warehouse one way, finance can look at data in
the data warehouse another way, and sales can look at data in the
data warehouse yet another way. And yet all of the organizations are
looking at the same data and there is reconcilability of data.

The ability to serve different communities is one of the most
important characteristics of the data warehouse. The way that the
data warehouse serves the different communities is through the
creation of data marts. Figure 10.1.11 shows that the data warehouse serves as a basis for data in the data marts and shows that
there are different data marts for different organizations. The data
warehouse and its granular data serve as a basis for the data found
in the data marts. The granular data in the data warehouse is summarized and otherwise aggregated into the form that each data
mart requires. Note that each data mart and each organization
will have their own way of summarizing and aggregating data.
Stated differently, the data mart for finance will be different from
the data mart for marketing.

Data marts are best based on the dimensional model, as shown
in Figure 10.1.12. In the dimensional model are found fact tables
and dimension tables. Tables and dimension tables are attached
together to form what is known as the "star" join. The star join is designed to be optimal for the informational needs of a department.

Data marts and the data warehouse combine to form an architecture, as shown in Figure 10.1.13. The integration of data occurs

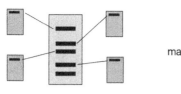

the dimensional model

Data marts are built on the basis
of the dimensional model

Figure 10.1.12

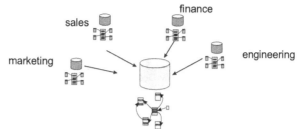

The dimensional model serves the data mart environment
and the relational model serves the data warehouse environment

Figure 10.1.13

as data is placed in an integrated, historical fashion in the data warehouse. Once the foundation of data is built, the data is passed into the different data marts. As data is passed into the data marts, data is summarized or otherwise aggregated.

There is another data structure that sometimes appears in data architecture, and that structure is one known as the "operational data store" (ODS). Figure 10.1.14 depicts an ODS.

The ODS has some characteristics of the data warehouse and some characteristics of the operational environment. The ODS can be updated in real time, and the ODS can support high-performance transaction processing. But the ODS also contains integrated data. In many ways the ODS is a "half way" house for data. Figure 10.1.15 shows the ODS.

The ODS is an optional data structure for corporations. Some corporations have need of an ODS; other corporations do not need the ODS. As a rule, if an organization does significant amounts of transaction processing, it will need an ODS.

The type of data that is found in the data marts usually includes what is known as a "key performance indicator" (KPI). Figure 10.1.16

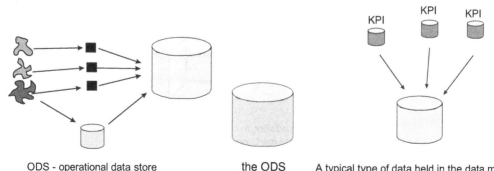

ODS - operational data store

the ODS

A typical type of data held in the data mart is the KPI

Figure 10.1.14

Figure 10.1.15   **Figure 10.1.16**

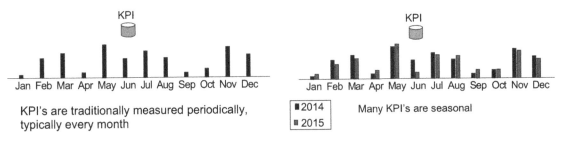

KPI's are traditionally measured periodically, typically every month

Figure 10.1.17

■ 2014
■ 2015

Many KPI's are seasonal

Figure 10.1.18

illustrates that data marts usually contain one or more KPIs. Every corporation has its own set of KPIs. Some typical KPIs might include:

- Cash on hand
- Number of employees
- Product order backlog
- The sales pipeline
- New product acceptance
- Inventory for sale

KPIs are typically measured on a monthly basis. Figure 10.1.17 shows such a periodic measurement of KPIs. There are lots of reasons to measure KPIs on a monthly basis. One value is the ability to spot trends as the trends are happening.

There is a problem with spotting trends on KPIs on a monthly basis, and that problem is that many KPIs are seasonal. By looking at a month-by-month trend line, the trend may not be accurate. To spot seasonal trends it is necessary to have a measurement of KPIs over multiple years, as shown in Figure 10.1.18.

In addition to having KPIs, data marts oftentimes house what are termed "cubes." Figure 10.1.19 shows that cubes often appear in data marts or in conjunction with data marts. A cube is

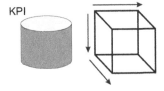

In addition to housing KPI's, data marts are also in the form of cube technology or online analytical processing (OLAP) technology

Figure 10.1.19

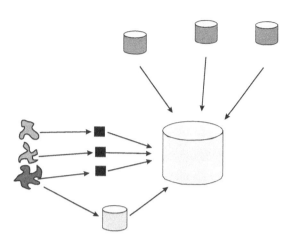

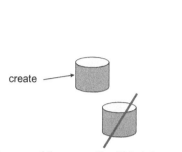

create

Because of the ease with which data marts can be created, it is often easier to create a new data mart than it is to maintain an existing data mart

modern information architecture for the operational environment

Figure 10.1.20

Figure 10.1.21

an arrangement of data that allows data to be examined from different perspectives.

One of the characteristics of data marts is that they are relatively easy and fast to create. Because of the ease of creation, most organizations build new data marts rather than do maintenance to existing data marts. Figure 10.1.20 shows that data marts are created rather than maintaining older data marts that need to have new requirements. The long-term effect of constantly creating new data marts is that after a while the organization is supporting many data marts that aren't being used.

Because data marts contain KPIs, there is great propensity for change. That is because KPIs are constantly changing. Every time the focus of a business changes, so change its KPIs. One day the business is interested in profitability. In this case KPIs focus on revenue and expenses. The next day the business focuses on market share. The KPIs now relate to new customers and customer retention. The next day the focus changes to meeting competition. The KPIs now change to looking at product acceptance and product differentiation.

As long as the business changes (and business change is simply a fact of life), KPIs also change. And as long as KPIs change, data marts change.

The generic architecture for the data architecture component of the operational environment is depicted in Figure 10.1.21.

PERSONAL ANALYTICS

In every corporation there are two levels of decision making – the corporate level of decision making and the personal level of decision making. The corporate level of decision making is a formal and even regulated environment. The personal level of decision making is informal.

There is a big difference between the corporate level of decision making and the personal level of decision making. The corporate level of decision making is where there are contracts, management decisions, and even compliance regulations. There is responsibility to the shareholders at this level of decision making.

The other level of decision making is the personal level of decision making. The personal level of decision making is off the cuff, individual, and informal. There usually is not any audit trail here. Personal decisions are made spontaneously and the needs for personal decision making are fluid, changing as often as every minute.

The personal analyst can look at data – any data – through the facilities of the personal analytical environment. The analyst can look at corporate data or personal data. The analyst can look at data in his or her time frame. There is no time constraint on doing personal analysis.

Figure 11.1.1 shows the two kinds of decision making.

Personal decision making is fluid and dynamic. The ideal tool for personal decision making is the personal computer. The personal computer is affordable, able to be relocated, and versatile. The personal computer is able to be refocused at the drop of a hat. There is little or no need for formal systems analysis or development of the personal computer. The analyst just sits down and jots down what is useful and relevant about what needs to be analyzed. Of course the personal computer does not have the speed and capacity of the larger corporate computers. The personal computer is not capable of processing the amount of data that a corporate computer can process. But that is of little concern to the individual analyst. Figure 11.1.2 shows that the personal computer is the best tool available for the individual doing personal analysis.

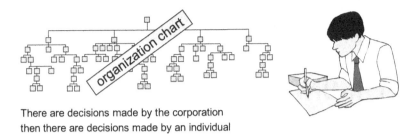

There are decisions made by the corporation
then there are decisions made by an individual

Figure 11.1.1

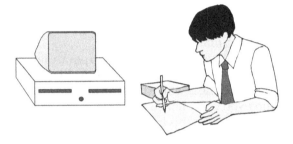

The personal computer is the ideal technology to use for
personal decision making

Figure 11.1.2

The most popular tool available to the personal analyst is the
spreadsheet. The spreadsheet – as measured by number of licens-
es – has to be the most ubiquitous tool for analysis that there is.
There are millions and millions of spreadsheets on personal computers around the world. At a Midwest bank recently, it was estimated that for the 2000 employees at the bank's one site, there
were 4,000,000 spreadsheets that had been created in order to
make banking decisions. Figure 11.1.3 shows that the spreadsheet
is the analytical tool most used on the personal computer.

There are great advantages to the spreadsheet. The largest advantage is the autonomy the spreadsheet provides the individual analyst. The analyst can do anything he or she wants with the
spreadsheet. The analyst can enter any formula, can enter any
data, and can change any data that he or she wishes to. There is no
one telling the analyst what to do or how to do it.

A second advantage of the spreadsheet is that the spreadsheet
is immediate. The analyst needs no special preparation time in order to start using the tool. The analyst just sits down and starts to
use the spreadsheet. The analyst can use the spreadsheet to help
formulate and structure what needs to be analyzed.

The ubiquitous tool on the personal computer is the spreadsheet

Figure 11.1.3

A third advantage of the spreadsheet is its ability to be flexible. The spreadsheet can be changed to suit almost any kind of analysis.

Another advantage of the spreadsheet is its cost. Oftentimes the cost of the spreadsheet is born when the personal computer is purchased and there is no further charge for the usage of the spreadsheet.

For these reasons and many more, the spreadsheet has found its way into many different environments. Figure 11.1.4 shows the advantages of the spreadsheet.

But there are some disadvantages to the spreadsheet. The first disadvantage is that the spreadsheet can be changed at will. Anyone building and managing a spreadsheet can place any value at

There are many advantages to the spreadsheet

Figure 11.1.4

any time into the spreadsheet and the spreadsheet won't complain. This means that the source of data going into the spreadsheet is not able to be audited. If an analyst wishes to give him- or herself a raise, as far as the spreadsheet is concerned, the raise has been granted. This, of course, may not be a reflection of reality. But the spreadsheet does not know or care. Making corporate decisions that are governed by management, contracts, legislature, and shareholders is not advisable when the source of data is a spreadsheet because of this lack of integrity of data.

Another disadvantage of the spreadsheet is that the systems that are created on the spreadsheet are not created with the discipline and the rigor of the corporate-based systems. It is always easy to change a system created on a spreadsheet. But where rigor and discipline of processing are required, that ease of a change in functionality is a liability, not an asset.

Figure 11.1.5 shows that there are some drawbacks with the spreadsheet.

Decisions are made at both the corporate level and the personal level. But the impact of the decisions is very different. Decisions made at the corporate level affect the budget and the policy of the corporation. Personal decisions influence how an individual does

But there are some restrictive advantages to the spreadsheet as well

Figure 11.1.5

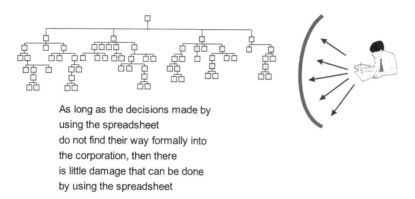

As long as the decisions made by
using the spreadsheet
do not find their way formally into
the corporation, then there
is little damage that can be done
by using the spreadsheet

Figure 11.1.6

his or her job. But when the day comes where corporate decisions are being made using personal tools, there is a fundamental problem. Figure 11.1.6 shows that personal decisions should only indirectly influence corporate decisions.

Stated differently, when individuals use their tools on a personal basis and convince themselves and perhaps others of a course of action or a change in policy, the individual then must convince the corporation. But the person doing the individual analysis is not in a position to directly interface the corporate data and systems with the personal data and systems. In a way, the personal analytical systems become an analytical "sandbox" as depicted in Figure 11.1.7.

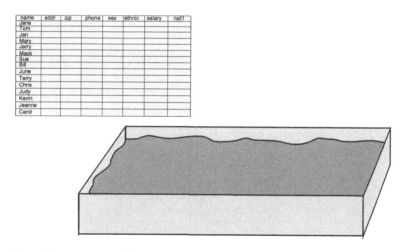

There is a very good fit between the sandbox and the spreadsheet

Figure 11.1.7

In the sandbox, the personal analyst can do anything – can use any data or any algorithm, can process with no fear of impacting others. But at the end, when the analyst has gained insights from the sandbox experience, the analyst must then institutionalize the results and insight into the corporate systems infrastructure.

So there is a very real and beneficial effect on corporate system from personal analytical decisions. However, the impact is indirect not direct.

12.1

A COMPOSITE DATA ARCHITECTURE

There are many reasons why developers love architecture. And one of the most compelling reasons why people love architecture is that – among other things – architecture embraces the whole. At some points architecture delves into detail. But in every architecture there is a master blueprint (or blueprints). This blueprint shows how everything fits together. And it is no different with data architecture. With data architecture (like all other architectures), there is a need for a comprehensive blueprint.

Blueprints are interesting in that there are different kinds of blueprints. For a large building, there will be one blueprint that focuses on power, such as electricity, gas, and so forth, for the building. There will be another building focusing on structural integrity and so forth. Taken together these different blueprints form a complete picture of the structure.

If you are building a one-story, one-room log cabin in the forest, you don't need much of a blueprint. But if you are building a large, complex expensive multistory building in the middle of a city, you need blueprints. There is much to be considered when it comes to building a multistoried structure in the middle of a modern city. And there is the same complexity and expense when it comes to a modern information infrastructure for technology and data.

Figure 12.1.1 shows one such blueprint – the composite infrastructure for information systems. The composite architecture is a depiction of the different components of the architecture and how they are juxtapositioned.

There are several features of the composite architecture that are of note:

- Timeliness of data. In general the fresher data is the closer data is to the interactive environment. The older data is the more it migrates to the archival environment.
- The essence of the interactive environment is the execution of applications. The essence of the data warehouse/data vault environment is integration of data.

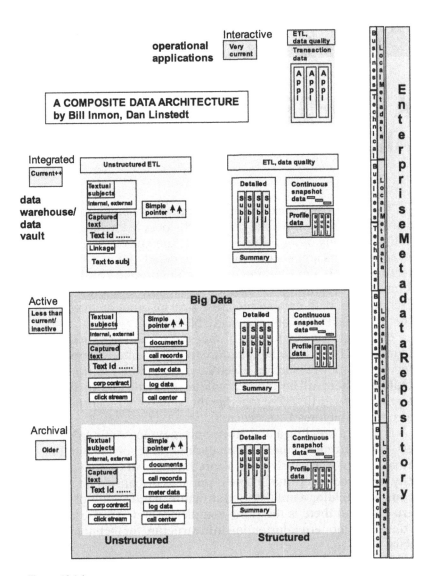

Figure 12.1.1

- The Big Data component is broken into two major sections – the analytical Big Data section and the archival section.
- Metadata stretches across the different environments with impunity. True enterprise metadata looks across data wherever it is at. Metadata is no great respecter of different physical or other boundaries of data
- There are different levels of metadata throughout the composite architecture.

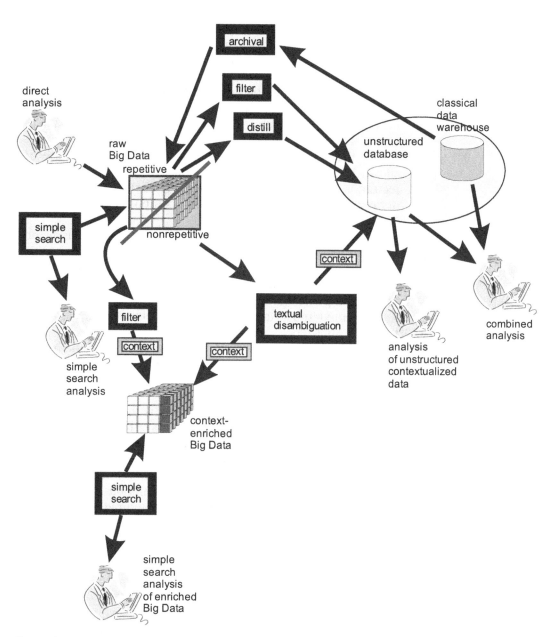

Figure 12.1.2

- The composite architecture depicts the detailed, bedrock data of the corporation (i.e., data in the system of record). There is other data – summarized data, aggregated data – that exists that is not reflected in the composite architecture. (Data marts are not reflected in the composite architecture.)

- There is a fundamental difference between data types in the composite architecture. Unstructured data (i.e., nonrepetitive data) is not directly mixed with transaction-based data (i.e., repetitive data).

The composite architecture is able to reflect how the different types of data can be combined into a single architecture. As such the composite architecture is a large-scale blueprint of data in the corporation.

But there are many aspects of the architecture that are not shown in Figure 12.1.1. Another aspect to the composite architecture is shown in Figure 12.1.2. In Figure 12.1.2 the dynamics of how the major components of the composite architecture are "wired" together are shown.

Figure 12.1.2 shows that the raw Big Data environment is divided into two major types of data – repetitive data and nonrepetitive data. The nonrepetitive is where the vast majority of the business value is. The nonrepetitive data flows into textual disambiguation. After flowing into textual disambiguation, the data is:
- Formatted into a standard database structure
- Contextualized

After the data passes through textual disambiguation, the contextualized data then passes either back to Big Data in a contextualized state, or the data passes into a standard database management system (DBMS).

The other flow of data from Big Data is the flow from repetitive data into either the distillation process or the filtering process. From the filtering and/or the distillation process, the data flows into the database environment.

The reverse flow of data from the data warehouse to Big Data shows the archiving of data from the data warehouse as data has its probability of access drop. Once the unstructured database/data

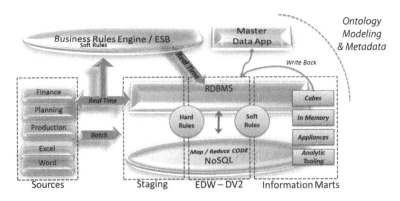

Figure 12.1.3

warehouse is created, the data can be analyzed (Figure 12.1.3). In the standard database environment, data can be analyzed where:

- Only structure data is analyzed.
- Only unstructured data is analyzed.
- Structured and unstructured data are analyzed together.

Data Vault 2.0 Architecture is based on three-tier data warehouse architecture, shown in Figure 12.1.3. The multiple tiers allow implementers and designers to decouple the enterprise data warehouse from both sourcing and acquisition functions and information delivery and data provisioning functions. In turn, the team becomes more nimble and the architecture is more resilient to failure and more flexible in responding to changes. NoSQL is added to the architecture so that the business can leverage their current investment in their relational platform, while also incorporating the new technology needed to handle Big Data. The methodology provides standards around hard and soft business rules in order to provide base-line standards which enable utilization of automation tooling.

GLOSSARY

4GL Fourth-generation language; a computer language optimized for ease of use

acronym resolution The process of expanding acronyms into their literal meaning

active data dictionary An automated metadata management facility that is tightly and interactively woven into the development and analysis process

actuary A professional mathematician trained in the art of studying life expectancy and accident probabilities

address The location of a unit of data

algorithm The instructions that govern the flow of activity in a procedure

alternate spelling A different way of forming a word pattern

Amazon.com A successful dot-com retailer company

analog A type of computing driven by sensory perceptions and signals, as opposed to a digital computer

anchor data in a DIS The key attribute(s) of a DIS

application A computerized system dedicated to solving or empowering a specific business function

archival processing The activities surrounding older and/or inactive data

ATM Automated teller machine; a "money machine"

attribute A value of data that is distinguishable from other values

backflow of data The movement of data from the data warehouse to the operational environment

BASEL II A governing body for financial activities and transactions

batch processing The collection of transaction into "batches" that are processed collectively

bell curve distribution A "normal" statistical distribution of activities and points of data that is roughly in the shape of a bell

BI Business intelligence

blather Email message generated internally that have no business relevance

block of data A large physical unit of data that can contain records of data

blog A personal diary that is open for the public to scrutinize

boilerplate Text that is copied verbatim for the purpose of serving as a general template

byte A basic unit of storage, usually 8 bits in length

call center A facility of the organization where an agent of the organization can engage in conversation with other people

call level detail record The detailed record of telephone conversations containing the information about who made a call, to whom the call was made, when the call was made, and how long the call lasted

cardinality The number of occurrences of two units of data that participate in a relationship

CDC Changed data capture; the incremental changes to a database are captured and stored, then retransacted or logged onto another database

cell of a spreadsheet A basic unit of data found in a spreadsheet

CIF Corporate information factory; the data warehouse–centric architecture that contains operational sources of data, ETL, an ODS, and data marts

class I ODS An ODS whose latency is measured in one second or less

class II ODS An ODS whose latency is measured in four hours or less

class III ODS An ODS whose latency is measured in 24 hours or less

clickstream data Automated measurements of the activity occurring on a website

comments A field of data containing free form text

compliance Business rules enforced by legislation or some other governing body

content enriched Big Data whose content has been contextualized

context The surrounding environment that gives definition to a word

contextualization The process of identifying the context of a word

convenience field An element of data placed in a structure in order to simplify and/or expedite analytical processing

core An early form of storage for storing data available to the CPU; core operated under the principles governed by the hysteresis curve.

corporate data The entire body of data of the corporation

CPU Central processing unit; the high-speed processing heart of the computer

CRT Cathode ray tube; a display device; a screen

Cullinet An early DBMS vendor selling a networked database management system

current valued data Data whose accuracy is as of the moment of access; online data

curve of usefulness The curve that indicates that the fresher data is, the more likely it is to be useful

DA Data administrator; a job classification whose responsibilities include the management of corporate metadata

DASD Direct access storage device; a mechanical device that holds electronic-based data

dashboards Data visualization tools that display the numbers, metrics, and scorecards on a single screen, making it easy for a business person to get information from difference sources and customize the appearance

database A structured collection of units of data organized around some topic or theme

data cleansing The process of finding and fixing errors and inaccuracies in data

data degradation The propensity of the integrity of data to diminish over time

data dictionary A repository of the metadata useful to the corporation

data flow diagram A schematic indicating the direction of the movement of data

data governance The activities necessary to the management of integrity of data

data life cycle The recognition that as data ages, that data takes on different characteristics

data mart A subset of a data warehouse that's usually oriented to a business group or team

data mining Analysis of large quantities of data to find patterns such as groups of records, unusual records, and dependencies

data model An abstraction of data

data quality The properties of data embodied by the "Five C's": clean, consistent, conformed, current, and comprehensive.

data profiling An essential part of the data quality process; this involves examining source system data for anomalies in values, ranges, frequency, relationships, and other characteristics that could hobble future efforts to analyze it.

data scientist An individual dedicated to the study of patterns found in data

data virtualization The process of retrieving and manipulating data without requiring details of how the data formatted or where the data is located

data visualization Presenting data in a visual way, such as with graphs and charts, helps business people glean insights they might not otherwise see; dashboards use the concept of data visualization to present data for analysis. IT is often a part of self-service BI, but is only as effective as the quality of the data it draws upon.

data warehouse A subject-oriented, integrated, nonvolatile, time-variant collection of data in support of management's decisions

DB2/UDB Database management system by IBM

DBA Database administrator; individual charged with the physical integrity of data

DBMS Database management system; system software that manages the storage and access of data on disk storage

DC Data communications; technology that manages messages generated as part of transaction processing

Demarco, Tom An early pioneer along with Ed Youdon specializing in structured systems development

dependent data mart A data mart whose sole source of data is the data warehouse; a dependent data mart is a component of the corporate information factory

dimensional modeling A generally accepted practice in the data warehouse industry to structure data intended for user access, analysis, and reporting in dimensional data models

direct access of data The ability of a database management system to directly find data, as opposed to having to sequentially search for data

DIS Data item set; the mid level of a data model

disk storage Physical media used for storing values of data

distillation The process of analyzing a large number of records (usually Big Data records) and producing a single result

document A basic unit of textual data

documentation Verbiage describing a system, application, database, procedure, etc.

document fracturing In textual disambiguation, the process of sequentially processing text looking for text that satisfies, such criteria as stop word processing, stemming, and homographic resolution

dormant data Data captured electronically but used very infrequently

download The movement of a bulk amount of data from one environment to another

DSS environment The environment where analysis is conducted

DW 2.0 The second-generation data warehouse architecture

EAI enterprise application integration; consolidating and integrating the applications that exist in an enterprise. The goal is usually to protect the investment in legacy applications and databases while adding or migrating to a new set of applications that exploit the Internet, e-commerce, extranet, and other new technologies.

EDI Enterprise data integration; an end-to-end data integration philosophy. It simply means that an organization has chosen a platform or strategy that enables them to integrate unlimited amounts of disparate timely data accurately and with confidence.

elapsed time of processing The length of time it takes for a process to execute

electronic text In a form where the words of the text are recognized by the computer

ELT Extract/load/transform; the process of extracting, loading, and transforming data. The problem with ELT is that many organizations only extract and load the data, but fail to transform the data.

email Messages from one party to another carried on an electronic medium

encoding The process of encryption of text into a form unrecognizable by an outsider

end user analyst A person charged with doing analytical processing against data and/or systems

enterprise metadata Metadata whose scope is the entire enterprise

entity A broad classification of data

ERD Entity relationship diagram; a logical description of how the major subject areas of the corporation fit together

ETL **Extract/transform/load**; the process in which data is taken from the source system, configured, and stored in a data warehouse or database. ETL tools automate data integration tasks.

exception processing The practice of identify and processing statistical outliers

executable code A program that has been compiled and resolved and is ready to be placed into execution

existing system x A system that is up and running

exploration warehouse A facility designed exclusively for statistical, analytical processing

extract program A process whose purpose is to read a file, find data, then move the data to another file

external data Data whose source is outside of the system of the organization

fact table The data structure where basic facts in a star join are stored

file A collection of records

file structure The organization of the collection of records

flat file A collection of records where the structure of each record is identical

foreign key An attribute used for distinguishing a record that participates in a relationship with another table

functional decomposition The process of reducing a large function or process into smaller finer functions

generic data model A data model of an industry, rather than of a specific company; a generic data model can be used as a template that can be customized for a given company within the industry that has been modeled.

Google A dot-com company that has indexed the Internet

granularity The level of detail found in a record of data

great divide The division of Big Data between repetitive data and nonrepetitive data

GUI Graphical user interface

Hadoop Technology designed to house Big Data; a framework for managing data

hashing algorithm An algorithm converts data values into an address

heuristic process An iterative process, where the next step of analysis depends on the results attained in the current level of analysis

hierarchical DBMS A database management system whose relationship between records is based on the parent/child relationship

HIPAA Health Insurance Portability and Accountability Act; the law protecting medical privacy

HIPO Hierarchical input/output; a chart showing the input to a process, the output from the process, and a brief description of the processing that occurs in the process

Hollerith punched cards An early means of storing data, typically containing 80 columns

homograph A word or phrase whose interpretation depends on the person who originally wrote the word or phrase

homographic resolution The process of contextualizing data based on the identity of the person who uttered the text

IBM 360 A machine that standardized operating systems; with the IBM 360 line, there was compatibility of processing across different machine types. A revolutionary technology that changed the face of computing.

IDMS A network DBMS by Cullinet

image A picture, such as a real estate photo of a house for sale, or an x-ray

impact analysis An estimation of the work and disruption that would be caused by a change to a system

IMS Information management system; a hierarchical DBMS by IBM

independent data mart A data mart whose source data comes directly from legacy systems, rather than being sourced by a data warehouse

index A database showing the address of a database record based on a value found in the record

inline contextualization The technique of inferring context by establishing a beginning delimiter and an ending delimiter

integrity of data The assurance that data is correct and accurate as stored

Internet The system by which data is stored and is made available to a large audience

in-memory analytics Leveraging advances in memory to provide faster and deeper analytics by querying a system's random-access memory (RAM) instead of disks; in-memory analytics' architectural options include in-memory analytics in the BI tools, as part of the database or on the BI appliance platform.

I/O input/output operation; the activity or reading or writing a record to disk storage. I/O operations happen in terms of mechanical speeds.

IT The information technology organization; the organizational entity charged with building and managing applications and technology systems

iterative process A process that is done in short finite steps, where there are many steps, but where each step is taken quickly

join The process of merging two or more tables on the basis of a common key

key An identifying attribute of data

Kimball, Ralph The thought leader centered on the dimensional model of data

KPI Key performance indicator; a measurement made periodically by the organization that examines important variables

language The text that is used to communicate with the computer; some languages are optimized for ease of use and other languages are optimized for speed of processing.

legacy systems The older systems used to run the business of the corporation as it was defined 10 or 20 years ago

lineage of data The "family tree" of data; data is transformed in many ways as it passes through a system. The lineage is a record of the transformations of data from the moment it enters a system until it is used in analysis.

link The mechanism by which two systems or two environments form a common relationship

Linux An operating system

load utility A utility provided by a DBMS vendor in which data is efficiently loaded into the DBMS

log tape A sequential record of the activities that have occurred inside a system; sometimes called a "journal" tape. The primary purpose of a log tape is for backup and recovery of a system.

logical data model A data model based on inferred relationships

machine cycle A full cycle of processing inside a computer

magnetic tape An early sequential storage mechanism

maintenance backlog The backlog of program and system redevelopment that occurred in the early days of programming

manual processing The mode of processing where work is done by human beings

mapping The instructions to textual ETL as to how to interpret a document or type of document

MapReduce A language for processing Big Data

master file A predecessor to database; a storage structure where the early system of record was stored

MDM Master data management; the set of processes used to create and maintain a consistent view; also referred to as a master list of key enterprise reference data. This data includes such entities as customers, prospects, suppliers, employees, products, services, assets, and accounts. It also includes the groupings and hierarchies associated with these entities.

memory The high-speed storage that is available to the computer; memory is accessed and processed in terms of electronic speeds.

metadata The classic definition of metadata is "data about the data."

ODS Operational data store; a type of database often used as an interim area for a data warehouse. Unlike a data warehouse, which contains static data, the contents of the ODS are updated through the course of business operations.

meteorological data Data downloaded from a satellite regarding weather patterns on earth

Microsoft A software vendor primarily of desk top technology

MPP Massively parallel processing; a type of operating system capable of handling large volumes of data

multiplex The ability of a system to share memory

named-value processing One of the two primary processing paths for textual ETL; named-value processing includes standard index processing, inline contextualization, custom variable processing, and other forms of processing

naming conventions The means by which names are assigned to a variable inside the building of a system

narrative Prosaic text

network The means by which electronic communications occurs between two or more nodes

networked DBMS A DBMS whose primary relationship between records is a networked relationship

nibble Half a byte

NLP Natural language processing; the notion that the context of text can be inferred from the text itself

node A processing location in a network

nonlinear format A format of text or reported values where the text or variables are arranged in a nonlinear format

nonrepetitive data Data whose records have no predictable pattern of structure or content; typical nonrepetitive records include email, call center data, warranty claim data, and insurance claim data.

non volatile data Data that once written cannot be changed; sometimes called "snapshot" data

nonrepetitive data Data whose contents do not repeat from unit to unit

normalization The process of organizing data at its detailed level into according to its existence criteria

OCR Optical character recognition

ODS Operational data store; a data structure that contains some of the properties of the data warehouse and some of the properties of the operational system. As a rule, the ODS is an optional structure that is found at some companies and not at others.

OLAP (online analytical processing) This technique for analyzing business data uses cubes, which are like multidimensional pivot tables in spreadsheets. OLAP tools can perform trend analysis and enable drilling down into data. They enable multidimensional analysis, such as analyzing by time, product, and geography. The major types of OLAP processing are MOLAP (multidimensional) and ROLAP (relational). HOLAP (hybrid) processing combines them.

OLTP Online transaction processing; the environment where online transaction processing is executed

online response time The length of time from the moment an operator initiates a transaction until that transaction returns output to the user

ontology A logical relationship of elements participating in a taxonomy

operating system The technology that controls the computer and all its operations

operational BI Analytical processing based on data generated by operational processing

operational environment The processing center where day-to-day transactional processing is supported

Oracle A large database vendor

oxide The surface of the storage medium where bits are stored

paper tape A very early form of storage

parallel management of data The processing approach where multiple machines are run in tandem with each other so that the elapsed processing time is reduced

parent/child relationship A hierarchical relationship of data for every parent node, there can be from 0 to n children nodes.

Pareto chart A method of displaying data values over time and classification

parsing The process of reading text and finding contextualized value that resides in the text

passive data dictionary A repository of data where the storage of metadata may or may not be used in the development and analytical process

pattern analysis The analysis that seeks to find recognizable patterns in the occurrence of points of data

PC Personal computer; a laptop or desktop device for personal computing

physical characteristics of data The physical dimension and configuration of a unit of data or data structure

physical model The physical definition of the shape and structure of data (as defined to the DBMS)

pointer A reference to another entity or the address of another entity

Poisson distribution The right-hand side of a bell curve as measured from the zero axis

postprocessing The processing that optionally can occur after text has passed through textual ETL

predictive analytics An advanced form of analytics that uses business information to find patterns and predict future outcomes and trends; determining credit scores by looking at a customer's credit history and other data is a typical use for predictive analytics.

preprocessing The editing that can precede textual processing

probability of access The mathematical statement of the likelihood that a unit of data will be accessed

program A procedure embodied in code

proper text Formal text as taught by a teacher of language (as opposed to slang, shorthand, notes, comments, etc.)

proximity analysis An analysis based on the closeness of words or taxonomies to each other

public accounting firm An organization charged with commenting on the compliance of a publicly traded corporation to accounting standards and rules

punched cards An early form of storage that had many disadvantages

query A procedure executed by a computer program in search of qualified data

record A unit of data that typically contains keys and attributes

record locking A means of ensuring transaction integrity during update processing

recursion The type of relationship where part of the definition makes a reference to the item being defined

referential integrity The process of relating data together in a disciplined manner

relational model A form of data where data is normalized

release of software Commercial software is controlled by releases of different versions of software. In a new release the software vendor will have added new functionality and will have fixed bugs and errors in the older release.

repetitive data Data whose units repeat in terms of structure and even content

report decompilation The process of reading a report and reducing the report to a normalized database; in general report decompilation is a nonlinear process because of the complexity of the format of the report.

reporting The process of collecting data from various sources and presenting it to business people in an understandable way.

repository A place where important corporate metadata is stored

requirements A statement of what is needed in the functionality of a system

reservations systems A system where corporation makes general reservations for services and products, such as an airline, hotel chain, or car rental organization

response time The measurement of time from when a transaction is initiated until the first of the transaction output is returned to the user

Roman census approach The method of moving processing to the data rather than moving data to the processor

SAP An ERP application software company

Sarbanes-Oxley Act A law requiring information compliance for publicly traded corporations; passed because of the misdeeds of Enron Corporation

SAS A company specializing in statistical analysis software

schema The means by which a pattern of data is identified

sequential analysis of data A process in which data is accessed sequentially

scorecards Performance management tools that help managers track performance against strategic goals

SDLC System development life cycle; the development life cycle based on the contributions of Ed Yourdon and Tom DeMarco

security The means by which data is protected

self-service BI An infrastructure that allows BI consumers to get the information they need without the help of the IT group

shared memory An arrangement of processors in which up to four processors share the same memory (see multiplexing)

shorthand The practice in transcription of not writing down actual words but writing down shortened symbols for those words

silicon A raw material much like sand that can be shaped into many different end products, such a semiconductors, beer bottles, and body parts

Silicon Valley The location where original technological innovation starts; in the Northern California, San Jose, Santa Clara, Mountain View vicinity

siloed systems The practice of building application system that have no interface or exchange of other application systems, where there is common data between those systems

SKU Stock keeping unit; in retailing the practice of tracking a record of each unit of inventory

SLA Service level agreement; the agreement within the corporation governing response time of transaction systems and "up time," the amount of time the system is up and available

slang Improper language; language that is used improperly, such as the word "ain't."

SME Subject matter expert; a person who thoroughly understands the business or a particular aspect of a business

snapshot record A record of data taken at a moment in time that cannot be updated

snowflake structure The dimensional modeling approach where more than one star schema are joined together

source code The uncompiled version of code

spam Unwanted, unsolicited email generated outside the corporation

spider-web systems The early architecture where applications grew in a siloed manner

spreadsheet The primary tool found in the personal computing environment

SQL The language interface for relational systems

SQL Server The DBMS built and managed by Microsoft

staging area A location where data that is to be transformed is held in abeyance waiting for other events to occur

star schema "Star join"; a fact table and its related dimension tables

statistical analysis The process of looking at a large number of values and evaluating the values mathematically

stemming The reduction of words to their root. For example, the stem of moving, moved, mover, and move is "mov."

steward The person in charge of the integrity of a type of data in the corporation

stop word A word in a language that is needed for communication but not needed to convey information. In English there are stop words such as "a," "and," "the," "to," and "from."

structured data Data that is managed by a database management system

SWU Standard work unit; the process of creating small modules that can flow efficiently and without bottlenecks

subdoc processing The recognition by textual ETL of the logical grouping of sections of text

synonym In grammar, a word that is a substitute for another word

System R A statistical processing software package

system of record "Single version of the truth"; the building of systems where there is integrity of data; there is one and only one location where any given unit of data is created, updated, and deleted from

taxonomy A classification of text

Teradata A database software company

text Words; language

textual analytics Analysis based on a foundation of text

textual disambiguation The process of reading text and formatting text into a standard database format

textual ETL See textual disambiguation

time variant Data that cannot be updated and whose value is accurate as of some one moment in time

transaction A computerized process that conducts business, usually updating or creating values

transaction processing environment The location and equipment where transaction processing for a corporation takes place

Tweet A short message sent over the Internet

uniprocessor A computer that has only one processor

UNIX An operating system

unstructured data Data whose logical organization is not apparent to the computer

unstructured data warehouse A data warehouse whose source of data is unstructured data

user The individual engaging in computation

video Media where there is moving action and accompanying audio

voice recognition The technology that allows voice to be converted to an electronic format

VVV Volume, variety, velocity, which are the original characteristics of Big Data

waterfall development The SDLC, so called because any one development activity must be done before the next activity can begin and because the output from any one level of activity becomes the input into the next level.

Yourdon, Ed An information technology pioneer who started the "structured" movement

INDEX

Printed in the United States
By Bookmasters